An Introduction to Early Mo

Edinburgh Textbooks on the English Language

TITLES IN THE SERIES INCLUDE

An Introduction to English Syntax
Jim Miller

An Introduction to English Phonology
April McMahon

An Introduction to English Morphology: Words and Their Structure
Andrew Carstairs-McCarthy

An Introduction to International Varieties of English
Laurie Bauer

An Introduction to Middle English
Jeremy Smith and Simon Horobin

An Introduction to Old English
Richard Hogg

An Introduction to English Semantics and Pragmatics
Patrick Griffiths

An Introduction to Early Modern English

Terttu Nevalainen

Edinburgh University Press

© Terttu Nevalainen, 2006

Edinburgh University Press Ltd
22 George Square, Edinburgh

Reprinted 2008

Typeset in 10.5/12 Janson
by Servis Filmsetting Ltd, Manchester, and
printed and bound in Great Britain by
The Cromwell Press, Trowbridge

A CIP record for this book is available from the British Library

ISBN 0 7486 1523 7 (hardback)
ISBN 0 7486 1524 5 (paperback)

Contents

List of figures and tables

To readers

This book is designed for undergraduates in English, who probably all have some previous knowledge of Early Modern English through their familiarity with Shakespeare. The book may be used on a ten-week course focusing on English from 1500 to 1700 which introduces the language of the period in general. It will also be of interest to linguistics undergraduates studying the structural development of the English language.

The organisation of the book loosely follows the other history of English volumes in the ETOTEL series. The order of presentation is cumulative. It starts by looking at the linguistic evidence available from the Early Modern period, and provides a short introduction to electronic collections of Early Modern English texts. Chapters on spelling and vocabulary follow. These areas of the language are easily accessible to most readers, and they were also of particular concern to speakers of Early Modern English. The next two chapters on morphology, nouns and verbs, feed into the discussion of syntax. Phonology comes last, after vocabulary and grammar, in order to minimise the amount of new information and allow reference to concepts relevant to pronunciation, such as native and borrowed lexis. The final chapter examines the sociolinguistics of Early Modern English: how it varied socially, and how it spread in the British Isles and was transported to North America.

The reader is expected to have some basic linguistic terminology, but all the key terms are defined and illustrated as they appear. The chapters begin by placing the issues to be discussed in a wider context, and end with exercises based on the preceding text, texts in the Appendixes or other easily available sources such as *The Oxford English Dictionary*. Straightforward questions for review have also been included. All the exercises can be used in class, as essay topics or homework assignments.

Many people have helped me in this textbook project. I would like to thank Heinz Giegerich for inviting me to embark on it in the first place, and Sarah Edwards at Edinburgh University Press for her support and patience during the writing process. At an early stage Jeremy Smith kindly gave me access to the typescript of the Middle English volume, and later I was able to benefit from the other volumes published in the ETOTEL series.

Over the years, my students of the History of English in Helsinki and Cambridge have provided me with feedback on many of the ideas and exercises included in this book. My warmest thanks go to Helena Raumolin-Brunberg and Matti Rissanen for their comments on various parts of the draft version, and to Derek Britton for his careful reading of the phonology chapter. I owe a special debt to Sylvia Adamson for reading through and commenting on the first complete draft of the volume.

Rod McConchie and Mark Shackleton made the text more readable, and Reijo Aulanko and Samuli Kaislaniemi helped me with the references. Last but not least, my gratitude to the Research Unit for Variation and Change in English, funded by the Academy of Finland and the University of Helsinki, for providing me with both financial assistance and a busy but stimulating working environment.

1 The Early Modern English period

Historical development proceeds not by stages but by overlaps.
(Wrightson 2002: 24)

1.1 Periods of English

The English language has been greatly transformed over the centuries. Three major periods are usually distinguished in its history: Old English (before c. 1100), Middle English (c. 1100–1500) and Modern English (after c. 1500). Many historians divide the Modern English period further into Early and Late Modern English with 1700 as a dividing line. To appreciate the extent of transformation the language has undergone, we only need to take a look at the three Bible translations (Genesis 1: 3) in (1). Their original spelling has been retained but modern punctuation has been added.

(1a) God cwæð ða: Gewurðe leoht, & leoht wearð geworht. (literally: 'God said then: Be light, and light was made.' Ælfric, early 11th century)

(b) And God seide, Liȝt be maad, and liȝt was maad. (John Wycliffe, 1380s)

(c) And God said, Let there be light: and there was light. (*Authorised Version*, 1611)

Ælfric's Old English version in (1a) needs glossing, because otherwise it will make no sense to a modern reader. It contains the word *God*, which is found unchanged in Present-day English, but the other words are no longer recognisable. By contrast, a modern reader might well recognise all the words in Wycliffe's Middle English translation in (1b) although the way some of them are spelled looks odd. Finally, the Early Modern English text of the *Authorised Version* in (1c) does not present any difficulties to speakers of Present-day English.

If Early Modern English is so like Present-day English, why single it out as a distinct period in the history of English? We could, of course, argue that there is the need to find a convenient end-date for the traditionally recognised period of Middle English, which was clearly different from Present-day English. But the Bible translations suggest that this line of argument may not help us determine the end point of the Early Modern period. In order to do that we need more evidence. Periods in language history are usually approached by looking at language-internal facts, as we have done above, or by focusing on language-external factors in the history of the language community. Let us start from the linguistic end, which will be our primary concern in this book, and return to external matters in the final chapter.

In principle, we can place the historical stages of a language on a scale from the most archaic to the least archaic. To do so, a variety of features characteristic of the language need to be analysed. Comparing English with its Germanic relatives, Roger Lass (2000) considered ten features. He graded them by giving one point for features like the presence of the infinitive ending (*singen* 'to sing') and a zero for its absence (*sing*) (for a complete list, see Note 1 at the end of this chapter).

(2) Archaism ranking of Germanic languages

Rank	Language(s)
1.00	Gothic, Old Icelandic
0.95	**Old English**
0.90	Old High German, Modern Icelandic
0.85	
0.80	
0.75	
0.70	
0.65	
0.60	Middle High German, Modern German, Middle Dutch
0.55	
0.50	
0.45	
0.40	
0.35	**Middle English**, Modern Swedish, Modern Dutch
0.30	
0.25	
0.20	
0.15	Afrikaans
0.10	
0.05	
0.00	**Modern English**

The scale of archaism Lass arrived at is given under (2) with the most archaic languages at the top and the least archaic ones at the bottom of the rank scale running from one to zero (Lass 2000: 30).

The scale confirms what we saw in (1): that Modern English is further removed from Old English than it is from Middle English or, for that matter, from Modern Swedish. The scale also suggests that there is no unambiguous cut-off point that would mark the boundary between Middle and Early Modern English: would it be at 0.25, 0.15 or 0.05, for instance? However, if we add up the features for individual Middle English texts, some of them such as the *Ormulum* and *The Owl and the Nightingale* come closer to the Old English end of the continuum while Chaucer best represents the kind of language marked as Middle English on the scale. Textual comparisons like this suggest that Middle English is not really one entity either but is quite diffuse in linguistic terms.

This is also more generally true of linguistic periods. Language change is no different from other historical developments in that it does not proceed in stages but rather by overlaps. Dividing language history into periods has nevertheless proved useful for scholarly purposes. It helps us focus on the various levels of language, such as spelling, vocabulary, grammar and pronunciation simultaneously over a given stretch of time. By doing so we can reconstruct the linguistic resources available to a community or to a notable individual such as Geoffrey Chaucer (1340?–1400) – a typical representative of Middle English.

As this book concentrates on the English language between 1500 and 1700, we could perhaps select William Shakespeare (1564–1616) as a typical representative of the language of the period. His usage has been documented in many grammars, the first two written in the late nineteenth (Abbott 1870) and early twentieth centuries (Franz 1939). If we tried to place Shakespeare on the above scale of archaism, however, he would be ranked at zero, and so indistinguishable from Present-day English. Unlike Chaucer, who displays all the following features, Shakespeare has none of them. His nouns do not take a dative ending (as in *in londe* for 'in (the) land'), his adjectives do not inflect within the noun phrase (*the gode man* for 'the good man'), and his verbs have no infinitive ending (*loven* for 'to love'). As far as person and number marking are concerned, Shakespeare systematically marks the third-person singular – just as we do today – and occasionally the second, whereas Chaucer could mark the first (*I sitte*), the second (*thou seyst*) and the third (*he gooth*) as well as the plural (*they maken*). So it seems we cannot distinguish Shakespeare's English from our own on the basis of these simple criteria of archaism. In order to do that, we need to refine our analysis.

1.2 Shakespeare – our contemporary?

The following sections will discuss spelling and grammar at three points in time between 1500 and 1700. Some of the lexical and semantic changes that have taken place over time will be considered in 1.2.4.

1.2.1 Spelling and grammar around 1600

That Shakespeare's spelling and grammar are not those of Present-day English is shown by the extract from *The Merry Wives of Windsor* in (3). Some of the spelling differences are fully regular, such as the use of the letter <v> word-initially for <u> (*vpon*) as well as <v>, and the letter <u> word-internally (*haue, loues*). Other spellings are less predictable: we can find, for instance, the word *letter* capitalised, and *hee* and *he* used as alternative forms.

> (3) *Nim.* And this is true: I **like not** the humor of lying: hee **hath** wronged mee in some humors: I should haue borne the humour'd Letter to her: but I haue a sword: and it shall bite vpon my necessitie: he loues your wife; There's the short and the long: My name is Corporall Nim: I speak, and I auouch; **'tis** true: my name is Nim: and Falstaffe loues your wife: adieu, I **loue not** the humour of bread and cheese: adieu.
>
> *Page.* The humour of it (quoth'a?) **heere's a fellow frights** English out of **his** wits. (HC, William Shakespeare, *The Merry Wives of Windsor*, 1623: 44.C2)

The major grammatical differences are marked in bold. Shakespeare does not use the verb *do* in all cases where Present-day English requires it (*I like not, I love not*). Although he only marks person in the third-person singular forms of verbs in (3), and so is not archaic in this respect, his usage varies between two endings, *-th* and *-s* (*hath* v. *loues, frights*).

Similarly, some of his contracted forms are basically modern (*there's, heere's*), but others are not (*'tis* rather than *it's*). The construction *here's a fellow frights* ('frightens') could also occur in colloquial speech today with the modern verb, but requires the subject pronoun *who* in Standard English (*a fellow who frightens*). In *out of his wits* Shakespeare uses the historical neuter possessive form *his* with reference to *English*, where we now use *its*. This new form was first attested in print in 1598, only a year later than *The Merry Wives* is believed to have been written. The text in (3) comes from the First Folio edition (published in 1623) but preserves the older form.

1.2.2 Spelling and grammar around 1500

There are equally a number of features in Shakespeare's spelling and grammar that differ from the language current a hundred years earlier. Let us compare (3) with the 'merry tale' in (4), which was printed in 1526. Alongside the regular *v*/*u* spellings, this passage displays the medieval convention of marking a nasal consonant with a tilde (~) put over the preceding vowel, as in *marchāte* ('merchant'), *Lōdon* ('London'), *mā* ('man') and *ĩ* ('in'). The abbreviation *y* stands for *that*, and there are a number of spellings that can make words hard for a modern reader to recognise (e.g. *hert* 'heart', *beddys* 'bed's', *persone* 'parson').

> (4) A rych couetous marchāte ther was y^t dwellyd in Lōdon **whych** euer
> gaderyd money & coud **neuer** fynd in hys hert to spend **noght** vppon
> hym self **nor** vppon **no** mā els/ **whych** fell **sore** syk/ & as he lay on
> hys deth bed had hys purs lyeng at his beddys hed/ & had suche a loue
> to hys money that he put his hand in his purs & toke out **therof** .x. or
> .xii. li *ĩ* nobles & put them in his mouth/ . . . wherefore the curate
> asked hym what he hadde in hys mouthe that letted hys speche/ Iwys
> mastere persone quod the syk man muffelynge I haue nothyng in my
> mouth but a lyttyll money because I **wot not** whether I shall go I
> thoughte I wolde take some spendyng money wyth me for I **wot not**
> what nede I shall haue **therof**/ (HC, *A Hundred Mery Talys*, 1526: 30–1)

The passage in (4) shows certain grammatical choices that were part and parcel of English around 1500 but no longer common a hundred years later. One of them is the use of the pronoun *which* to refer to humans: *a rych couetous marchāte... whych*. It persisted in the King James Bible (1611) (*Our Father, which art in heaven*), but had mostly been replaced by *who* by that time.

The text in (4) also contains an instance of multiple negation: *neuer ... noght ('nothing') ... nor ... no*, current in most kinds of English until the end of the Middle English period. It lost ground in the sixteenth century, but Shakespeare and his contemporaries could occasionally have two negatives in constructions with *nor* and *neither*, as in *this is no mortall busines, nor no sound* (*Tempest*). The merry tale in (4) also looks back to Middle English in that it lacks *do* in negatives (*I wot not* 'I do not know') and has adverb forms such as *sore* instead of *sorely* (*sore syk* 'sick') and *therof* rather than *of it*.

1.2.3 Spelling and grammar around 1700

Continuing with the tradition of merry tales, let us compare the texts in (3) and (4) with the jest in (5). It appeared in print in 1687, and became part of the diarist Samuel Pepys's collection of 'Penny Merriments'. As is typically the case with small publications of this kind, we do not know when exactly these 'Canterbury Tales' had been penned by the *Chaucer Junior* who claims their authorship. But the language displays a number of features characteristic of the second half of the seventeenth century. Apart from the use of capitals to highlight important nouns (*Gentleman, Horse, Gentlewoman*, etc.), the spelling looks quite modern. Only the verb forms *vext* and *reply'd* differ from their modern spellings. Similar contractions are found in Shakespeare, for example, *humour'd* in (3), indicating that the vowel in the <ed> ending was no longer pronounced at the time.

> (5) A married Gentleman coming through Canterbury, his Horse threw him, which a young Gentlewoman seeing, fell **a laughing**; the Man being terribly vext that she should laugh at his fall, angerly said, Madam, pray **admire not** at this, for my Horse always stumbles when he meets a Whore; she sharply reply'd, have a care then Sir, you do not meet your Wife, for then you will certainly break your neck. (HC, *Penny Merriments*, '*Canterbury Tales*', 1687: B1v.–B2r.)

The grammar in (5) is also much closer to Present-day English than in (4). The intensifying adverb *terribly* ends in -*ly*, and the negative clause *you do not meet* contains *do*. But there is also evidence to suggest that the passage is not Present-day English: the auxiliary *do* is optional, as it is not used in *admire not*. Similarly, the construction (*fell*) *a laughing* contains the relic of a preposition ('on'), found in some regional dialects today. Grammatical differences like this do not prevent the modern reader from grasping the syntactic relations in an Early Modern English text. More problems may be created by semantic and lexical differences, which can obscure its meaning.

1.2.4 Meaning changes

We have been looking at examples of what we might call 'humorous' texts, but the word *humour* itself has meant different things at different times. Originally a technical term, it goes back to ancient and medieval physiology, and denotes any of the four basic fluids of the body (blood, phlegm, choler and melancholy or black bile). These were believed to determine a person's physical condition and mental disposition. As a focal cultural concept the term acquired many derived senses, including, according to the *Oxford English Dictionary*, 'inclination or liking, esp. one having no apparent ground or reason; mere fancy, whim, caprice, freak, vagary'. *Humour* became so popular in the late sixteenth and early seventeenth centuries that its abuse was made fun of in 'humours comedies', for instance, in Ben Jonson's *Every Man in his Humour* and *Every Man out of his Humour*. In *The Merry Wives*, Corporal Nym's excessive use of the term is illustrated by *the humor of lying, in some humors, the humour'd Letter* and *the humour of bread and cheese* in (3).

The early sixteenth-century text in (4) contains other culture-bound and obsolete expressions. A *noble* was an English gold coin, which by 1550 was worth six shillings and eight pence. At the time *curate* could be used to refer to any clergyman with the spiritual charge of a parish; here it is used synonymously with *parson*. In *letted hys speche* the verb *letted* does not mean 'allowed' but its opposite, 'hindered', 'impeded'. The word continues life in tennis, and in the legal phrase *without let or hindrance*. In (4) the merchant's speech begins with *Iwys* (*iwis*), an adverb meaning 'certainly', 'indeed', 'truly'. It can be traced to an Old English word meaning 'certain', although some sources also relate to *I wot* ('I know').

The late seventeenth-century extract in (5) contains fewer obsolete words. The *Oxford English Dictionary* tells us that the adverb *angerly*, meaning 'with anger or resentment', was replaced by *angrily* from the seventeenth century onwards. The politeness marker *pray* in **pray admire not at this** goes back to *I pray you* (or *thee*), and corresponds to Present-day English *please*. The verb *admire*, which to a modern reader may look out of place in (5), has gained positive senses in the course of time, meaning gazing on with pleasure or holding in respect. Here it retains its original sense 'wonder or marvel at', 'be surprised'.

1.3 Evolution and standardisation

Some scholars date the beginning of the Early Modern English period from the effects of the Great Vowel Shift (GVS), a series of sound changes affecting the quality of all Middle English long vowels. The first changes had taken place by 1500, and the shift was completed in the south in the course of the seventeenth century. As a result of the GVS, words like *meet* and *see*, Middle English /meːt/ and /seː/, for instance, came to be pronounced /miːt/ and /siː/. As these examples show, Present-day English spelling does not reflect the outcome of the sound change because the principles of spelling conventions had largely been fixed before the chain shift was completed. Changes in the various domains of language clearly proceed at different rates.

Language historians are prepared to accept the fact that named periods such as Middle and Early Modern English are delimited by conventional but basically arbitrary cut-off points. The major linguistic developments of a period may coincide part of the time, but need not last throughout the period, or form the beginning and end-points for it. The Early Modern English period is marked by a number of such developments, both gains and losses. In grammar, the auxiliary *do* is introduced to negative and interrogative clauses; the relative pronoun *which* is replaced by *who* with reference to humans; and the second-person singular pronoun *thou* and multiple negation disappear from most contexts of use. Some of these changes are shared by most varieties of English, while others have come to be associated with the rise of the standard language. A case in point in the second category is the demise of multiple negation, constructions like *they **didn't** find **nothing*** giving way to *they didn't find **anything***.

In general, it is helpful to think of *standardisation* as a sociolinguistic process which expands the range of the uses to which a language is put, but restricts its internal variability. The usage of a given region or group of people becomes the basis for these new uses, especially in writing. As the process advances, this variety also undergoes at least some degree of conscious elaboration, and is codified in grammar books and dictionaries. The final stage of the process of standardisation typically involves the prescription of 'correct usage'.

In English the process of standardisation began in the late Middle Ages with the expansion of the vernacular to many functions earlier occupied by French or Latin. The first nationwide attempts to regularise English spelling came in the fifteenth century. However, as we saw in example (4), above, texts displayed a great deal of spelling variation even in the sixteenth century. Although they may have had few distinct regional dialect features, they do not fulfil the modern norm of each word having a single spelling. Even Shakespeare spelled his name in several different ways. However, in order to make written English better suited for new uses in the Early Modern period, for instance, as the language of learning, it also became subject to some conscious elaboration. This is particularly obvious in the lexical borrowing from Latin, either directly or via French.

The end point of the Early Modern period has often been put at 1700, before the standardisation of English entered its extensive codification stage in the eighteenth century. Or it has been pushed to 1800, by which time the standardisation process had reached the peak of its prescriptive stage. Many norms of Standard English were explicitly codified in such eighteenth-century landmarks as Samuel Johnson's *A Dictionary of the*

English Language (1755) and Robert Lowth's *A Short Introduction to English Grammar* (1762). There was also a growing body of literature in the eighteenth century stigmatising certain pronunciations. They included /h/-dropping in words beginning with this sound such as *hand* and *heart*.

However, viewing Early Modern English simply as a period leading up to Standard English does not do justice to the linguistic reality of the time. This book will describe the English language between 1500 and 1700. The variety to be focused on could be called 'General English' following Alexander Gil, an early seventeenth-century schoolmaster, who will be discussed in Chapter 2. This General English may be characterised as the common variety that people from different regional backgrounds oriented to especially in writing. It was variable and changed over time. As such, it provided the basis not only for the standard but also for many non-standard mainstream dialects of Present-day English.

1.4 Summary

The texts analysed in this chapter suggest two main conclusions. First, the Shakespeare extract is more recognisably modern than the 'merry tale' dating from the early sixteenth century. This is particularly evident in spelling and grammar. Similarly, the late seventeenth-century jest proves more modern than *The Merry Wives*. Taking these texts as representative of the language between 1500 and 1700, the traditional Early Modern English period, we can conclude that Early Modern English evolves with time. Just as some Middle English texts come closer to Old English than others, earlier Early Modern English texts are relatively more archaic than later texts.

The second conclusion is that there does not appear to be any one set of linguistic features that could be used to mark the beginning and the end of the Early Modern period. Spelling, pronunciation, grammar and vocabulary do not change hand in hand but evolve at varying paces. This will become more evident in the following chapters, which will discuss the major linguistic changes in Early Modern English showing just *how* different it was from Middle English, on the one hand, and from Present-day English, on the other.

Note

1. Lass's features encompass the following: (1) root-initial accent, and (2) at least three distinct vowel qualities in weak inflectional syllables (see section 9.5 of this book); (3) a dual; (4) grammatical gender (see section 6.3.1); (5) four vowel-grades in certain strong verbs (section

7.1.2); (6) distinct dative in at least some nouns; (7) inflected definite article; (8) adjective inflection (section 7.2.1); (9) infinitive suffix; and (10) person and number marking on the verb (section 7.1.1) (Lass 2000: 26). Few of the features are found in Early Modern English; for Middle English, see Horobin and Smith's *An Introduction to Middle English* (2002).

Exercises

1. Review and find examples of the linguistic features and developments used in this chapter in characterising the Early Modern English period.

2. Go back to Nym's usage of *humour* in (3), and compare it with the senses of the noun *humour* and the adjective *humoured* in the complete edition of *The Oxford English Dictionary* (OED). Which of the OED senses are illustrated by (3)? Alternatively, compare Nym's usage with that of other Shakespearian characters in *The Harvard Concordance to Shakespeare* (Spevack 1973). How representative of Shakespeare in general is Nym's range of meanings?

3. Some of the words in the 'merry tale' in (4) may be unrecognisable merely because of their non-standard spelling. One way to overcome the problem of spelling variation is first to skim through the text and then reread it word by word. When you come across any unfamiliar words or meanings, look them up in *The Oxford English Dictionary*, using either the complete printed edition or the electronic version. How many words did you need to look up?

Further reading

There are only two book-length introductions to Early Modern English, Charles Barber's (1976, 2nd edn 1997) and Manfred Görlach's (1991). Both describe the same period, 1500–1700. Barber's book is detailed but highly readable, and it draws its illustrative material mostly from literary texts. Görlach's more concise but no less informative volume contains an appendix with a wide selection of Early Modern English texts of various kinds. There are several introductions to the language of Shakespeare, among them Hussey (1992), Adamson et al. (eds) (2001), Blake (2002) and Hope (2003). *The Harvard Concordance to Shakespeare* compiled by Spevack (1973) is a useful tool for looking up Shakespeare's words in their dramatic contexts.

Volume 3 of *The Cambridge History of the English Language* (1999, ed. Roger Lass), is a comprehensive reference work covering English from 1476 to 1776. It contains chapters on orthography and punctuation

(Salmon), phonology and morphology (Lass), syntax (Rissanen), lexis and semantics (Nevalainen), regional and social variation (Görlach) and literary language (Adamson). Collections of research articles on Early Modern English include those edited by Salmon and Burness (1987), Kastovsky (1994) and Rydén et al. (1998).

2 Sources for the study of Early Modern English

2.1 Range of evidence

Early Modern English provides the modern student with much ampler textual and metalinguistic materials than any earlier period. For the first time, we have contemporary analyses of the pronunciation, grammar and vocabulary of English, and can read descriptions of its regional and social varieties in teaching manuals and textbooks of different kinds. All this information is valuable in that it gives the modern reader and researcher a window on the period and its linguistic concerns.

Precious though this contemporary metalinguistic evidence may be, it is not enough to provide a detailed picture of the language of the period. There are several reasons for this. The material that has come down to us is often insufficient, or it may be conflicting and therefore hard to interpret, especially where phonetic details are concerned. Early Modern English pronunciation was typically discussed by teachers and spelling reformers, who did not have the use of an International Phonetic Alphabet, but had to devise their own transcription conventions. In an age without recording equipment and no one standard pronunciation this was a great challenge.

The problem faced by early English grammarians was quite the opposite. There was a grammar model that was in common use throughout Europe, the traditional teaching grammar based on Latin. It was this model that Early Modern English schoolboys were taught in grammar schools, where they studied the classical languages. It also provided the framework that English grammarians followed in their first descriptions of their mother tongue. But as English was grammatically different from an inflectional language like Latin, the exercise often proved artificial, introducing non-existent categories and contrasts into descriptions of English, while at the same time omitting relevant grammatical distinctions. Section 2.3 will discuss and illustrate some of these grammars. Latin also contributed prominently to the first monolingual English dictionaries. The majority of them were so-called 'hard-word' dictionaries designed for the benefit of those who did not have access to a classical education. They reflected the worries concerning the suitability of English as an official and literary language. These linguistic anxieties will be discussed in Chapters 3 and 4.

It is obvious that to supplement these contemporary accounts, language historians will have to study evidence on actual language use. And as was shown in Chapter 1, it is not enough to consult just one author from the middle of the period, for we need both earlier and later material to place the language in a broader context. This *diachronic* evidence on language use provides the background against which linguists can evaluate long-term historical trends in English, and modern readers can appreciate the creativity of their favourite Elizabethan, Jacobean or Restoration authors. Section 2.4 will briefly illustrate the wide range of Early Modern English texts that have come down to us. Some electronic selections of these texts (*corpora*) available for the study of the changing language of the period will be introduced in section 2.5.

2.2 Comments on varieties of English

In their *Introduction to Middle English*, Horobin and Smith note that the Middle English period is 'notoriously the time when linguistic variation is fully reflected in the written mode' (2002: 33). The reason for this was that, with the dominant roles assumed by French and Latin in public life, the vernacular was parochially rather than regionally or nationally focused. In fact, scribes copying texts could modify them to reflect local dialect use. This was no longer true of Early Modern English, which had gained most of the earlier functions of Latin and French. With the rapid standardisation of spelling in the sixteenth and seventeenth centuries, fewer and fewer texts are localisable.

Despite the regularisation of spelling especially in the printed word, variation of course does not disappear from Early Modern English and its daily use. A wealth of contemporary commentary on linguistic variability emerges in various kinds of writing such as teaching grammars, works on rhetoric and early proposals for spelling reforms. Although most of these accounts are neither comprehensive nor systematic, they reveal the wide spread of regional and social differentiation in Early Modern English.

In *Logonomia Anglica* (1619), written in Latin, the London schoolmaster Alexander Gil briefly describes the principal dialects of Early Modern English: the General, the Northern, the Southern, the Eastern, the Western and the Poetic (see Figure 2.1). Except for the General and

Figure 2.1 The dialects of Early Modern English according to Gil (1619).

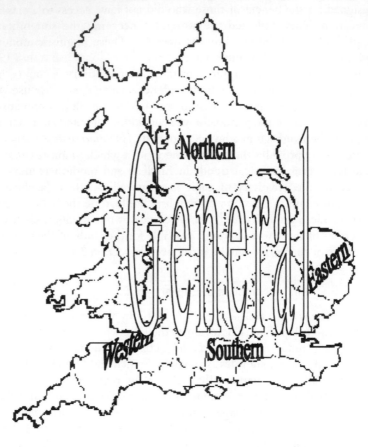

the Poetic, similar distinctions appear in Middle English dialectology (Horobin and Smith 2002: 51). The differences between Early Modern English dialects relevant to Gil's concern as a spelling reformer are largely to do with pronunciation, but he also takes up some morphological features. These include *gang* for *go* and *hez* for *hath* in the Northern dialect, which Gil, himself originally a Lincolnshire man, considers the purest and most ancient among English dialects. Two of the features he uses to distinguish the Southern dialect from the rest are the use of *Ich* for *I*, as in *cham* for *I am*, and initial fricative voicing, the use of /z/ for /s/ (*zing* for *sing*) and of /v/ for /f/ (*vill* for *fill*).

Eastern dialect speakers are said to attenuate their speech, diphthongs in particular. Gil also associates this feature with affected female speakers he calls Mopseys (see section 9.3.2, below). The Western dialect differs most from the rest having, for instance, /i/ prefixed to past participles (*ifror* for *frozen; idu* for *done*). It is condemned by Gil as having 'the most barbarous flavour, particularly if you listen to rustic people from Somerset, for it is easily possible to doubt whether they are speaking English or some foreign language' (1619 [English transl. 1972: 103]).

Gil makes a division between dialects spoken by country people and those spoken by persons of genteel and cultured upbringing, who are said to have 'but one universal speech, both in pronunciation and meaning'. However, the pronunciation of this General dialect (*Communis dialectus*) is also 'sometimes ambiguous' (1619 [1972: 104]). While Gil strongly advises against learners imitating country dialects, this is permitted in the Poetic dialect – especially if the poet opts for the Northern variety. Variable though it was, the language of the educated upper ranks hence served as the model for Gil's introduction to English. The textbook also advocated a more speech-like spelling system, which may have had some impact on the spelling of Gil's most famous pupil, the poet John Milton.

Gil is not the only textbook writer to discuss social and regional variation in Early Modern English in terms of prestige. An often quoted passage on prestige language comes from *The Arte of English Poesie* (1589: 120–1), a handbook of rhetoric specially intended for young poets in search of patronage. The author, George Puttenham, encourages his readers to imitate 'the vsuall speach of the Court, and that of London and the shires lying about London within lx. myles, and not much aboue'. A poet should specifically aim at the language of 'the better brought vp sort'. It has the aristocratic authority of the Royal Court while at the same time being, according to Puttenham, 'the most vsuall of all his countrey'; it also has aesthetic value ('well sounding'), and is deemed suitable as a literary medium (i.e. *English Poesie*).

An earlier proposal to the same effect was advanced in the mid-sixteenth century by John Hart, the London orthoepist, who was faced with the problem of finding a consistent basis for a spelling reform. He hoped to develop a spelling system that would reflect the spoken language of the time better than the conservative norm which was becoming fixed in the sixteenth century. Like Puttenham after him, in his *Methode* (1570: IIIb) Hart looks up to 'the Court and London, where the flower of the English tongue is vsed'. Hart's spelling reform will be introduced in Chapter 3.

Puttenham (1589) contrasts this language of 'the better brought vp sort' with country dialects referring to their speakers as the 'poore rusticall or vnciull people'. He discourages the aspiring poet from imitating their speech, as well as the speech of 'of a craftes man or carter, or other of the inferiour sort, though he be inhabitant or bred in the best towne and Citie of this Realme'. As the least worthy of all dialects, Gil (1619) mentions thieves' cant, which he denounces as a 'venomous and disgusting ulcer of our nation . . . For that detestable scum of wandering vagabonds speak no proper dialect but a cant jargon which no punishment by law will ever repress, until its proponents are crucified by the magistrates, acting under a public edict' (1619 [1972: 104]).

2.3 Early grammars

It may sound paradoxical that many of the English grammars published between 1500 and 1700 were written in Latin. A number of them were, however, intended for foreign learners of English, and it was therefore appropriate to use Latin, which was still the international *lingua franca* of learning. English learners mostly studied the structure of their mother tongue in order to be able to master Latin. Latin grammatical categories constituted the basis for language learning throughout Europe at the time, and they were also followed by English grammarians and educationalists. So Roger Ascham, a tutor of Princess Elizabeth, takes it for granted that '[a]fter the childe hath learned perfectlie the eight partes of speach, let him then learne the right ioyning togither of substantiues with adiectiues, the nowne with the verbe, the relatiue with the antecedent' (*The Scholemaster* 1570: 1). The original is reproduced in Figure 2.2.

Not that there were that many English grammars published in the Early Modern period. Only four appeared in the sixteenth century, and thirty-two in the seventeenth. This is a modest crop in comparison with the over 200 grammars that appeared in the eighteenth century (listed by Michael 1970: 588–94). The early grammars also differed from their eighteenth-century counterparts in that they were not overtly prescriptive. They described the grammar of English using Latin-derived categories but did not label some forms or structures as 'correct' and dismiss others as 'incorrect' – or in eighteenth-century terms, 'affected', 'barbarous', 'censurable', 'improper', 'inadmissible', 'vulgar', and so on. Early Modern English school grammars professed to exclude regional dialects but did not rule out variation in the General dialect. Clearly it was more diffuse than the Late Modern standard variety codified in eighteenth-century grammars.

In fact, the first English grammar to be compiled in English, William Bullokar's *Pamphlet for Grammar* (1586), gives alternative realisations for

Figure 2.2 *The Scholemaster* by Roger Ascham (1570).

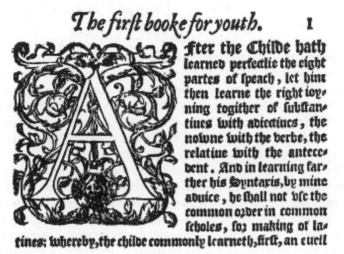

forms undergoing change at the time. Let us consider three examples that illustrate Bullokar's recognition of linguistic variability. When he lists the forms of *Indicative mood present-tense singular* with the verb *love*, he gives two second-person plural pronouns, *ye* and *you* (Bullokar 1586: 25):

(1) *I lou*   Plural   *we*
    thu louest   *ye, or you*   *lou.*
    he loueth   *they*

In Bullokar's time the object form *you* was in the process of spreading to the subject function and had already replaced *ye* in many contexts. The traditional subject form *ye* was preserved in literary and religious texts such as the Bible. Bullokar records both but does not suggest that one of them is better or more grammatical than the other. He also inserts this note into the margin: *Est, and eth, are formatiue endings of the present tense: eth sometime changed into z.* This observation documents another ongoing change. The third-person singular suffix -*(e)th* was receding and being replaced by -*s*, often pronounced, as Bullokar indicates, as voiced /z/. The incoming form was originally a northern feature (note Gil's *hez* for *hath*, above), but it also came to be adopted by southerners in the course of time. The third example of Bullokar's tolerance of variability comes from his discussion of the present-tense forms of the verb *be*.

(2) $\left.\begin{cases} I\ am \\ thu\ art \\ he\ iz \end{cases}\right.$ Plural $\left.\begin{cases} we \\ ye\ or \\ they \end{cases}\right.$ be or ar.

Here, too, he provides alternative forms, *be* or *are* for the present-tense indicative plural. *Be* is the southern dialect variant used indiscriminately for the indicative and the subjunctive mood, whereas *are* was originally a northern dialect form only used in the indicative, never in the subjunctive. By Bullokar's time it had already become common in the south, but as with *ye* and *-eth*, discussed above, the traditional forms were still found both in formal writing and in many rural dialects.

Bullokar is conservative in that he systematically records the second-person singular pronoun *thou*, which was receding from general use at the time. *Thou* was current in regional dialects but, in most cases where one person was being addressed, *you* would have occurred in the General dialect. However, in grammar books the distinct singular form was also needed for practical purposes: the students were taught to recognise its position in the pronominal paradigm, which helped them classify the corresponding Latin form.

The emphasis of early English grammars was indeed on the recognition and classification of forms, the traditional parts-of-speech analysis. The exercise appended to Paul Greaves's *Grammatica Anglicana* (1594) gives an idea of this time-honoured approach to grammar teaching (3). The English text to be analysed is a verse riddle. Part of the analysis, given in Latin, is translated into English on p. 19.

(3) *I was as small as any straw,*
  When first I gan to grow:
  Then growing to a riper age,
  My shape was changed so.
  Then tooke they me out of my place
  Where I was borne and bred:
  And when they saw my shape was turnd,
  They straight cut of my head.
  This being done, then did I drinke,
  Whereby such force I had,
  I made sworne brethren deadly foes,
  I made true lovers glad.
  And this did I, and ten times more,
  I have and must doe still:
  Yet did I nothing of my selfe,
  But all against my will.

I] primitive demonstrative pronoun: sg. *I, Me*, pl. *We, Us.*

Was] anomalous preterite form. *Am*, first person, singular number.

As] native adverb.

Small] singular adjective, singular by virtue of the noun: no formal number distinction made.

Straw] singular noun, pl. *strawes*, *e* inserted for ease of utterance.

When] native adverb.

First] enumerative adverb, from a numeral adjective.

Gan] anomalous preterite form of *gin.*

To] Prepositive adverb attached to the infinitive.

Grow] present infinitive with the anomalous preterite *Grew.*

Then] native adverb.

Growing] present participle of *grow* formed by adding *ing.*

To] prepositive adverb attached to the noun *age.*

A] singular cardinal numeral, in speech always preceding a consonant.

Riper] comparative grade of *ripe*, the superlative of which is *ripest.*

Age] singular noun: pl. *Ages.*

My] derived pronoun, always attached to a noun.

Changed] regular thematic form of *change* formed by adding *d.*

So] native adverb . . .

(Greaves 1594: 59–61)

It is obvious that Greaves does not always make the same part-of-speech distinctions as would be made today. His category of adverb, for instance, is broader comprising conjunctions (*when, as*) and prepositions (*to*). He does not have the article category – Latin does not need it – but analyses *a* etymologically as a numeral (*one*). On the other hand, he distinguishes, by virtue of the number of the noun, between singular and plural adjectives (*small*), although there is no distinction in English. These analyses and the terminology they are couched in go back to earlier and contemporary Latin grammars, which were by no means uniform either.

By the end of the Early Modern English period many of the analyses and terms familiar to us have found their place in English grammars. So John Wallis's *Grammatica Linguae Anglicanae* (1653) refers to such parts of speech as articles (*a/the*), prepositions and conjunctions, and no longer assigns case and number distinctions to English adjectives.

Both Greaves and Wallis wrote their grammars with foreign learners in mind. Wallis's grammar is often remembered by its *shall* and *will* rule, which specifies that, to indicate the future (*prediction*), *shall* is used in the first person and *will* in the second and third person. But in his account of tense forms of irregular verbs, for instance, Wallis falls in with the variationist tradition and provides alternative expressions evaluating them merely in terms of frequency ('less commonly', 'less often'). He allows as many as three past tense forms for verbs such as *abide* (*abode*, *abidd*, *abided*) and *thrive* (*throve*, *thrive*, *thrived*) (1653: 107–8). By comparison, the anomalous preterites listed by Greaves (1594: 19) show no more than two forms. Evidence like this suggests that variation had not necessarily decreased with time in the General dialect described by sixteenth- and seventeenth-century school grammars.

2.4 Texts and genres

The testimony of the early grammars is valuable as it provides us with Early Modern English speakers' accounts of their own language – albeit with an overlay of Latin. But people rarely speak and write exactly like grammar books, even if these tried to cater for alternative ways of saying the same thing. The wide range of texts available from the Early Modern period reveals that people used much more varied language than could be captured by traditional school grammars modelled on Latin. This is not to say that every gentleman, let alone gentlewoman, would have mastered the full range of contemporary kinds of writing. This was obviously not the case, but thanks to the advent of printing and improved literacy, the selection of Early Modern English texts and genres is considerably broader than the textual evidence for Middle English.

Looking at Early Modern English textual resources, the modern reader will, however, soon notice that not all the genres we are accustomed to were available in the Renaissance and Restoration. The novel is one of them. The merry tales that served as illustrations in Chapter 1 represent one of the older genres of fiction that preceded the modern novel, which appeared in the late seventeenth century. Letter-writing in turn provided the format for epistolary novels such as Samuel Richardson's *Pamela* (1740). The traditional genre of letter-writing also influenced new non-literary genres. They include newspapers, which owe a great deal to other contemporary news media, particularly to chronicles, newsbooks and pamphlets. However, it was newsletters commissioned by eminent individuals that probably contributed most to the genre both in England and on the Continent. The first official English newspaper, *The London Gazette*, started to appear in the 1660s.

In the sixteenth and seventeenth centuries domestic news passed by word of mouth or private letter more quickly than it could be printed. Before the appearance of the first printed news-sheets in England in the 1620s and even long after this, foreign news was also circulated in manuscript newsletters. The newsletter genre can be illustrated by the

Newdigate Newsletters dating from the last quarter of the seventeenth and beginning of the eighteenth century. Most of them were addressed to Sir Richard Newdigate in Warwickshire. They were issued three times a week by the Secretary of State's office and dealt with foreign and domestic matters. The extract in (4), from the 8th of January 1675, confirms the modern media studies truism that bad news makes good news.

(4) The King of Poland desireing a nearer Correspondence **wth** this Crowne then has bene formerly, & haveing sent Over to desire his **Maty** to be godfather to his Daughter, his **Maty** was prepareing to send an Envoy ExtraOrdnary thither to stand for him, when the last post brought news **ye** young Princess was dead.

The Indians in new England Continue to doe **ye** English much mischeife, Even to that degree that all trade is in a maner interupted, and by a vessell arived yesterday from Virginia Wee have advice that **ye** Indians had risen there likewise to **ye** Number of 5 or 600 & that they had kil**d** severall of **ye** English.

(ICAME, *Newdigate Newsletters*, 8 January 1675: 273)

The modern editor of the originally hand-written letters has retained the original spelling and punctuation. He has lowered but not expanded the superscripts, which represent abbreviations, spelling *wth* for *w^{th}* ('with'), *Maty* for *Ma^{ty}* ('Majesty', referring to Charles II), *ye* for *y^e* ('the'), and *kild* for *kil^d* ('killed'). Abbreviations like these go back to the writing conventions of medieval manuscripts. As we will see in Chapter 3, the official newsletter in (4) resembles private letters of the period in that its spelling is less regular than the orthography of printed publications. But handwritten and printed texts also share many late seventeenth-century conventions, including the frequent use of capitals for a rhetorical effect to mark content words, typically nouns, but also other parts of speech.

The evidence provided by irregular spellings has been used by scholars trying to determine how the writer might have pronounced a particular word. However, as pointed out earlier, much of the written data became so regularised in the Early Modern period that it is not easy to draw any hard and fast conclusions on the actual pronunciation of texts on the basis of spelling. Although not fully standardised, the spelling of the letter in (4) tells us as much, or as little, about how it might have been pronounced at the time as any Present-day text. But we do have private letters and other documents written by barely literate people, whose spelling is so irregular that something may be inferred about their pronunciation. More texts like this can be found from the sixteenth century than from the seventeenth.

The description of phonological variation in Early Modern English also owes a good deal to drama. Representations of dialectal speech can be found in comedies and tragedies throughout the Early Modern period. The south-western variety disparaged by Gil (1619) was in fact a stock-in-trade stage dialect in early comedies. The dialogue between Hodge and Tib in (5) is drawn from *Gammer Gurton's Needle*, a verse play from the mid-sixteenth century assigned to William Stevenson.

> (5)   *Hodge.* **Cham** agast by the masse, **ich** wot not what to do
> **Chad** nede blesse me well before **ich** go them to
> Perchaunce some felon sprit may haunt our house indeed,
> And then **chwere** but a noddy to venter where **cha** no neede,
>
> *Tib.* **Cham** worse then mad by the masse to be at this staye
> **Cham** chyd, **cham** blamd, and beaton all **thoures** on the daye,
> Lamed and hunger storued, prycked vp all in Jagges
> Hauyng no patch to hyde my backe, saue a few rotten ragges.
>
> *Hodge.* I say Tyb, if thou be Tyb, as I trow sure thou bee,
> What deuyll make a doe is this, betweene our dame and thee.
> (HC, *Gammer Gurtons Nedle*, c. 1560: 7–8)

Most of the time Gammer Gurton's servants Hodge and Tib both use the south-western pronoun *ich* for *I*, and contracted forms such as *cham* for *ich am*, *chad* for *ich had* and *chwere* for *ich were*. The fact that this is stage dialect becomes evident when Hodge reverts to the use of the first-person form *I* in collocations such as *I say* and *I trow*.

The passage also contains the speechlike form *thoures*, a contraction for *the hours*. Colloquial contractions such as this are not a specifically south-western feature, but occur commonly throughout the country, and will be discussed in more detail in section 9.5. Moreover, not all typical south-western features are recorded by the author of *Gammer Gurton's Needle*. If Gil (1619) is to be trusted, /i/ continued to be prefixed to past participles in this dialect area. Tyb's speech contains several instances of past participles (*chyd* 'chided', *blamd* 'blamed', *beaton* 'beaten', *lamed*, *storued* 'starved', *prycked vp*), but none of them takes the old prefix. The author may have omitted it because he could be sure that the stage dialect was recognised as such by the audience – or that actors could be trusted to imitate it well enough.

The omission could also have been dictated by the verse form of the play, which could not accommodate any extra syllables. Be that as it may, a verse play and verse in general can often provide the linguist with some information on words that must have sounded alike. The rhymes in (5) include *do*: *to*, (*in*)*deed*: *need*, *staye*: *daye*, *Jagges*: *ragges*, and *bee*: *thee*. They hold no surprises for the modern reader but neither do they give much indication as to the actual pronunciation of the vowel sounds in question. Is the vowel in *do* and *to* an /o/ or an /u/ sound, for instance? Or are *deed* and *need* pronounced with an /eː/ or an /iː/? In questions like this contemporary orthoepic evidence is needed.

At least one detail in (5) may strike the modern reader as grammatically odd. This is the second line ending in *them to* ('to them'), where the preposition *to* has been postponed to fill up the rhyme position. Syntactic liberties like this make verse texts generally less well suited for the study of historical syntax than prose texts.

2.5 Corpus resources

One way to study the changes that have taken place in earlier English is to make use of electronic text collections which have been specifically compiled for that purpose. A number of Early Modern English corpora are available. Some of them cover the entire period, others just parts of it; some contain many different genres (multi-genre corpora), while others consist of only one genre such as personal correspondence or pamphlets (single-genre corpora). An advantage in using an electronic corpus is the easy access it provides to the structure and use of the language, and to changes that take place in them across time. As processes of language change are typically gradual, corpora also provide the information of frequency of use needed for making diachronic comparisons.

Below at (6) is a computer-generated list (*concordance*) which presents all instances of the two subject forms, *ye* and *you*, of the pronoun *you* that Roger Ascham uses in a passage of *The Scholemaster* (1570), one of the texts included in the *Helsinki Corpus of English Texts* (HC). Each line begins with information encoded in the electronic text and contains the period of writing (E1=1500–1570), text category (IS=secular instruction), and page reference to the source text. This line concordance shows that the author preferred the traditional subject form *ye* in seven cases out of nine, but also used the incoming *you* twice. Evidence like this confirms the variable usage recorded by Bullokar in (1) and (2), above.

(6)	E1 IS/ 183:	him, and saie here	ye	do well. For I assure
	E1 IS/ 184:	the best allurements	ye	can, to encorage him to
	E1 IS/ 214:	your selfe, whether	ye	wold, that your owne son
	E1 IS/ 215:	in aige, if euer	ye	thinke to cum to this
	E1 IS/ 215:	I am cum vnto, lesse	ye	meete either with
	E1 IS/ 215:	But will	ye	see, a fit Similitude of

El IS/ 215:   to worthinesse, if euer **ye** purpose they shall cum
El IS/ 214: som happines: and whan **you** do consider, what
El IS/ 215:   in yougthe, I was, as **you** ar now: and I had

This section will introduce the *Helsinki Corpus*, which has provided a much used resource for exploring Early Modern English over the last couple of decades. Many of the illustrations found in this book come from this corpus compiled at the University of Helsinki. The Early Modern English section of the corpus divides the period into three subperiods, 1500–1570, 1570–1640 and 1640–1710. This division is arbitrary but makes it possible to compare the language in successive stretches of time. As suggested in Chapter 1, there were important linguistic differences between the first half of the sixteenth century, Shakespeare's time around the turn of the seventeenth century, and the second half of that century.

The *Helsinki Corpus* is sensitive to genre continuity across time in that basically the same set of genres has been sampled for the corpus from each Early Modern English subperiod. Altogether fifteen genres have been included in the corpus, ranging from some of the most formal kinds of writing available such as the *Statutes of the Realm* to the most informal kinds such as comedy. Most of the genres are public and appeared in print (autobiographies, handbooks, philosophical and educational treatises and histories) but some private writings such as personal correspondence and diaries were also available from the whole period. Most of the HC genres represent typical written communication, the printed ones in particular, but language composed for oral delivery (plays and sermons) was also gathered, as was material originally produced in the spoken medium (trial proceedings). In sum, the corpus consists of texts that represent different communicative needs and situations. A mini-corpus consisting of short extracts sampled from the sources of the HC is provided in Appendix 1, and some longer texts are given in Appendix 2.

However, as the Bible translations in Chapter 1 show, it may sometimes be enough to study just one genre to see how English was transformed with time. Let us make a comparison of the three Early Modern English translations of Boethius's *De Consolatione Philosophiae* included in the HC. That several translations of this medieval philosophical treatise were made available within a space of 200 years might be a reflection of the rapid pace of linguistic change at the time. Another reason for multiple translations could be the Renaissance fascination with classical texts. A large body of Latin and Greek texts were translated into English after the introduction of the printing press. The Boethius excerpts in (7) come from the translations made by George Colville (1556), Queen Elizabeth I (1593) and Richard Preston (1695). Colville's and Preston's versions both appeared in print, but Queen Elizabeth's work was not originally intended for publication.

(7a) Hetherto it suffyseth that I haue shewed the maner and forme, of false **felicite** or **blessednes**, which if thou beholdeste perfetlye, it restythe to declare from henceforthe, whyche is the very true **felicitie**.

BOE: Truelye I do se, that **ryches** cannot be satisfied with suffysaunce, nor **power** wyth **kyngedomes**, nor reuerence with **dygnities**, not **glory** with nobilitie or gentles, nor myrth with **pleasures**. (HC, George Colville (trans.), *Boethius*, 1556: 68)

(7b) 'Hitherto hit sufficeth to shewe the forme of gileful **felicitie**, wiche if you Clirely beholde, the ordar than must be to shewe you the true.' 'Yea I se,' quoth I, 'that ynough suffiseth not **riches**, nor **Power king-domes**, nor honor **dignities**, nor **glory** the prising, nor Joy the **plea-sure**.' (HC, Elizabeth I (trans.), *Boethius*, 1593: 57–58)

(7c) Let it suffice that I have hitherto described the Form of counterfeit **Happiness**: So that if thou considerest well, my Method will lead me to give to thee a perfect Draught of the true.

Boet. I now see plainly that Men cannot arrive at a full Satisfaction by **Riches**, nor at **Power** by enjoying Principalities or **Kingdoms**, nor at Esteem and Reverence by the Accession of **Dignities**, nor at Nobility by **Glory**, nor at true Joy by carnal **Pleasures**. (HC, Richard Preston (trans.), *Boethius*, 1695: 124)

It is immediately evident that the three renderings of the same passage do not match in terms of length and phrasing. Queen Elizabeth's manu-script version is by far the shortest and most compact. It is therefore interesting to find that the three translations nevertheless share a number of words. Looking at nouns we find *riches, power, kingdoms, dignities, glory* and *pleasure(s)* in all three. This suggests that no major changes had taken place in the use of these words in contexts like this over time.

But there are also items on which the translators differ. What Colville translates with two words as *felicite or blessednes* is rendered as *felicitie* by Queen Elizabeth and *happiness* by Preston. *Blessedness* and *happiness* are original English words formed by means of the ending *-ness*, while *felic-ity* is a Middle English loan from French. *Blessedness* also goes back to Middle English but *happiness* is more recent, first attested in this sense in the sixteenth century. Elizabeth prefers *felicity*, but occasionally uses *blessedness* and *happiness*. Although hardly conclusive, this evidence suggests that *blessedness* was gradually being replaced by *happiness* as the English equivalent of the Latin *felicitas*. *Blessedness* clearly betrays its religious origins ('the state of being blessed, especially with Divine favour' according to the OED), while *happiness* goes back to the more secular adjective *happy* meaning 'fortunate' and 'prosperous'.

2.6 Summary

This chapter has introduced some data sources available for the study of Early Modern English. Discussions of the vernacular appear in a variety of sixteenth- and seventeenth-century works ranging from handbooks of rhetoric to school grammars and spelling guides. Looking at sixteenth- and seventeenth-century grammars as evidence of Early Modern English usage, we find that many of them, especially the earlier ones, are too closely tied to their Latin models to do full justice to the structure of English. Throughout the Early Modern period, grammars nevertheless give much valuable information on spelling, pronunciation, word classes and word-formation before the era of prescriptive grammar. Along with other teaching materials used at the time, they also provide contemporary views on regional and social variation of the vernacular.

The ultimate source of information on actual usage is of course the wealth of Early Modern texts that have survived. They cover a wide spectrum of written genres from the more formal kinds, such as statutes and official documents down to informal, such as jests, comedies and private letters. Many new forms of writing were introduced in the course of the Early Modern period, including newspapers. The study of textual variation will give us an idea of the variability and richness of the linguistic expression of the time. Reflecting the widening range of genres in the Early Modern period, electronic corpora such as the *Helsinki Corpus of English Texts* have proved useful tools for this work.

Exercises

1. Discuss and illustrate contemporary commentators' views on the range of regional and social variation in Early Modern English (section 2.2).

2. Ute Dons (2004) compares Early Modern grammarians' accounts with the actual linguistic usage of the period as revealed by studies of text corpora. She finds that despite the Latin descriptive models they impose on English, the grammars contain a large number of accurate

statements on usage, and her conclusion is that beginning with the first grammars 'the authors developed a growing awareness of typically English features' (2004: 252). Find support for Dons's findings by reviewing the evidence presented in section 2.3.

3. Compare the spelling of the late seventeenth-century newsletter in (4) in section 2.4 with one of the printed texts (play, travelogue, sermon or educational treatise) in Appendix 1 from the same period. In particular, discuss the use of abbreviations and capitalisation in the two extracts.

4. What Colville translates as *myrth* at the end of his Boethius translation in (7a) is rendered as *joy* by Queen Elizabeth (7b) and Richard Preston (7c). Use evidence from the OED to find reasons for the translators' different choices. Consider particularly the chronological span given for sense 2 of *joy* and senses 1 of 4 of *mirth*.

Further reading and study resources

The English grammatical tradition from the sixteenth to the eighteenth century is discussed by Michael (1970), Vorlat (1975) and Dons (2004), and the Latin impact on English grammar and style by Partridge (1969). *A Dictionary of English Normative Grammar 1700–1800* (Sundby *et al.*, 1991) records the eighteenth-century prescriptive reaction to Early Modern English usage with sources such as the King James Bible (1611) and Shakespeare heading the list of quotations of 'bad grammar'.

The electronic *Helsinki Corpus of English Texts* is available from the Oxford Text Archive (OTA at http://ota.ahds.ac.uk) and the International Computer Archive of Modern and Medieval English (ICAME, Bergen, Norway, at http://helmer.aksis.uib.no/icame.html). They also provide the corpus manual online; it specifies the coding conventions and lists all the source texts with bibliographical details (Kytö (comp) 1996). For more information on the Early Modern English section of the corpus, see also Nevalainen and Raumolin-Brunberg (1993). The Scots counterpart of the HC is the *Helsinki Corpus of Older Scots* (HCOS; Meurman-Solin 1995), also available from the ICAME and the OTA.

Corpora consisting of many genres such as the *Helsinki Corpus* provide information on usage-based differences in language variation and change. This information can be supplemented by corpora that enable the study of user-based variation. One such resource, compiled for the study of Early Modern English in its social context, is the *Corpus of Early English Correspondence* (CEEC; see Nevalainen and Raumolin-Brunberg 2003, Nurmi 1999). The ICAME and the OTA distribute a sampler version of this corpus (CEECS). The *Newdigate Newsletters*, compiled by

Philip Hines, Jr, are also available from these data archives, as is *The Lampeter Corpus of Early Modern English Tracts*, which contains tracts and pamphlets published between 1640 and 1740. It can also be accessed online at http://www.tu-chemnitz.de/phil/english/chairs/linguist/real/independent/lampeter/lamphome.htm.

In this book, examples cited from electronic corpora are indicated by their abbreviations (HC, CEEC, etc.) in the reference line, which in addition gives the writer, title and date of the text. Further details are provided by the corpus manuals. The editions cited that are still in copyright are also listed in the reference section at the end of this book.

The growing number of electronic data sources for the study of Early Modern English ranges from the *Michigan Early Modern English Materials* (http://www.hti.umich.edu/m/memem/) (Bailey et al. 1975) to the commercially available Chadwyck-Healey *Literature Collections* (LION) (http://collections.chadwyck.co.uk/) and *Early English Books Online* databases (EEBO) (http://eebo.chadwyck.com/home). The large *Oxford English Dictionary* quotations database, 2.4 million quotations altogether, can also be searched for words, like a corpus. For dictionaries, see Chapter 4, and for the use of corpora in language study, for example, Biber et al. (1998).

3 Towards a standard language

3.1 Middle English legacy

Standard language has been defined as one that shows maximal variation in function and minimal variation in form. Maximal variation of function means that a language community uses its language for all purposes, both locally and nationwide. In the late Middle Ages this was not the case with England, as the country was not ruled in English but in French and Latin. They were used as prestige (*High*) varieties, while English was mostly used locally and at home as an informal (*Low*) variety. In sociolinguistic terms the situation was one of *diglossia*: co-occurring languages served different functions in the community.

3.1.1 Chancery Standard

In 1066, the Norman Conquest had replaced English with French as the medium of administrative, literary and religious writings in England. Latin, as the international *lingua franca* throughout the Middle Ages, continued to be used in law and the administration and as the language of the Catholic Church and higher education. For the first two centuries after the Conquest, English was mostly used for local purposes and as a spoken variety, but in the fourteenth century it began to gain ground supralocally as a written medium. In the early fifteenth century, French considerably declined in official use. The kind of English that replaced it as the first nationwide written model was the idiom of the government documents issued by the King's writing offices at Westminster, including the Privy Seal and Signet Offices and the Chancery.

When English began to be written more widely in the late Middle Ages, it was done by men with little training in writing their mother tongue. The royal clerks working in the central administration were accustomed to writing in Latin and French, which had established written forms, while dialectal variation was freely expressed in English.

The English written by these clerks represented southern usage, but it also displayed many northern dialect features. The language of the documents they produced is often referred to as the *Chancery Standard*. It falls short of the standard-language requirement of 'minimal variation in form', but does represent a move towards it.

Even the commonest words could be spelled in a number of different ways in Middle English. This vast amount of orthographic variation is recorded in *A Linguistic Atlas of Late Mediaeval English* (LALME; McIntosh et al. 1986). A word such as *through* could have anything up to 500 variant forms ranging from *thurgh*, *thorough* and *þorowe* to barely recognisable forms such as *drowgȝ*, *yhurght*, *trghug* and *trowffe* (Smith 1996: 68, 76). Compared with this, the fourteen spellings of *through* found in a corpus of fifteenth-century official documents shows a considerable reduction (Fisher et al. 1984: 392).

Although these official documents were linguistically quite variable, they achieved two goals. First, they recognised English as a medium in which the nation could be governed, and so conferred upon the vernacular a role as a High variety on a par with Latin and French. Secondly, in producing documents in English, the Westminster writing offices came to select the kind of English that was to serve as a *reference dialect* in the process of standardisation of the written language. However, had the city of York continued as the seat of government, as it had been some hundred years earlier, the choice would probably have been in favour of a northern reference variety rather than a southern one.

3.1.2 Early printing

Chancery texts spread in manuscript form. It was not until towards the end of the fifteenth century that the printing press was introduced into England when William Caxton set up his press at Westminster in 1476. Being able to reproduce a text in exactly the same form any number of times spreads written-language norms widely and efficiently. In this way the printing press became a vehicle for language standardisation.

Although English had been in administrative use well over fifty years before the introduction of the printing press, it was not fixed enough to satisfy the needs of the printer and translator. Caxton complains about the variability of English in a famous passage in the preface to *Eneydos*, his translation of Virgil's *Aeneid*, in 1490. Part of it is cited in (1), where he also considers, but rejects, the idea of using earlier English as his model.

> (1)   and fayn wolde I satysfye euery man / and so to doo toke an olde boke
>   and redde therin / and certaynly the englysshe was so rude and brood

that I coude not wele vnderstande it. And also my lorde abbot of west-
mynster ded do shewe to me late certayn euydences wryton in olde
englysshe for to reduce it in to our englysshe now vsid / And certaynly
it was wreton in suche wyse that it was more lyke to dutche than
englysshe I coude not reduce ne brynge it to be vnderstonden / And
certaynly our langage now vsed varyeth ferre from that. whiche was
vsed and spoken whan I was borne / For we englysshe men / ben borne
vnder the domynacyon of the mone. whiche is neuer stedfaste / but
euer wauerynge / wexynge one season / and waneth & dyscreaseth
another season / And that comyn englysshe that is spoken in one shyre
varyeth from a nother. (Reprinted in Bolton 1966: 2)

Caxton finds that English has changed beyond recognition in the course
of time: the early texts he had read were 'more lyke to dutche [German]
than englysshe'. He was nearly seventy when he wrote the preface, and
notes that English has also changed during his lifetime. And judging by
the range of regional variation, the language would certainly continue
to change. Caxton solves the problem of variability by steering a middle
course between the 'ouer rude' and the 'curyous' ('intricate', 'subtle'),
and concludes that 'the comyn termes that be dayli vsed' are easiest to
understand.

As Caxton would have predicted, the English language changed a
great deal between 1500 and 1700; but dialect levelling also took place.
Most of the texts preserved from this period form part of a mainstream
variety, which cannot be readily localised. This is particularly true of
spelling, which is easier to standardise than most other aspects of language such as pronunciation. But as modern readers would not accept
any of the texts in Chapter 1 as fully standard, there is more to the
process of standardisation than the selection of a reference dialect and
the cutting of optional variation – Caxton's 'over-rude' and 'curious'. As
vernaculars continue to vary and change, standards have to be fixed. This
is where *codification* comes into the picture. Standard norms are codified
gradually through the production of spelling books, dictionaries and
grammars.

3.2 Fixing the form: spelling standardisation

3.2.1 Layers of history

When Old English began to be written down, the Latin alphabet was not
ideally suited for the purpose. Matters were complicated after the
Norman Conquest with the application of French spelling conventions

to English. As spelling systems also tend to be conservative, they often record earlier stages of the language. In Caxton's spelling in (1) there are a number of words ending in <e> that reflect the stage of English that had inflectional endings, first reduced to -*e* and later on to zero (*wolde, toke, olde, boke*). This meant that historically disyllabic words had become monosyllabic. When the vowel in these words was long, the final silent <e> was later often reinterpreted to mark its length.

Whatever phonemic fit there was between spelling and pronunciation in the fifteenth and sixteenth centuries was further upset by ongoing sound changes in the southern pronunciation system. This is significant because the first national models for spelling, the royal writing offices and early printing presses, were based in the capital and referred to the southern rather than the northern dialects for spelling norms. What is more, those responsible for creating norms for the written language were familiar with French and Latin and could turn to these languages for spelling authority. Recreating connections between words borrowed from Latin and French, they introduced etymological spellings into English. Many of these found a permanent place in print, and subsequently in the dictionary of Standard English, including *debt* (< ME *dette*, L *dēbitum*), *doubt* (< ME *doute(n)*; L *dubitāre*), *indict* (< ME *endite(n)*; L **indictāre*), and *victuals* (< ME *vitailes*, L *victuālia*). In some cases etymological spellings led to spelling pronunciations, as in *adventure* (< ME *aventur*; L *adventūra*) and *advice* (< ME *avis*; L **advīsum*) (Salmon 1999: 28).

3.2.2 The sixteenth century: reform or custom?

Fixing English spelling in its present-day form was virtually completed in print by about 1650. The process was astoundingly rapid if we look at the Caxton excerpt in (1), and bear in mind that even the basic principles of spelling continued to be debated by orthoepists and grammarians in the sixteenth century. There was no agreement as to whether English spelling ought to be *phonemic*, reflecting pronunciation as closely as possibly, or *logographic*, distinguishing words pronounced alike (*homophones*) by spelling them differently. The phonemic principle is followed in (1) in a number of short words such as *and, man, not* and *it*. But Modern English also follows the logographic principle in keeping apart the spelling of *flower* and *flour*, *rain* and *reign*, *scene* and *seen*, and many others.

In the sixteenth century there were many advocates of a more phonemic spelling system, most notably, John Cheke, Thomas Smith, John Hart and William Bullokar. Hart first presented his proposal in *The Opening of the Unreasonable Writing of Our Inglish Toung* (1551) and almost two decades later in *An Orthographie* (1569) and *A Methode* (1570). He drew attention to the many spelling practices that did not match the pronunciation of his time: superfluous letters occurred in words such as *authorite* (the letter <h>), *condempned* (<p>), *eight* (<g>) and *people* (<o>), and unnecessary variation was found in homophones like *sunne* 'sun' and *sonne* 'son'.

Hart criticised the use of the silent word-final <e> to indicate a long preceding vowel in words like *spake*, *take* and *before*, whereas in words spelled with double consonants (as in *sunne* and *sonne*), this final <e> created an extra syllable. He was also troubled by the use of one letter to represent two different sounds, <g>, for instance, representing /g/ in *geve* ('give') but /dʒ/ in *gentle* (some of the letter symbols he proposed are shown in Figure 3.1). Hart ended his list of spelling 'vices' by noting that in words like *fable* and *circle* the final <e> was misplaced, since the words were pronounced *fabel* and *cirkel* (Hart 1551 [1955: 122–3]).

Although it did have an impact on some contemporaries, Hart's proposal for a spelling reform failed to gain general acceptance. Among those who put it into practice was Thomas Whythorne, a musician and courtier, who wrote his autobiography (c. 1576) following some, but not all, of Hart's phonemic conventions. The passage in (2) is an excerpt from Whythorne. Many of the principles he adopts from Hart (1569) have to do with how to represent vowel length.

(2)   Heer yow shall vnderstand by þe way, þat I did kovenant with þe said ʒentilman and wẏf, þat I wold be with þem but by þe week, and also þat I wold be ywzed az A frend, and not A servant, whervpon þei did not only allow mee to sitt at þeir ṭabull, but also at þeir own mes, az long az þer weṛ not any to okkiupy þe room and plạs þat weṛ A great deall my betterz. (Thomas Whythorne, *The Autobiography of Thomas Whythorne*, c. 1576 [1961: 94])

Whythorne refrains from using the final <e> to indicate a long preceding vowel but marks long vowels either by doubling them (*heer, week, mee, room*), or by using a dot above or underneath the vowel (*wẏf, ṭabull, weṛ, plạs*), as suggested by Hart. He deviates from Hart in that he doubles a consonant in order to signal that the preceding vowel is short (*shall, sitt, ṭabull, okkiupy, betterz*). Whythorne also continues the tradition of using the letter thorn <þ> for the voiced initial fricative (in *þe* 'the', *þat* 'that', *þei* 'they', *þem* 'them', *þer* 'there', and so on). But he follows Hart in writing the letter yogh <ʒ> for /dʒ/ (*ʒentilman*); <z> instead of <s> to indicate the voiced sibilant (*az, ywzed* 'used', *betterz*); and <k> instead of <c> for the velar stop /k/ (*kovenant, okkiupy*).

Figure 3.1 Some consonant symbols proposed by John Hart (1570: Bij).

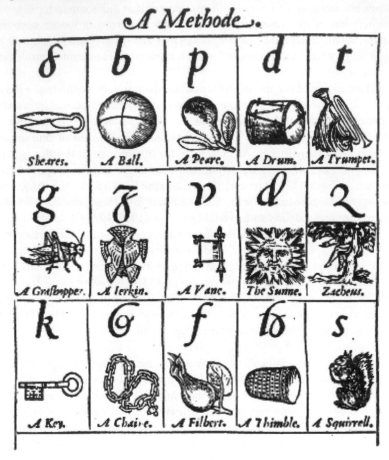

Whythorne does not, however, follow Hart as far as his *punctuation* is concerned (unlike the spelling, the punctuation of (2) is not fully original but some marks were added by the editor of the manuscript, who wanted to make it easier for a modern reader to follow). Like many writers at the time, Whythorne made use of commas and full stops, but mostly commas, without much capitalisation.

Hart (1551 [1955: 157–61]) introduces seven basic punctuation marks related to the structure and functions of sentences: the comma (*incisum*), the colon (a *joint*), the full stop or period (the *point*), the question mark (the *asker*), the exclamation mark (the *wonderer*), parentheses or round brackets (the *clozer*) and square brackets (the *note*). Except for the greater frequency of the colon, their functions come close to the way they are understood today. The *point*, for instance, is said to mark the end of a full sentence.

The apostrophe, however, (the *tourner*) is discussed under accents rather than punctuation (*pointing*) because it signals the omission of a vowel. Hart illustrates it with 'writ th'articles plaine t'understand: for write the articles plaine to understand' (1551 [1955: 153]). It is noteworthy that the apostrophe does not mark the possessive -*s*, which is a later innovation. Hart's system of punctuation largely went back to the continental models introduced into England in the early sixteenth century. The system was adopted with some modifications by printers and educators in the following decades.

Despite its supporters, the general idea of a spelling reform based on the phonemic principle met with staunch opposition. Richard Mulcaster, an influential London schoolmaster, denounced the idea in his *Elementarie*, a popular guide for teachers which he published in 1582. His reasons for doing so were practical: there was too much variation in speech, especially in regional dialects, to recommend pronunciation as a basis for orthography. Appealing to Quintilian and other classical authors, Mulcaster relied on established usage to provide the basic guidelines for spelling, maintaining that '[t]he vse & *custom* of our cuntric, hath allredic chosen a kinde of penning, wherein she hath set down hir relligion, hir lawes, hir priuat and publik dealings' (1582: 98).

Mulcaster bases his principles of spelling on the traditional alphabet and suggests that the use of each letter of the alphabet should be governed by general orthographical rules. He basically rejects the use of 'superfluous' letters and so, for instance, the doubling of consonants to indicate a short preceding vowel in words like *putt*, *grubb* and *ledd* for *put*, *grub* and *led*. But while he approves the use of double <oo> in *soon*, he prefers the use of final <e> to mark vowel length in *seme* ('seem') and *sene* ('seen'). Final <e> is also found useful in distinguishing word pairs such as *made* and *mad* and *stripe* and *strip*. To homophones such as *light* he assigns the same spelling (1582: 111, 118).

Mulcaster also expressed the need for a monolingual English dictionary to supply the 'right writing' of words. To provide his readers with something to go by, he appended to his book an alphabetical spelling list of more than 8,000 common English words. Over half of them are identical with modern standard spelling. If we discard the common convention of using <i> for both <i> and <j>, and <v> word-initially and <u> medially for both the vowel and the consonant, the proportion is even higher (Barber 1997: 86).

3.2.3 The seventeenth century: public and private

In the seventeenth century, the advocates of a phonemic spelling system lost their battle against custom. Textbooks for reading and spelling like Mulcaster's had a direct impact on how English orthography was taught and learned. Edmund Coote's *The English Schoole-Maister* (1596), which contained a spelling-book with exercises and a hard-word dictionary, was one of the most popular textbooks of the time and went through more than fifty editions in the seventeenth century. It is, however, telling of the process of spelling standardisation that Coote's spellings do not always match with Mulcaster's. Coote writes, for instance, *seem* and *seen*, and not *seme* and *sene*.

By 1650, the printed word was already characterised by a remarkable degree of orthographic uniformity. A fixed spelling system had become an area of technical specialisation in the printing trade, and these print-ers' standards were imposed on manuscripts to be published. There are only a few conventions to distinguish late seventeenth-century print from ours. They include the frequent use of contracted forms of past tense and past participle verb forms (*'d* for *-ed*); of the spelling *-ick* for the suffix *-ic* and *-or* for British English *-our*; and of capitalisation to signal content words, especially nouns, often for expressive foreground-ing (see the Preston extract (7c) in Chapter 2).

Needless to say, even after the standardisation of the printed word, a good deal of spelling variation continues to be found in private writings, letters and diaries. These private texts display both phonemic variation and idiosyncratic spellings. Besides, what looks like an idiosyncratic spelling can in some cases be a phonemic realisation of a regional pro-nunciation of a word. We may recall that part of the argument in favour of traditional spellings had been regional and social variation in English pronunciation. For this reason Alexander Gil, the promoter of the General dialect, argued that 'writing will have to conform not to the pro-nunciation of ploughmen, working-girls, and river-men, but to that used by learned and refined men in their speech and writing' (1619 [1972: 87]).

The text excerpt in (3) comes from a letter written in 1686 by Jane Pinney to her husband the Reverend John Pinney. The Pinneys lived in Dorset.

(3) My dare
heare yo^u see what yor dafter doe write that shee have . . . yor
writetinges, that is true but what doe thay sicknifie unles old pimer had
given him mony in consederation of it yo^u most com and take bands of
her and her housban if yo^u can get thim to give yo^u bands be fore it

runes to fare; for shee is wth childe and how can you neglecke such
athinge as this what doe yoᵘ knō how god may deale wth her such alit-
till cretuare and old to, and then her husband shall arest yoᵘ for all yoᵘ
are worth. (HC, Jane Pinney, 1686: PINNEY 39)

Many traditional spelling features are found in Jane Pinney's letter. She
frequently indicates a long vowel or diphthong in monosyllabic words
by a word-final <e>. Apart from such modern standard spellings as *write*,
true, *take* (*be*)*fore* and *are*, she extends this convention to *dare* ('dear'), *doe*,
shee, *fare* ('far'), *childe* and *deale*. She writes a single consonant before a
short preceding vowel in many cases such as *what*, *that*, *is*, *but*, *what*, *had*,
it, *get* and *god* and, non-standardly, in *unles* and *com*. But the two conventions cross, for instance, in (*a*)*thinge* and *shall*, which both contain a short
medial vowel.

Phrase-level phonological processes may be at work in Pinney
running the unstressed indefinite article *a* after *such* together with the
following word in *athinge* and *alittle*. There are also a number of spellings
– mostly content words – that look simply idiosyncratic, including
writetinges for 'writings' and *sicknifie* for 'signify'. However, the idiosyn-
cratic-looking form *dafter* for 'daughter' was quite common in the seventeenth century. It can be related to other words like *laughter* and *slaughter*,
today both are spelled like *daughter*, but only *slaughter* rhymes with it.
Laughter by contrast is now pronounced like Jane Pinney and many of her
contemporaries must have pronounced *daughter* (see 9.4).

3.3 Elaborating the functions: borrowing and codification

As we saw in Chapter 2, the range of genres available from the Early
Modern period is considerably wider than from Middle English. English
had developed into a High variety, and was in the process of becoming
the only one for most kinds of communication. This widening functional
range called for conscious elaboration of the language. It also gave rise
to linguistic insecurity as many speakers and writers had doubts whether,
in William Caxton's words, this 'rude and symple englyssh' would have
the literary qualities needed for the expansion (Jones 1953 [1966: 5]).

The influence of classical models, particularly Latin, was all-
pervasive throughout the Early Modern period, especially in the sixteenth and early seventeenth century. Latin provided a repository of
technical terminology for new domains of use, such as science. Writers
recognised the Renaissance literary ideal of lexical variation known as
copiousness or *copy* (*copia verborum*), which encouraged borrowing for the
sake of lexical richness. The ideals of classical rhetoric were followed in

matters of style and grammar. So the classical Latin sentence was often 'imitated so far as (and sometimes beyond what) the mechanics of the English sentence would permit' (Gordon 1980: 77).

3.3.1 Elaboration and insecurity

The functions of English became more elaborate in the sixteenth century although it had yet to make its way into higher education and scholarship. The Reformation radically changed the language of the Church from Latin into English as the Bible and the *Book of Common Prayer* were published in the vernacular in the sixteenth century. The Bible was now for the first time translated not from Latin but from the original biblical languages, Hebrew and Greek.

William Tyndale, whose translation of the New Testament appeared in a revised form in 1534, opted for basic structural simplicity in order to be understood by ordinary people. In an age of religious turmoil, however, he was charged with supposed heresies in his choice of religious terms. These included the Greek *ekklesia*, traditionally translated as *church* but rendered by Tyndale as *congregation*, which was said to misrepresent the institutional aspect of the Church. He was eventually arrested on a heresy charge and burnt at the stake, but his work was to become of foundational value to later biblical translations, in particular, the *Authorised Version* or King James Bible (1611). Many of Tyndale's terms including *Jehovah, Passover, scapegoat* and *atonement* have lived on, as have his phrases, such as *the powers that be* (Romans 13), *the salt of the earth* (Matthew 5), and *a law unto themselves* (Romans 2) (McGrath 2001: 75–9). The *Authorised Version* also contains Tyndale's version of Genesis 1: *Let there be light: and there was light.*

While many philosophers and scientists including Francis Bacon (1561–1626) and Isaac Newton (1642–1727) continued to publish in Latin (Newton's *Philosophiae Naturalis Principia Mathematica* (1687), for example), the vernacular was also increasingly used for literary and scientific purposes in translations and original works. In both cases, writers were faced with the same problem as Caxton and Tyndale of finding English expressions and terms for those familiar from other languages.

The extract in (4) from *The First Principles of Geometrie* (1551), the first scientific treatise of geometry in English, shows how Robert Record coped with the problem. He first gives the Greek and Latin equivalents for a term, but then makes a point of translating it into English. Had his terms been accepted, we would now be talking about *threelike triangles* instead of equilateral ones. However, as Chapter 4 will show, coining native words for foreign terms was not taken for granted at the time.

(4) There is also an other distinction of the names of triangles, according to
their sides, whiche other [either] be all equal as in the figure E, and that
the Greekes doo call *Isopleuron*, and Latine men *aequilaterium*: and in
english it may be called a *threlike triangle*, other els [or else] two sydes bee
equall and the thyrd vnequall, which the Greekes call *Isosceles*, the Latine
men *aequicurio*, and in english *tweyleke* may they be called, as in G, H, and
K. (HC, Robert Record, *The First Principles of Geometrie*, 1551: B3r.)

The issue of how to enrich English was part of sixteenth-century
writers' concern for the adequacy of their mother tongue as a literary
medium. To meet the needs of creating English vocabulary for new concepts and new registers, masses of words were borrowed from the classical languages either directly or via French. These words were not
directly accessible to those without classical education – not everybody
glossed their loan words as carefully as Record did his native coinages in
(4). This situation created linguistic insecurity among the less educated,
including the majority of women.

The remedy lay in monolingual English dictionaries. The first in the
long line of these 'hard-word' dictionaries was compiled by Robert
Cawdrey, and appeared in 1604. Its title begins: *A Table Alphabeticall, con-
teyning and teaching the true writing, and vnderstanding of hard vsuall English
wordes, borrowed from the Hebrew, Greeke, Latine, or French, &c.* On the title
page Cawdrey specifies his intended readership by noting that the words
were:

gathered for the benefit & helpe of Ladies, Gentlewomen, or any other vnskil-
full persons, Wherby they may the more easilie and better vnderstand many
hard English wordes, which they shall heare or read in Scriptures, Sermons, or
elswhere, and also be made able to vse the same aptly themselues.

In practice, Cawdrey relied heavily on the list of hard words published
by Coote in *The English Schoole-Maister* (1596).

Classical borrowing became the subject of a public controversy in the
sixteenth century as new loan words were frequently introduced not
only because of necessity but also for the purpose of ostentation. These
learned neologisms, known as *inkhorn terms*, were debated and their
affected use was ridiculed by Shakespeare, Jonson and other contemporary writers. This strand of borrowing continued well into the seventeenth century in popular publications such as *The English Dictionarie*
(1623) compiled by Henry Cockeram. He anglicised a large number of
the Latin entries in two contemporary Latin–English dictionaries and
introduced more 'refined and elegant' terms for ordinary words. He

proposed that *length* could be replaced by *Longitude* or *Proceritie, friend-ship* by *Amity, fruitfulness* by *Fertility* or *Fecundity* – and *happiness* by *Felicity*.

In this intellectual climate it is no wonder that classical models influ-enced the grammar of many sixteenth-century humanist writers: Thomas More (today best known for his Latin work *Utopia*), John North, the translator of Plutarch, Richard Hooker (*Of the Lawes of Ecclesiasticall Politie*), and many more. This classical influence continued in the seven-teenth century in authors like John Milton. The illustration in (5) of a complex sentence modelled on Latin comes from Thomas Elyot's edu-cational treatise *The Boke Named the Gouernour* (1531).

> (5) And therfore **the great kynge Alexander**, whan he had vainquisshed Ilion, where some tyme was set the moste noble citie of Troy, beinge demaunded of one if he wold se the harpe of Paris Alexander, who rauisshed Helene, **he** therat gentilly smilyng, **answered that** it was nat the thyng that he moche desired, **but that** he had rather se the harpe of Achilles, wherto he sange, nat the illecebrous dilectations of Venus, but the valiaunt actes and noble affaires of excellent princis. (HC, Thomas Elyot, *The Boke Named the Gouernour*, 1531: 26)

Heavy subordination and a delayed verb are hallmarks of these *periodic* sentences. In (5) the subject (*the great kynge Alexander*) and the verb (*answered*) are separated by subordinate clauses, some further embedded in others. The subject is resumed by the pronoun *he* closer to the verb. The verb takes an object, which consists of two co-ordinate clauses (*that ... but that*). Other clauses with intricate parallels are embedded in them. The use of parallel and antithetical structures of this kind was encour-aged in sixteenth-century expositions of rhetoric.

Classical influence declined towards the end of the seventeenth century, as stylistic ideals changed after the Restoration. Some critics, however, continued to express doubts about the potential of English to achieve the highest literary standards. Joseph Addison wrote about Milton's *Paradise Lost* in *The Spectator* (1712) as follows:

> (6) if his *Paradise Lost* falls short of the *Æneid* or *Iliad* ... it proceeds rather from the Fault of the Language in which it is written, than from any Defect of Genius in the Author. So Divine a Poem in *English*, is like a stately Palace built of Brick. (Görlach 1991: 40)

Critical voices like this suggest that the struggle of English for a High language status was not completely won by the end of the Early Modern period.

3.3.2 Codification

Unlike word-lists appended to reading manuals, which listed common words, dictionaries contained definitions of 'hard vsuall English wordes', and so contributed to the *codification* of the borrowed lexical element in English (see 4.1.3). The number and volume of monolingual English dictionaries grew in the course of the seventeenth century, and came to encompass a wide range of contemporary lexical variation with the spelling to a large extent standardised. This was taken for granted, for instance, by Edward Phillips, the compiler of *The New World of English Words* (1658). In his preface he noted that: 'As for Orthography, it will not be requisite to say any more of it, then may conduce to the Readers direction in the finding out of words.' The only thing he thought needed mentioning was his use of <e> to render both Latin <æ> and <œ>, as in <preparation> for <præparation> and <Amebean> for <Amœbæan>.

In contrast to orthography, as we saw in Chapter 2, the codification of English grammar only gained momentum in the eighteenth century. But the ideology of standardisation itself goes back to the preceding centuries. One side of it was manifest in the linguistic insecurity and talk about the inadequacy of the vernacular associated with the functional expansion of the language. At this point, the norm that English was compared with was supplied by Latin and other continental languages with a longer and more versatile literary tradition.

The first complaints about the 'misuse' of the English language began to appear in the late seventeenth century. Combined with improved literacy and the expanding functions of the vernacular, language change had a major role to play in raising the public awareness of linguistic variability. After the restoration of the monarchy in 1660, writers often compare the English of earlier authors with their own. John Dryden (1631–1700), for instance, discusses 'incorrect' constructions in Ben Jonson writing less than a hundred years earlier, and takes great care in revising his own usage according to the stylistic ideals of the Restoration. To Dryden is attributed, for instance, the rule that a sentence should never end with a preposition.

Unlike French or Italian, Standard English was not codified by a language academy, although a number of appeals to that effect were made after the Restoration. The Royal Society, a national scientific society founded in 1662, even set up a special committee in 1664 with the aim of improving the English language. The committee included John Dryden, John Evelyn and other men of letters, but it failed to produce any concrete results. The same fate befell all later appeals for an English counterpart of the French Academy, including Jonathan Swift's famous public letter, *A Proposal for Correcting, Improving and Ascertaining the English Tongue* (1712). In the eighteenth century the legislative task of how English should be used was left to private individuals – compilers and publishers of prescriptive grammars, dictionaries, textbooks and usage guides.

3.4 Summary

Two major processes of standardisation took place in the Early Modern period. First, the vernacular was extended to practically all domains of language use. This functional expansion of English to administrative, religious, scholarly and literary contexts led to its linguistic elaboration, especially to lexical intake from foreign prestige languages such as Latin. The other development associated with the written language was the regularisation of spelling. After the first, highly variable national models in the fifteenth century and various proposals for spelling reforms in the sixteenth, spelling was largely regularised in the printed word by the mid-seventeenth century following, in Mulcaster's words, the 'use and custom' of the country rather than its speech.

The explicit codification of Standard English grammar was left to the eighteenth century, as were the prescriptive practices associated with standard-language ideology. For these reasons, the Early Modern English to be described in the following chapters is not a fixed standard language but a more diffuse mainstream variety of English, Gil's General dialect, based on southern and central rather than northern regional dialects. It is unlocalisable in its written form, and lexically and stylistically enriched by foreign models, yet grammatically to a large extent unregulated by prescriptive forces.

Exercises

1. Rewrite the Caxton passage in (1) using modern spelling, punctuation and capitalisation.

(Some words in the passage may need glossing: *fayn* = *fain* 'gladly', 'willingly'; *shewe* 'show'; *euydences* = *evidences* 'documents'; *dutche* = *Dutch* 'German'; *ne* 'nor'. Notice Caxton's alternation between forms like *another* and *a nother*, *wryton* and *wreton* ('written'), and *vsid* and *vsed* ('used'). But his spelling of *englysshe* ('English') is consistent throughout the passage!)

2. Compare a passage in a modern edition of a Shakespeare play with the same passage in the First Folio of 1623 noting the various ways in

which the spelling and punctuation have been modernised for the benefit of the modern reader. You may use the First Folio passages in example 3 in Chapter 1, and example 1 in Chapter 4. How consistent is the spelling in the First Folio? What are the major differences in the punctuation of the First Folio and the modern edition?

(In many modern editions the *Merry Wives* passage cited in Chapter 1 can be found in act 2, scene 1, and the *Hamlet* passage cited in Chapter 4, in act 2, scene 2.)

3. Calculate an 'index of modernity' by comparing the spelling of any two texts in the two Appendices. In order to be able to compare your findings directly, begin by marking off a passage containing exactly 100 words in each text. Then, for each text, draw up a list of all the word-forms whose spelling differs from Present-day English in the 100-word passage. How many such spellings did you find? Discuss your findings in terms of the types of text you selected (early *v.* late, formal *v.* informal, originally printed *v.* written by hand, and so on).

4. When Daniel Defoe made his proposal for an English counterpart of the French Academy 'to polish and refine the *English* Tongue' he wrote:

'[i]nto this Society should be admitted none but Persons Eminent for Learning, and yet none, or but very few, whose Business or Trade was Learning . . . In short, There should be room in this Society for neither *Clergyman, Physician,* or *Lawyer*' (1697: 234). Find evidence in section 3.3 of developments in Early Modern English that might have prompted Defoe's negative opinion of the learned professions.

Further reading

The language situation in medieval England is described by Horobin and Smith (2002, Chap. 3), and the local written norms of Middle English by Samuels (1963). *An Anthology of Chancery English*, compiled by Fisher et al. (1984), illustrates fifteenth-century government usage; for a critical evaluation of the 'Chancery Standard', see Benskin (2004). The Caxton passage in (1) is reprinted, for example, in Bolton (1966: 2), an anthology of primary material from 1490–1839.

For the process of spelling standardisation, see Scragg (1974) and Salmon (1999). Attitudes to Early Modern English are discussed by Jones (1953) and Barber (1997, Chap. 2); both of them give comprehensive accounts of the Inkhorn Controversy, which revolved around the introduction of loan words in the sixteenth and early seventeenth centuries. The events and processes leading up to the King James Bible are described by McGrath (2001). Adamson (1999) traces the various strands of classical influence in Early Modern literary language. For a discussion of the ideology of standardisation, see Milroy and Milroy (1999: 24–46), and for further developments in the Late Modern period, Görlach (2001).

4 Old words and loan words

4.1 Continuity and change

As we have seen, one of the chief linguistic concerns in the Early Modern English period was vocabulary building. But how did the speakers' and writers' conscious efforts to enrich the vernacular affect the basic lexical resources of their language? In this chapter we will adopt a broader view of Early Modern English lexis by placing these innovations against the backdrop of the more enduring patterns of vocabulary in the language. This 'common core' will be related to the ways in which the English word stock grew by means of borrowing from other languages in the Early Modern era. Chapter 5 will in turn focus on the language-internal aspects of vocabulary enrichment, word-formation and meaning change. Let us begin, however, by taking a closer look at the notion of *vocabulary* as an inventory of *words*.

4.1.1 Counting words

People sometimes think that the impact of a book or the greatness of an author can be measured by the number of words used. Before this notion can be adequately examined, we need to know what is actually meant by a *word*. A fundamental distinction can be made between a word as an element in a text (*word 1*), an entity separated from other words by spaces, and a word as an entry in a dictionary (*word 2*). Words as text elements are the building blocks out of which phrases and sentences are constructed. Taken together, Shakespeare's works consist of 884,647 words of this kind or, more specifically, *word-form tokens*, since the most frequent ones are of course repeated hundreds of times.

Using the simple orthographic definition given above and excluding the names of the speakers, there are altogether fifty-seven words in the text extract in (1). However, as many of them occur more than once – *my*, *he* and *words* three times – we can count each word-form only once to get

45

the number of different *word-form types*, which amount to forty-seven. In all, Shakespeare's works contain only 29,066 word-form types (Spevack 1973: v).

> (1) *Pol.* How say you by that? Still harping on my daughter: yet he knew me not at first; he said I was a Fishmonger: he is farre gone, farre gone: and truly in my youth, I suffred much extreamity for loue: very neere this. Ile speake to him againe. What do you read my Lord?
>
> *Ham.* Words, words, words.
> (William Shakespeare, *Hamlet*, 1623: 2.2)

Words are listed in dictionaries because they have different meanings. A dictionary entry (*word 2*) is headed by the *base form* of a word. Since all the different forms of a word have the same basic meaning, they are not listed as separate entries. So dictionaries include, for instance, separate entries for the noun and verb *love* and the adjective *lovely*, but not for the plural form of the noun (*loves*), or the past tense (*loved*) or past participle forms (*loved*) of the verb, or the comparative and superlative forms of the adjective (*lovelier, loveliest*). The term *lexeme* is used to distinguish a word as a meaning-bearing unit from the grammatical scatter of its word-forms. A dictionary therefore supplies its readers with an inventory of the *lexemes* of a language, which is what we think of when talking about new words being added to a language. When no confusion arises, *word* will be used in this technical sense in this chapter.

It is estimated that Shakespeare's works contain roughly 17,750 lexemes (Scheler 1982: 89). Vocabulary statistics obviously crucially depend on what is counted, but as far as lexemes are concerned, some scholars have calculated that while Chaucer's vocabulary equals that of the *Authorised Version* of the Bible, it is only one third of Shakespeare's (Burnley 1983: 133). There may be various reasons for this, beginning with the lexical elaboration of the English language in the Early Modern period discussed in the previous chapter. We could also argue for an author's lexical creativity by referring to the number of *new words* (*neologisms*) he or she has coined. This is, however, trickier than counting word forms and lexemes in an author's works.

In order to know what is new we need to have an idea of the contents of the lexicon of the language in the period under study. Unfortunately there is to date no Early Modern English Dictionary to match the Old and Middle English Dictionaries. *The Oxford English Dictionary* remains the principal source for Early Modern English but its coverage is uneven at times. Shakespeare's works have been almost exhaustively mined for the OED while Thomas Nashe's and Thomas Wyatt's, for instance, have not (Schäfer 1980: 65). This complicates studies of lexical creativity in the past. At the same time it is true that few writers, especially before the electronic age, have had access to anything like a full lexical inventory of their mother tongue. Some words may therefore have been coined more than once.

Despite all these reservations, few scholars would doubt that Shakespeare indeed stands out as an exceptionally innovative writer. Some estimate that out of the 17,000–18,000 lexeme types attested in the Shakespeare corpus, one in ten was coined by him (Shipley 1977: 28)! This count includes *compound words* which consist of two or more lexemes that form a new one. The parts of a compound are normally recognisable, such as *love* and *letter* in *love-letter*, defined by the OED as 'a letter written by a lover to the beloved, and expressing amatory sentiments'. But since compounds have a meaning of their own, not always predictable from their parts, they are listed in dictionaries. Established compounds such as *fishmonger* in (1) are often written solid as one word.

As the number of new words attributed to Shakespeare looks very high, we must assume that many of them followed well-established patterns – otherwise they would not have been comprehensible to theatre-goers in Elizabethan and Jacobean London. One of his favourite new adjective patterns is the type *green-eyed (jealousy)*, *marble-hearted (fiend)*. The word-formation resource Shakespeare exploits here is *affixation*: a phrase consisting of an adjective and a noun (*green eyes*, *marble heart*) is turned into an adjective by adding the suffix *-ed* ('having green eyes', and so on). He also makes use of the other patterns of forming new lexemes available to speakers of Early Modern English; they will be discussed in Chapter 5.

As the comparison of Shakespeare's lexeme types (17,750) and his word-form tokens (about 885,000) reveals, however, there must be a good deal of lexical repetition in his texts. It is the commonest words in English that also recur in the dramatist's language. Even creative geniuses share the common core of their mother tongue with their contemporaries.

4.1.2 The common core

The *common core* of English consists of frequent everyday vocabulary used in all registers in speech and in writing. This core, which largely goes back to Old English, forms the backbone of the language. It includes the names of everyday objects and actions; terms for family and social relationships; the commoner verbs, adjectives and adverbs; and the central *grammatical* or *function words* (articles, pronouns, prepositions, conjunctions and auxiliary verbs). The ten most frequent word-form tokens in a million-word corpus of Standard Present-day British English are all grammatical: *the, of, and, to, a, in, that, is, was* and *it* (Hofland and Johansson 1982). It is interesting to see that the top ten most frequent word-forms in the Early Modern English section of the *Helsinki Corpus of English Texts* are the same as in the Present-day corpus except that they include *I* but not *was*. These words are all native Germanic in origin.

In the course of time, the core vocabulary has also absorbed a number of loan words but, according to some estimates, roughly 50 per cent of the core vocabulary items of English remains Germanic (Scheler 1977: 73). The ten most frequent *lexical* or *content* verbs (lexeme tokens) in a large corpus of Present-day British and American speech and writing are: *say, get, go, know, think, see, make, come, take* and *want* (Biber et al. 1999: 373). All go back to the native Old English stock except for *take*, which is a Scandinavian loan word in late Old English and *want*, another word of Scandinavian origin, first attested in Early Middle English.

If we compile a similar top ten for the last Early Modern English period (1640–1710) in the *Helsinki Corpus*, the ten most frequent lexical verbs in order of frequency are: *say, make, come, go, know, see, take, think, tell* and *give*. As in the Present-day study, *do* is excluded, as it is more typical as an auxiliary than as a main verb. Incidentally, the Shakespeare extract in (1) also has two instances of the lexemes *say* and *go*, and one of *know*. The Early Modern English list based on the *Helsinki Corpus* contains two lexemes, *tell* and *give*, which do not show up in the Present-day list. *Give*, (the eleventh most frequent verb in the Present-day data) also goes back to Old English, although the initial /g/ may be attributed to Scandinavian influence on northern Middle English. *Get* and *want* do not appear among the Early Modern English top ten, although both are frequent in the data.

These high-frequency verbs mostly come from three principal semantic domains: activity verbs (*come, go, make, get, give, take*), communicative verbs (*say, tell*), and mental verbs (*know, think*). In Present-day English they are proportionately more frequent in conversational data than, say, in fiction, newspapers and academic writing (Biber et al. 1999: 373). Long-term evidence like this illustrates the primacy of speech over writing as a means of human communication. It partly explains how a sizable part of the common core can reach back to the earliest stages of a language.

Another lexical domain that is interesting to look at in this context is *proper names*. Although these do not strictly speaking belong to the core vocabulary of English, they display considerable diachronic continuity. The most popular names given in England between 1538 and 1700 are listed in (2) in descending order of frequency, with *John* and *Elizabeth* as the most frequent male and female names, respectively. There is naturally some regional and diachronic variation in this material compiled by Scott Smith-Bannister (1997: 135–44), but not much attributable to factors like the name-givers' social status, for instance. The most frequently given names are remarkably stable across time with rather more change in girls' names than in boys'. This stability could be explained by the fact that children were commonly named after their parents and godparents, girls somewhat less frequently than boys.

(2) **Top ten Early Modern English names (1538–1700)**

John	Elizabeth
William	Mary
Thomas	Anne
Richard	Margaret
Robert	Jane
Edward	Alice
George	Joan
James	Agnes
Henry	Catherine
Nicholas	Dorothy

By way of comparison, the ten most common first names, all male, of the members of the American Congress born between 1721 and 1960 were: *John, William, James, Thomas, Charles, George, Robert, Joseph, Henry* and *Samuel* (Kjellmer 2000: 144). As many as seven of them also appear among the Early Modern English top ten in (2); only *Charles, Joseph* and *Samuel* do not. In England these three names gained in popularity in the seventeenth century with especially Joseph and Samuel in the ascendant after 1620. The Congress statistics suggest that the Early Modern English pattern of giving names to boys continued across the Atlantic after the Declaration of Independence in 1776.

4.1.3 Extension and specialisation

As pointed out in Chapter 3, it was the non-core vocabulary that caused concern in the Early Modern English period when the vernacular came to be extended to new written-language functions. As it was important to consolidate the newly created technical vocabulary, its codification began quite early. Well over 100 publications, monolingual glossaries and specialist dictionaries appeared between 1475 and 1640 alone, including translators' glossaries, which were typically appended to texts translated from Latin dealing with medicine, religious instruction, education and polemics.

These specialist terminologies, 'terms of art', were compiled in various fields ranging from alchemy and architecture, cant and classics, to law, logic and military fortification. Legal terms, for instance, became more accessible to law students and lay people alike with the publication of the first English law dictionary, John Rastell's *Exposiciones terminorum legum anglorum* (1523–4). It translates into English the definitions of some 160 Anglo-French legal terms in current use at the time. The work proved very popular, and went through thirty editions in the course of 300 years. The first edition includes many terms that continue in technical use today, including *accessory, burglary, contract, felony, treason* and *voucher. Burglary* is defined as follows:

> (3) Burglary is when one breketh and enterith into a nother mann*es* howse in the nyght to the entēt to stele goodis ī which case though he bere away nothyng yet it is felony and for that he shalbe hangid/ but the brekyng of an house in the day for suche entent is no felony (John Rastell, *Exposiciones terminorum legum anglorum*, 1523: B2r.)

Specialist terms also appeared prominently in seventeenth-century hard-word dictionaries such as John Bullokar's *The English Expositor* (1616), Thomas Blount's *Glossographia* (1656) and Elisha Coles's *An English Dictionary* (1676). The most wide-ranging of these three, Coles, contains terms in divinity, husbandry, physic (i.e., medicine), philosophy, law, navigation, mathematics and other arts and sciences, and also pays attention to dialect words and archaisms. However, it was not until the early eighteenth century that monolingual English dictionaries began to record the most common everyday words.

4.2 Borrowing

As the rise of 'hard-word' dictionaries such as Cawdrey's *Table* (see 3.2.1) testifies, borrowing had a great impact on Early Modern English vocabulary in general. The Renaissance promoted borrowing from Latin, and the revival of classical learning also intensified borrowing from Greek. Many Greek loans were filtered through Latin or French, and Latin loans through French, to the extent that the term *Latinate* could be used to cover all three.

4.2.1 Illustration: the year 1604

Let us turn to historical dictionaries to get a better idea of the extent to which borrowing is related to other methods of vocabulary building in Early Modern English. The words listed in (4) come from the record of the *Chronological English Dictionary* (CED) for 1604, the year when Cawdrey's hard-word dictionary appeared. As the CED is based on the *Shorter Oxford English Dictionary*, it only contains the main entries of the OED and therefore under-represents native means of word-formation such as compounding. But it can serve as a rough basis for comparing the various sources of new lexemes (altogether 179 recorded for the year 1604). The principal sources and their frequencies are also listed in (4).

(4) **Sources of new words recorded for 1604 in the CED**

Latin (*addiction, amability, assert, customary, hallucinate*...)	30%
French (*accommodation, chocolate, excitement, lemonade*...)	29%
Native Germanic (*affrighted, black eye, galled, hint*...)	20%
Spanish (*chinchilla, condor, dorado, guano*...)	6%
Native languages of Peru (*charqui, guanaco, quipu*)	2%
Greek (*Aganippe, idiosyncrasy*)	1%
Dutch (*polder, unravel*)	1%
Other languages (less than 1% each)	5%
e.g. Arabic (*Ottomite*)	
Italian (*becco*)	
Irish (*leprechaun*)	
Scandinavian (*fleer*)	
Etymology unknown (*blotch, gibber, hush, phew*...)	6%

The role of borrowing as one of the principal means of enriching Early Modern English is clearly borne out by the data. About 60 per cent of the new words recorded for 1604 come from Latin and French, whereas native Germanic patterns of word-formation only cover some 20 per cent of the new words. The etymology of a few words is unknown, but some, such as *hush/husht* and *phew*, imitate the sounds associated with the actions they denote.

In many cases a closer look at the words reveals a more complex history. It is not always easy to tell whether a word was borrowed straight from Latin or from Latin via French, or whether it was created by means of the productive word-formation patterns available at the time. So *addiction* is identified by the OED as an adaptation from the Latin *addic-tiōn-em* and its first citation is glossed as 'penchant' ('*Each man to what sport and revels his **addiction** leads him*' (*Othello* II. ii. 6). *Accommodation*, by contrast, is said to have been adopted from the French *accommodation*, it in turn being adapted from the Latin *accommodātiōn-em*. Its first citation and sense 'room and suitable provision for the reception of people' also go back to *Othello*: '*Such Accomodation and besort As leuels with her breeding*' (I. iii. 239). However, the verbs *addict* and *accommodate* were both recorded in the sixteenth century. We may therefore wonder whether it is possible that the English nouns were formed from these verbs by means of the ending -(*a*)*tion* independently of the Latin or French nouns.

Let us turn to Cawdrey for contemporary evidence on the issue. His *Table Alphabeticall* only consists of about 2,500 entries, but he does include both *accommodate* and *addict*. His paraphrase of the verb *accommodate* is 'to make fit to, or convenient for a purpose'. *Addict* to him is clearly a participle, because he gives it the senses 'given to' and 'appointed to'. We may conclude from Cawdrey's testimony that, in the senses cited, the nouns *accommodation* and *addiction* could hardly have been of common currency at the time, and derivation by means of -(*a*)*tion* is not a likely choice. Mulcaster, too, lists the verb forms *accommodat* and *addict* in his *Elementarie* (1582), but omits the nouns. It is therefore probable that the nouns were borrowed either from French or from Latin by using the same model as French, dropping the Latin inflectional ending (see 4.2.2).

Such ready-made models did not, however, exist for all languages. The loan from Irish now generalised as *leprechaun* 'a little man-like creature with magical powers' was first recorded as *lubrican* in 1604 by the OED: '*As for your Irish lubrican, that spirit Whom by preposterous charms thy lust hath rais'd In a wrong circle*' (Middleton, *Honest Whore*, Part 2; III. i.). The first instance in the OED of *leprechaun*, spelled as *leprehaun(s)*, dates to 1818.

The lack of fixed models can particularly be seen in oral borrowing from languages with no written form. A case in point is *rac(c)oon*, borrowed from the Powhatan (Virginia) dialect of Algonquian. According to the OED, it appeared in two plural forms as *rahaugcums* and *raugroughcums* in a narrative by Captain John Smith in 1608. In the illustrations from 1610 we find the forms *aracoune* and *arathkone*, and in 1624 *aroughcun* and *rarowcun*. The modern form *raccoon* is first attested in 1672.

4.2.2 Sources and anglicisation

Bearing in mind the difficulty of determining what is borrowed and how indirectly, the OED record nonetheless suggests that Latin was the most common source for Early Modern English loan words. Figure 4.1 shows the number of loans in Early Modern English identified as going back to

Figure 4.1 Early Modern English loans from Latin and French.

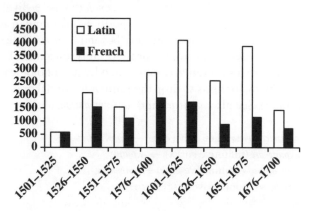

either Latin or French. The figures are drawn from a quantitative study by Jonathan Culpeper and Phoebe Clapham (1996: 218), who based their calculations on the immediate donor languages and first citations in the electronic version of the entire OED record.

The absolute frequencies of loans in Figure 4.1 suggest that, throughout the Early Modern English period, Latin contributed more new words to the English lexicon than French. Latin borrowing peaked between 1575 and 1675, when it contributed more than 13,000 new words. Overall, some 35 per cent of the new lexis recorded for sixteenth century in the OED was loans, overwhelmingly Latinate, and the figure rose to 40 per cent in the seventeenth century. So although the figures for 1604 in (4) clearly downplay the role of native means of word-formation they are indicative of the massive trend to Latinate borrowing at the time.

Early Modern English loans from Latin are mostly bookish. Some of them were short-lived, but a large number remained in the language as technical terms, while others made their way into general use. Most of the Latin loans are nouns, adjectives and verbs. In the Renaissance more loans go back to Latin directly than in Middle English, and their sources vary from Classical to Neo-Latin.

Nouns are often taken over morphologically unaltered in the nominative case, as in *augur, circus, interior* and *medium*. Technical terms preserve their original plurals: *formula – formulae, fungus – fungi, genius – genii, genus – genera*. Other Latin case forms are also borrowed, for instance, the ablative in *folio* (of *folium* 'leaf'), *proviso* ('it being provided'), *rebus* (pl. 'by things') and *via* ('by way of'). Verb forms are adopted as nouns in *caveat* ('let [him] be aware'), *deficit* ('it is wanting'), *exit* ('[he] goes out), *fiat* ('let it be done'), *ignoramus* ('we do not know'), *recipe* ('take'), *tenet* ('[he] holds') and *veto* ('I forbid'), and whole phrases in *facsimile* ('make' + 'like') and *factotum* ('do' + 'the whole'). Adverbs and prepositions are found in *alias* ('otherwise'), *alibi* ('elsewhere') *extra* ('outside', 'beyond'), *interim* ('meanwhile'), *item* ('thus') and *verbatim* ('word for word') (cf. Serjeantson 1961: 263–4).

Latin words are also often accommodated by morphological anglicisation. One way to do this is to drop the Latin inflectional or derivational ending, as in (5). See also *addiction* and *accommodation*, above.

(5) *constriction-em* (accusative case) → *constriction*
      expung-ere (infinitive suffix) → *expunge*
      immatur-us (nominative case) → *immature*
      terrific-us (nominative case) → *terrific*

Another common method of anglicising Latin nouns is to replace the Latin endings by terminations that had come into Middle English via French. They include the noun endings *-ity* (from L *-itās*), producing words like *immaturity* and *invisibility*, and *-ence*, *-ency*, *-ancy* (from *-entia*, *-antia*), resulting in words like *transcendence*, *delinquency* and *relevancy*. With adjectives these common adapted endings include *-able* and *-ible* (from *-ābilis*, *-ibilis*), as in *inviolable* and *susceptible*.

As in the case of Latin, most of the Greek loans are nouns, adjectives and verbs. Nouns predominate, and usually take the plural morpheme *-s*. Greek provided mostly technical terms in various fields ranging from *catastrophe* and *crisis* to *hyperbole* and *praxis*, from *dialysis*, *hypothesis* and *coma* to *cosmos*, *narcosis* and *psyche*.

At a time of intense borrowing of terminology, fields such as medicine, zoology, botany and theology gained most. Specialists who defended borrowing from Latin appealed to the lack of equivalent technical terms in English. The success of Latinate terminology may also be partly attributed to its lack of ambiguity. As will be shown in Chapter 5, native words tend to have many senses, but a borrowed technical term usually has only one. After the Restoration in 1660, Latin became unfashionable in general use, but continued to supply technical terminology. While basically promoting the use of English in the seventeenth century, the Royal Society openly endorsed the one-form one-meaning principle in technical terms. Many must also have shared Robert Boyle's view of 'the propriety' of retaining the terms used in the *lingua franca* of international science and scholarship.

But, as Brian Vickers points out, there is a downside to learned borrowing: 'Justifiable, even unavoidable though this neologising may have been, the effect was to create a strangely hybrid tongue' (1987: 20). In other words, while loan words can improve the lexical precision of English, they make the language more opaque when semantically related words bear no resemblance to each other. *Addicted* is not similar in form to *given to*, or *anatomy* to *cutting up*, for instance. As pointed out above, when lexical aids such as hard-word dictionaries were discussed, this lexical opacity was a problem to many. However, the ease with which the well-educated could switch from English to Latin and Greek even in their private discourse, is well evidenced by personal letters. Writing to his close friend and fellow churchman John Cosin in (6), Richard Mountague code-switches several times, even in the middle of the sentence (for example, *when he was chin deepe in lacu Lemanno*). Both men were fluent in Latin.

(6) Good Ihon, *Salutem in Christo.*
You did well to black lead your booke. I had not the patience, though I would have had the leysure, to read the blew-coate through. Casaubon the author of such bald stuff! *Credat Judaeus Apella.* Though his minde had ben that way 20 yeares since, when he was chin deepe *in lacu Lemanno*, yet his learning could not disgorge such dorbellismes. *Non vidi magis.* What this Abraham Darcie is I can not tell. (CEEC, Richard Mountague, 1624: COSIN, 32)

Unlike Latin, French loan words come from a living language, and reflect England's cultural and political links with France, as well as the impact of French immigrants. Sixteenth-century loans continue to reflect the earlier role of French as a language of administration and law, but much of the seventeenth-century intake can only be explained in terms of Anglo-French relations, which were revived during the Restoration. The large number of unanglicised loans in the latter half of the seventeenth century indicates the fashion among the cultivated upper ranks of introducing French words and phrases into ordinary conversation, a practice that language-aware writers like Dryden found particularly objectionable. In (7) John Cosin uses the French form *bonté*, not the anglicised form of the same word, *bounty*, which would also have been available to him in the same sense.

(7) It may well be that I am in this particular likewise beholden to Mr. Gayers, of whose generous freedome and *bonté* I have had divers testimonies heretofore. (CEEC, John Cosin, 1659: COSIN, 288)

In general, French loans do not depart greatly from their sources in form, although they often undergo some sound substitutions and stress shifts. Morphological anglicisation takes place with affixes which already have a corresponding English form, *contre-* changing into *counter-* (*counterpoint*), *-té* into *-ty* (*fidelity*), and verbs in *-er* taking the suffix *-ise* (*anathemise*). Unanglicised words may retain their original forms (*contretemps, naïveté*). In most cases loans retain their spelling and pronunciation as close to the original as allowed by English phonology. This trend reflects the changing functions of French loans from necessary terms used by all social ranks to marked foreignisms, which, as Görlach (1991: 168) remarks, became the hallmark of a prestigious and educated elite towards the end of the Early Modern period.

Sixteenth-century borrowings from French include military and naval terms, such as *colonel, pilot, cartridge* and *trophy*, as well as trade loans such as *cordon, livre, indigo, vase* and *portmanteau.* There are also loans that might be called 'social', including *bourgeois, genteel, esprit, madame, minion* and *vogue.* They become particularly frequent in the seventeenth century (*class, decor, beau, faux pas, liaison, malapropos, ménage, naïve, rapport, repartee*). Other areas where French borrowing made an impact are the arts and literature, dress, entertainment and food, giving, among others, *ballet, cabaret, champagne, denim* (< *serge de Nîmes*), *memoirs, nom-de-plume, rôle, crayon, soup* and *vinaigrette.*

Just like French, Italian supplied many loans related to Italian products (for example, *artichoke, majolica, parmesan*), arts and social customs (for example, *cameo, canto, carnival, cupola, duel(lo), fresco, madrigal, motto, piazza, stanza*). Loan words reflecting Italian life and society such as *gala, gambit, gusto, incognito, regatta* and *umbrella* accumulate in the second half of the Early Modern English period. Many architectural terms found a lasting position in English (*balcony, grotto, portico, villa*), as did musical terms such as *opera, recitative, solo* and *sonata.*

Beside native Spanish words, contacts with Spain introduced many loans of non-European origin into Early Modern English. Hispanic borrowing is characterised by trade terms and products (*anchovy, cargo, lime* (fruit), *sherry*), people and titles (*don, desperado, hidalgo, renegade, toreador*), military and political terms (*armada, embargo, junta*). American-based Spanish loans also relate to people (*cannibal, negro*) and food products (*avocado, banana, maize, potato, tobacco, tortilla* and *vanilla*).

4.3 Summary

Early Modern English borrowed heavily from the classical languages, Latin in particular, as well as from French and other Romance languages. Foreign borrowing provided the language with much needed technical terminology and increased its lexical variability. At the same time,

Latinate loans also increased the opaqueness of English vocabulary introducing semantically related words from different sources. Heavy borrowing did not, however, disrupt native continuity, the Germanic element remaining the backbone of English vocabulary even after the Early Modern period.

Exercises

1. There are fifty-seven *word forms* in the Shakespeare quotation in (1). The number falls to forty-seven when only *word-form types* are counted. Make a list of these word-form types, and assign them to their respective *lexemes*. How many different lexemes did you find?

(Note that, despite their realisation, personal-pronoun forms such as *I, me* and *my* count as tokens of one lexeme, as do *he, him* and *his*, and so on. The contracted form *Ile*, by contrast, consists of two lexemes, *I* and [*wi*]*ll*.)

2. Compare the use of common-core words in formal and informal texts. Select two different kinds of text, for example, a sermon and a play, from the same period in Appendix 1, and calculate how many times the most frequent word forms *the, of, and, to, a, in, that, is, it* and *I* appear in the first 100 words of text in each. Are there any differences in the use of these common-core items between the texts?

3. Identify the Latinate (Latin, French, Greek) loan words in a 100-word passage of the first (Cecil) and the fourth (Harley) text in Appendix 2. Use the OED etymologies to determine their loan-word status. What general criteria can you derive for identifying loan words on the basis of your findings, for example, in terms of word-length and endings? How does the official letter differ from the private one in loan-word use?

4. A good many of Shakespeare's Latinate neologisms did not catch on. They include *unprovoke* (*Macbeth* II.iii.29), *outjest* (*King Lear* III.i.16), *super-dainty* (*The Taming of the Shrew* II.i.188), *immoment* (*Antony and Cleopatra* V.ii.166), and *rumourer* (*Coriolanus* IV.vi.48). Look up two of them in the OED and in a collected edition of Shakespeare to determine (a) what they mean, (b) how they are formed, and (c) how they are used by the dramatist. Why might they not have caught on?

(Note that *outjest* is found under *out-* (III.16) and *super-dainty* under *super-* (III.9a) in the OED; the rest of the coinages are listed as entries of their own, although in principle *unprovoke* and *immoment* could come under *un-* and *in-*, respectively.)

Further reading

The principles of analysing English vocabulary are outlined in Carstairs-McCarthy (2002). Nevalainen (1999: 336–42) discusses Early Modern English lexical statistics and their reliability, as well as Shakespeare's Latinate neologisms. Gordon (1980: 12–15, 85–94) extends the notion of lexical common core to the study of native continuity in English prose style. The stylistic implications of the English 'double lexicon', native and borrowed words, are explored by Adamson (1989), and Nurmi and Pahta (2004) provide a corpus-based account of patterns of code-switching in Early Modern English.

Early Modern English dictionaries are introduced by Stein (1985) and Starnes and Noyes ([1946] 1991), and other early lexical sources by Schäfer (1989). The *Lexicons of Early Modern English* database (LEME), compiled by Ian Lancashire, contains word entries from well over 100 monolingual English dictionaries, bilingual lexicons, technical vocabularies and other lexical works published between 1480 and 1700 (Lancashire 2003). Details about the sources of Early Modern English loan words are found in Barber (1976, 2nd edn 1997), Nevalainen (1999), Scheler (1977) and Serjeantson ([1935] 1961) – all heavily indebted to the OED.

5 Word-formation and semantic change

5.1 Word-formation

As noted in the previous chapter when looking at Shakespeare's lexical innovations, new words can be formed from existing ones by various word-formation processes. This applies to both native and borrowed word-stock. The benefit of word-formation as a means of vocabulary enrichment is that the resulting words are transparent in form. If they are based on established lexical elements, this transparency makes their meaning readily accessible to all. This was one of the reasons why many writers and translators in the sixteenth century were against excessive foreign borrowing and promoted native means of word-formation as the basis for creating new terminology.

Word-formation processes produce lexemes which can be characterised in terms of free and bound elements, or *bases* and *affixes*, respectively. Bases are free in that they can occur alone, while affixes cannot. The three basic word-formation processes both today and in Early Modern English are compounding, affixation and conversion:

(a) **compounding**: adding a base to another base: *picture* (noun) + *frame* (noun) → *picture-frame* (noun)

(b) derivation by means of **affixation**: adding an affix to a base:

(a) **prefixation** (L *prae-* 'before'): attaching a prefix to a base, usually without a change of word class: *mis-* + *spell* (verb) → *misspell* (verb)

(b) **suffixation** (L *sub-* > *suf-* 'under', 'close to'): attaching a suffix to a base, usually with a change of word class: *common* (adjective) + *-ness* → *commonness* (noun)

(c) **conversion** (zero-derivation): assigning the base to another word class without changing its form: *bottle* (noun) → *bottle* (verb) 'put in a bottle'

This classification also shows the basic typological change in English from *stem-formation* in Old English to *word-formation* as we know it today. In Modern English, lexemes are invariant when they serve as bases of word-formation. This was not the case in Old English, where the base could vary. The Old English noun *cyme* 'arrival', for instance, had been derived from the verb *cuman* 'come', and *dom* 'judgement' from the verb *deman* 'judge' (cf. *deem*); the verb *fyllan* 'fill' and the adjective *full* are also derivationally related (Hogg 2002: 104). This variation reflected historical sound changes. In the course of time stem variation was lost in derivational morphology and invariant lexemes were established as bases for word-formation. In this respect Early Modern English is modern as fixed base forms are used in all word-formation processes.

It is often assumed that an established word blocks the derivation from the same base of another word with the same meaning. In Early Modern English this strict economy principle was often relaxed. Synonymous operations were applied to one and the same base quite freely. There were four variants, for instance, of the verb 'to make longer': *length*, *lengthen*, *enlength* and *enlengthen*. The noun *throne* gave rise to as many as five verbs with roughly the same meaning, 'remove a ruler from his position of power': *disthronize*, *disthrone*, *dethrone*, *unthrone* and *dethronize*. Many of these multiple derivations were experimental and did not outlive the Early Modern English period. Some of those that did have become semantically differentiated; compare, for instance, the verbs *light*, *lighten* and *enlighten* (Görlach 1991: 180).

5.1.1 Compounding

Compound words behave like non-compounds in that they have a form and a meaning of their own. The plural of *picture-frame* is *picture-frames*, and not *pictures-frames*, as would be the case with two independent words, and the primary stress of the compound falls on the first element, *picture*. Dictionaries define this compound as 'a frame forming a border round a picture' – not, for instance, 'a frame consisting of pictures', although by some stretch of the imagination perhaps it could also take on that meaning (cf. *picture-book*, and *earth bank* in (1), below). All this holds for Early Modern English as well.

Compounds consisting of two nouns (N+N) are the most productive type of compounding in Early Modern English and today. They are also discussed by William Bullokar, the author of the first grammar of English to appear in English. He illustrates the process of compounding ('*compositions*') in his *Pamphlet for Grammar* (1586: 61) with a short passage of text containing a set of examples and their paraphrases:

(1) On an erth-bank ner medow-ground, I saw a hors-comb ly, Which I browht intoo a hors-mil that a ston-wal stood nih, And fynding thaer an elmen plank, I sowht for a wood-betl And woodn wedges, but found nawht, sauing a laten-ketl.

(Compositions and substantiue adjectiues resolued by prepositions of, for, or, with.)

On a bank of erth or erthn bank, ner ground for medow, I saw a comb for a hors ly, which I browht intoo a mil with hors, that stood nih a stonen wal, or wal of ston, and fynding thaer an elm-plank, or plank of elm, I sowht for a betl for wood, and wedges of wood, but found no-thing, sauing a ketl of laten.

Besides regular compounds consisting of two nouns (*earth bank, meadow ground, horse comb, horse mill, stone wall, wood beetle* and *latten kettle*) the passage illustrates 'substantive adjectives', nouns premodified by an adjective (*elmen plank, wooden wedges*). Bullokar's compounds are typical in that some of them, such as *horse comb* and *stone wall*, date back to Old English. *Meadow ground* is first recorded in 1523, and *horse mill* in 1530. Of *wood beetle* ('a wood-boring beetle') and *latten kettle* ('a kettle made of latten'), there is, however, no earlier mention in the OED. We may therefore assume that they have either passed by the dictionary compilers unrecorded or that they are simply lexical innovations the writer had formed using productive compounding rules.

Compound adjectives, also common in Early Modern English, typically consist of a noun and an adjective, as in *fireproof, lifelong, skin-deep* and *world-wide* ('as wide as the world'). Another productive pattern consists of a noun followed by a past participle. In these compounds the noun often has an adverbial function: *frost-bitten* ('bitten by frost'), *hand-made* ('made by hand'), *heart-felt, heaven-sent.*

Typical compound verbs consist of a particle and a verb. Their meaning is either concrete (*overcloud, undersign*) or, more frequently, abstract. Both *out* and *over* can have the abstract sense of 'outdo in V-ing': *outlive, outsell, overbid, overshine. Under* was often associated with the sense 'below a fixed norm or standard': *underbid, underrate, undervalue.*

5.1.2 Affixation

There were more than 120 affixes available in English in Shakespeare's time – many more than Chaucer had in the fourteenth century. As new loan words were integrated into Early Modern English, prefixes and suffixes adopted from foreign sources came to be applied to older loan words and ultimately to the native word-stock as well. It took some time before the affixes derived from loan words established themselves. Many of them continued to be associated with borrowed lexis. When non-native affixes were attached to long, polysyllabic loan words, they became even longer. It is therefore no wonder that they presented problems for those who had not had access to a classical education.

As noted above in 5.1, the process of *prefixation* resembles compounding in that it does not change the part of speech of a word, while *suffixation* can do that. It is also noteworthy that affixes often have more than one meaning, and two or more affixes can have roughly the same meaning both today and in Early Modern English. Some common Early Modern English affixes are listed and illustrated below (with Latinate forms in **boldface**). Just like today, there were more suffixes than prefixes.

Prefixes:

for forming nouns:
- *fore-*, ***pre-***, ***ante-*** ('before N'): *forecourt, preconception, antechapel*
- ***counter-***, ***anti-*** ('against N'): *counterplot; anti-king*

for forming adjectives:
- *un-*, ***in-***, ***dis-*** ('not A', 'the converse of A'): *unfit, inhospitable, discontent*

for forming verbs:
- *un-*, ***dis-***, ***de-*** ('to remove N'): *unburden, disburden, dethrone;* ('to reverse the action of V') *unload, disappear, deobstruct*
- *be-* ('to provide with N'; 'V completely, thoroughly'): *bestain, bedeck*
- ***en-/em-*** ('to put into N', 'to provide with N'): *enthrall, embody*
- *mis-* ('V wrongly, badly'): *mismatch, misname*
- *re-* ('V again, back'): *refill, reprint*

Suffixes:

for forming nouns:
- *-ing*, ***-ment***, ***-al***, ***-ation***, ***-ance/ence***, ***-ure*** ('the act, cause, result, state etc. of V-*ing*'): *landing, retirement, recital, formalisation, admittance, exposure*
- *-ness*, ***-ity*** ('the condition, quality, etc. of being A'): *wittiness, capability*
- *-er* ('someone who V-*s*'): *heeler, examiner*

for forming adjectives:
- *-ed*, *-ful* ('having N'): *dropsied, rose-lipped, beautiful*
- *-y* ('full of N', 'characterised by N'): *dirty, healthy*
- *-less* ('without N'): *matchless, stateless*
- ***-able*** ('fit for V-*ing*/to be V-*ed*'): *answerable, unavoidable*
- *-(**ic**)**al*** ('relating to N', 'having the character of N'): *arithmetical, whimsical, imperatorial*

• -*ing*, -*ive*, -*y* ('that V-*s*', 'capable of V-*ing*'): *persisting, persistive, crumbly*
for forming adverbs:
• -*ly* ('in an A manner'): *bawdily, domestically*
for forming verbs:
• -*en*, -*ate*, -*ify* ('make A', 'become A'): *brighten, facilitate, beautify*

Among the broadly synonymous negative prefixes, the native *un-* was the most productive, combining freely with native (for example, *un-English, unfit*) and borrowed bases (*undesirable, unfortunate*). Coming across a native prefix with a borrowed base, or vice versa, is much more likely in the works of Shakespeare than in the *Authorised Version* of the Bible. The only loan prefixes that Shakespeare never combines with native bases are *de-* and *pro-* ('the substitute of'); both were infrequent in Early Modern English (Garner 1987).

In view of the number of suffixes borrowed, it is significant that the most productive ones should be native: -*ness* and -*er* produce the most nouns in the period 1500 to 1700, and -*ed* and -*y* are the most frequently attested adjective suffixes (Barber 1997: 233–4). These calculations are based on the OED, and do not include words solely used in Scots or regional English dialects.

The suffix -*er* is in fact so frequent that it may be argued that it is fully productive and can go with any verb, and therefore ought to be discussed under *inflectional morphology* (see Chapter 6). It is a borderline case, but an argument for *word-formation* is that -*er* forms may develop meanings that cannot be predicted from the corresponding verbs: *pointer* denotes a dog breed as well as 'somebody who points', and *poker* can be either a person or an instrument (the card-game is a later loan word). The other extreme, the high productivity of -*er* in nominalisations, is illustrated by the extract in (2) from Bishop John Parkhurst's unflattering account from 1570 of a Norfolk mischief-maker. This man was:

(2) a break*er* off men headdes . . . a fetch*er* of writtes from London to trouble poore neyghboures, a deliuer*er* of a prisoner out of the stockes at Acle . . . a sett*er* on of promot*ers* to trouble men and to get away their monie . . . a pull*er* of[f] of Duitche women's kerchers openlie in the market at Yarmouthe. (John Parkhurst, *The Letter Book of John Parkhurst, Bishop of Norwich*, 1974–5: 60)

Derivation by native suffixes involves no change in the basic stress pattern or phonological shape of the base, but borrowed suffixes vary in this respect. The main stress may, for instance, be attracted to the syllable immediately before the suffix especially when the new suffix combines with a foreign base. These stress-affecting suffixes include -(*ic*)*al* and -*ity* (*económical, histórical, capability, feasibílity,* cf. 9.5).

5.1.3 Conversion

The word-formation process of conversion changes the word-class of a word. In this respect it resembles a typical case of suffixation. Compare the two nouns derived from the verb *remove* in Early Modern English: *removal* (1597) is formed by adding the suffix -*al* to the verb, and *remove* (1553) simply by means of conversion (*zero-derivation*). Although there are no particular signs of nouniness in *remove* when it is listed in the dictionary, it behaves syntactically like any other noun. Just like *removal*, it can take an article, appear in the plural, and complement a verb or a preposition, as in example (3).

> (3) Our horse alsoe came off with some trouble, beinge wearied wth the longe fight, and their horses tyred; yett faced the enimies fresh horse, and **by severall remoues** got off without the losse of one man, the enimie followinge in the reere with a great body. (CEEC, Oliver Cromwell, 1643: CROMWELL, 11)

There are few formal constraints on conversion in Early Modern English. Just like today, the only word-classes that cannot be readily formed by this means are *function words*; pronouns, prepositions and conjunctions, for instance. But function words themselves are freely converted to nouns (*the **ins** and **outs***) and to verbs (*to **near**, to **up***), or both (***but** me no **buts***).

In Early Modern English verbs are commonly produced from nouns and adjectives by means of conversion. As with verbs derived by suffixation, causation is an important semantic element in conversion verbs. The verb *invoice*, for instance, is first attested in 1698: (OED) '*When they are publickly **Invoiced**, it will be at their own Wills to make their Bargains* (FRYER *Acc. E. India & P.* 88)'. It has the following senses in the OED: 'to make an invoice of, to enter in an invoice' and 'to send or submit an invoice to a person'. Similarly, the verb *lump* means 'to put altogether in one lump, mass, sum, or group'; *dirty* 'to make dirty'; and *secure* 'to make secure or safe'. Conversion verbs may sometimes have even semantically opposite senses. The verb *skin*, for instance, is found to mean either 'to furnish or cover with skin' or 'to strip or deprive of skin'.

The potential for multiple readings in word coining might have been utilised by Shakespeare in Edgar's famous line in *King Lear.* 'He childed as I fathered!' (III.vi.113). Many critics interpret *childed* as a conversion verb and give it the dynamic reading 'he (being) turned into a child' or 'behaving like a child'. A parallel interpretation is extended to *fathered*. But the passage gets a very different meaning if *childed* is interpreted in an adjectival sense as 'having (cruel) children', and *fathered* as 'having a (cruel) father'. This reading analyses the words as adjectives formed from nouns by means of the *-ed* ending (cf. *dropsied*, *rose-lipped* in 5.1.2).

5.2 Semantic change

When new concepts need to be named, borrowing and word-formation are not the only solutions – an existing word can also undergo a change of meaning. Processes of semantic change are very common but often gradual, and therefore harder to pin down than word-formation processes. The meaning of a word can be *generalised* or can *specialise*, becoming more restricted in its sphere of reference. These processes typically lead to *polysemy*, when a word gains a new sense but retains the old one as well. But if there is a risk of confusion, one of the senses may be lost. This was, for instance, the case of *meat*, which in Early Modern English meant both 'food' in general and 'the flesh of animals used as food'. The general sense is intended in (4), but now only occurs in sayings like *one man's **meat** is another man's poison.*

(4) From *Yorke* I rode to *Doncaster*, where my horses were well fed at the Beare . . . Sir *Robert Anstruther* (I thanke him) not only paying for my two horses **meat**, but at my departure, he gaue me a letter to *Newarke* vpon *Trent*. . . (HC, John Taylor, *The Pennyles Pilgrimage*, 1630: 140.C1)

5.2.1 Outcomes of semantic change

Early Modern English semantic changes can often be related to the social and cultural developments of the time. Generalisation of titles took place when *Master* (*Mr*) and *Mistress* (*Mrs*), originally the titles of the lower gentry, came to be used when addressing people who did not own land, which was the defining feature of the gentry. As the change was gradual, one and the same person could be addressed by different titles even in the same context. Let us consider the case of Alice Lisle, prosecuted for high treason in 1685. She was the widow of John Lisle, former President of the High Court of Justice and a member of Oliver Cromwell's House of Lords. During the trial she was variously called *Lady Lisle*, *Mrs Lisle*, and plain *Alice Lisle*. She was addressed as *Alice Lisle* by the Clerk of Arraignments (5a), and *Mrs Lisle* by the Lord Chief

Justice (5b), but referred to as *Lady Lisle* by most of the witnesses, who included a baker and a farmhand (5c).

(5a) How sayest thou, **Alice Lisle**, art thou Guilty of the High-Treason contained in this Indictment, or not Guilty? (HC, *State Trials*, vol. 4, 1685: 106)

(5b) Look you, **Mrs. Lisle**, that will signify little; but if you have any Witnesses, call them, we will hear what they say. (HC, *State Trials*, vol. 4, 1685: 123)

(5c) When I came to my **Lady Lisle's** House, I went to the Bailiff that belong'd to my **Lady Lisle**. (HC, *State Trials*, vol. 4, 1685: 109)

The case in (5a), where Alice Lisle is addressed by a combination of first name and last name, is a formulaic expression; it is also the only time the pronoun *thou* is used when addressing her. *Mrs Lisle*, uttered by the Lord Chief Justice Jeffries in (5b), is basically an appropriate form because her father and husband were both born to the lower gentry. Following the common usage of her peers outside the court, however, the Justice also often refers to her as *Lady Lisle*. This form is preferred throughout the proceedings by her social inferiors such as James Dunne the baker in (5c), who may have wished to avoid showing any disrespect to her at a time when *Mrs* had become the default title for a woman regardless of her social status. We will return to address forms in 10.3.

Meaning generalisation also took place with many specialist terms in Early Modern English, including *humour* (see Chapter 1), which was a technical term in medieval physiology. The four humours of blood, phlegm, choler and melancholy made up the fluids of the body that were thought to govern a person's health and temperament. In the fifteenth and sixteenth centuries the term was generalised to refer both to a person's general disposition or temperament and passing moods (*be in a good humour*). It also gained the more specific senses of 'that quality which excites amusement' and 'the faculty of perceiving what is ludicrous or amusing'. The term lost its popular scientific application in the course of the seventeenth century, but continues as a medical term in the sense of 'bodily fluid' or 'semifluid', for example, with reference to the blood or lymph.

A similar layering of meaning can be seen in *phisicke*, as Cawdrey spells the word in his hard-word dictionary, defining it as 'medicine, helping or curing'. Early Modern people commonly talk about *taking physic* (and *physician* continues to be used in the sense of 'medical doctor' up until the present day). The word also had the broader sense 'knowledge of the natural world', in which sense it was rivalled by the longer *physics* from the late sixteenth century onwards. By the eighteenth century *physics* had won the upper hand and was established in the sense of 'natural science in general'. John Locke (1632–1704) still appears to have included the study of God and angels in the scope of physics, but in the eighteenth century it came to apply solely to the inorganic world.

Science retained its original sense of 'knowledge', but was also used of skill or mastery in any department of learning in Early Modern English. The *seven liberal sciences* could appear synonymously with the *seven liberal arts* with reference to studies in medieval universities, which consisted of the lower division, the *Trivium* (grammar, logic, rhetoric) and the upper division, the *Quadrivium* (arithmetic, music, geometry, astronomy); hence the title *Master of Arts*. Example (6) illustrates their parallel use by Francis Bacon around 1600. From the seventeenth century on, *science* also increasingly came to be associated with theoretical knowledge in contrast to practical skill denoted by *art*.

(6) Schollers in Vniuersities come too soone, & too vnripe to Logicke & Rhetoricke; **Arts** fitter for Graduates then children, and Nouices: For these two rightly taken, are the grauest of **Sciences**, beeing the **Arts of Arts**, the one for Iudgement, the other for Ornament: (HC, Francis Bacon, *Advancement of Learning*, 1605: 5r.)

Philosophy (lit. 'love of wisdom') continued to be used with reference to human knowledge of all kinds, as in (7), John Evelyn's description of a 12-year-old child prodigy. It was not until the nineteenth century that the separation of the physical from the mental in the field of human learning gave rise to the specialisation of *science* as 'natural and physical science', in contrast to *philosophy* as the study of human thinking and knowledge.

(7) There was not any thing in Chronologie, Historie, Geographie, The several systemes of Astronomers, Courses of the starrs, Longitudes, Latitudes . . . which he did not readily resolve & demonstrate his knowledge of . . . we asked him questions which could not be resolved without considerable meditation & judgement: nay, of some particulars of the Civil Lawes, of the Digest & Code: He gave a stupendous account of both **Natural**, & **Moral Philosophie**, & even in Metaphysics: (HC, John Evelyn, *Diary*, 1689–90: 898)

Lexical sets provide another angle on how meanings expand and contract. The names of the seasons illustrate both processes. English has always divided the year into four seasons with the core words *summer* and *winter* going back to Old English. However, in the course of the Middle English period the word *lent*(*en*) disappeared in its established sense of 'spring', and *summer* was for a while stretched to cover 'spring' as well (as in the song *Sumer is icumen in*). There were a number of new 'spring-words' between the fourteenth and sixteenth centuries including *ver*, *springing-time*, *springing* (*of summer*/*the year*), *prime-temps*, *seed-time*, *new time*, *spring-time*, *spring of the leaf*, and, from the early sixteenth century on, plain *spring* (Fischer 1994).

The traditional term for the third season, *harvest*, was lost by the end of the eighteenth century. The now current British English term *autumn* had been borrowed from French in the fourteenth century, and *fall*(*ing*) *of the leaf* and plain *fall* were introduced in the sixteenth century, presumably on the analogy of *spring*(*ing*). *Fall* became the standard American term for the third season. The specialisation of *spring* and *fall* as names for seasons dissociated them from their origins, making them *homonyms* of the other nouns derived from the same verbs (as in *take a fall*).

5.2.2 Mechanisms of semantic change

The basic mechanisms that produce semantic changes are *metaphoric transfer* and *contextual inferencing*. *Metaphoric transfer* operates on a perceived similarity, physical or functional, between the descriptive meanings of two words. Physical similarity was the basis for many plant names found in *The Grete Herball* (1526; see Rydén 1984), such as *bear's foot*, *goose-bill* ('the rote of it is lyke a goos byll'), *goosefoot* ('because the sede spredeth forkewyse as a goos fote'), *king's crown* and *priest's hood*. Functional similarity was involved in processes that produced terms such as *parasite*, 'an organism living in or upon another', which constitutes a metaphorical extension of its original sense 'one who eats at the table or at the expense of another'.

A combination of physical and functional motivation may lie behind the plant name *hare's palace* ('For yf the hare come vnder it/ he is sure that no beest can touche hym') (Rydén 1984: 36, 44). Technical terms created by metaphorical means may also be international loans. *Satellite*, a sixteenth-century loan-word meaning 'an attendant upon a person of importance' acquired the sense 'a small or secondary planet which revolves around a larger one' in the mid-seventeenth century. The OED notes that the Latin *satellites* was first applied in 1611 by Johannes Kepler to the secondary planets revolving round Jupiter, which had been recently discovered by Galileo Galilei.

The other basic mechanism of semantic change, *contextual inferencing*, is at work in *metonymy* ('name change'), a common mechanism as a result of which an entity gets the name of another entity inseparably associated with it. These associations can be of diverse kinds: part for whole (*the crown* being used for the wearer of the crown, the monarch); container for contents (*dish* 'a broad, shallow vessel to hold food' used for food ready for eating); concrete for abstract (*humour* 'bodily fluid' becoming the name for temperament, *spring/ fall* (*of the leaf*) designating the first and third seasons); and abstract for concrete (an action noun coming to denote the result of the action: (*an*) *etching, savings*). A word can have multiple metonymic meanings, as in (8), where *crown* also refers to the name of an inn with a sign depicting a crown.

(8) Justice *Markham* had reason to warrant his doings; for it did appeare, a Merchant of *London* was arraigned and slanderously accused of Treason for compassing and imagining the King's Death, he did say he would make his Sonne Heire of the **Crown**, and the Merchant meant it of a House in *Cheapside* at the Signe of the *Crowne*, (HC, *The Trial of Sir Nicholas Throckmorton*, 1554: 75.C1)

Contextual inferencing was also at work in the generalisation of titles discussed above. The process was driven by inferences based on external factors such the addressee's apparent wealth, and by social factors such as politeness: in order not to underestimate their interlocutor's social status, speakers preferred to err on the side of caution by upgrading it. Similarly, when people wish to appear polite and co-operative, they may promise more than they can perform. A case in point here is the adverbs *anon, by and by, directly* and *presently*, which all originally had the sense 'at once' but gained their 'blunted' senses 'soon', 'shortly' in Late Middle and Early Modern English; see (9).

(9) *Tom.* Well wench, what says thy Mistris? is she willing to forgive me my fault, and to let me go up Stairs to her.

Nan. You may **presently**, but not yet, for she is not awake, and being disturb'd, will be more froward. (HC, *Penny Merriments*, 1684–5: 271)

The application of a word can also generalise or specialise if evaluative information gets incorporated into its meaning. In Middle English, the noun *boor* simply meant 'peasant' or 'person living in the country'. In the sixteenth century it began to be used synonymously with 'rustic' and 'peasant with no refinement'. Having acquired this negative meaning aspect, it gained the more general sense 'a rude, unmannered person'.

Many adjectives similarly acquired connotations of disapproval in the course of the Early Modern English period including the following (original senses shown in brackets): *coy* ('quiet', 'modest'), *cunning* ('able', 'skilful'), *mediocre* ('of middling quality, neither bad nor good', 'average'), *obsequious* ('compliant', 'obedient'), and *vulgar* ('ordinary'; 'customary'). The older sense of *cunning* is shown in (10), an extract from a medical treatise published in 1602 (*Artificiall* in its title meaning 'professional', 'skilled').

(10) The sixt Intention Chirurgicall is, that in those *Strumas* that are fastened but to a thinne and slender roote, you shall binde them about and plucke them out. This last action (as it appeareth) is verie easily performed by a skilfull Operator or **cunning** Chirurgian: (HC, William Clowes, *Treatise for the Artificiall Cure of Struma*, 1602: 33)

A negative connotation is sometimes lost in the course of time, as we can see comparing the Present-day meanings of a number of words with their earlier senses. The following are some illustrations of this process (with the Early Modern English senses in brackets): *enthusiasm* ('supernatural inspiration', 'imagined divine inspiration'), *politician* ('crafty schemer', 'intriguer'), *precise* ('excessively scrupulous', 'puritanical'), and *shrewd* ('malicious', 'hurtful' 'cunning') (Barber 1997: 250–1).

5.3 Summary

In principle, word-formation does not make a basic distinction between loan words and native vocabulary in Early Modern English. Both provide material for compounding, affixation and conversion. A number of new affixes, both prefixes and suffixes, were introduced into Early Modern English from the Latinate section of the vocabulary. They made a sizable addition to the derivational resources of the language, but in most cases continued to be applied to borrowed rather than native vocabulary in the Early Modern period. At the same time, lexical statistics show that native affixes produced more new words than the numerous Latinate affixes.

Word-formation and borrowing from other languages increased the number of new words in Early Modern English. A new word could also result from semantic change in cases where the derived meaning was so different as to be no longer associated with its source; a case in point is *fall*, a verbal noun and the name of a season. More typically, however, semantic change led to polysemy in the lexicon, as words acquired new senses while at the same time retaining their earlier ones. As a result, older words now usually have more senses than more recent ones.

Exercises

1. Identify the lexemes formed by means of compounding and affixation in any two texts in Appendix 1. In some cases you might find it helpful to consult the OED.

2. Perusal of text corpora has shown that synonymous words, alternative ways of saying 'the same thing', are rarely used exactly alike or in the same context.

Discuss some synonymous derivations illustrated in this chapter, for example, the nouns *remove* and *removal* or the verbs *length* and *lengthen*. In each case, were the words interchangeable in Early Modern English according to the information given in the OED? If you have access to corpora such as the HC or electronic Shakespeare, look them up and compare their uses.

3. The more recent a word is, the fewer senses it is bound to have. According to one study, 40 per cent of the words first recorded in the fifteenth century have only one sense today. The figure for words that date to the seventeenth century is 60 per cent and, for those that go back to the twentieth century, as high as 98 per cent (Finkenstaedt and Wolff 1973: 108–10).

Find out how polysemous an old word can be by looking up the noun *hand*, *heart* or *house* in the OED. Concentrate on the primary senses marked with Arabic numerals under I (simple word), excluding phrases (under II) and attributive uses and combinations (under III). How many senses does the word have? Characterise the ways in which they have come about (metaphor, metonymy, and so on). What proportion of them were first attested in the sixteenth and seventeenth centuries?

4. Discuss changes in connotations of disapproval. Look up two of the words listed at the end of section 5.2 (*coy, cunning . . . politician, precise, shrewd*) and note their various senses. How dominant are those with negative associations in Early Modern English in the OED record? If you have access to the HC or some other Early Modern English corpus, find out which of the dictionary senses occur in the data.

Further reading

A good introduction to English word-formation can be found in Carstairs-McCarthy (2002), who also examines the role of history in shaping the way English vocabulary is structured. Quirk et al. (1985:

1515–85) provide a systematic inventory of currently productive word-formation processes, and Marchand (1960; use 2nd edn 1969) gives a comprehensive account of Present-day English word-formation on historical principles. Semantic change is discussed in general terms by Geeraerts (1997). Hughes (1988) is a lively discussion of semantic changes in a number of lexical sets in the history of English, and Lewis (1960; use 2nd edn 1967) contains in-depth histories of *nature, sad, wit, free, sense, simple, conscience* and *conscious, world* and *life.* More detailed surveys of Early Modern English word-formation and processes of semantic change are provided, with references, by Barber (1976; 2nd edn 1997), Görlach (1991) and Nevalainen (1999).

6 Nouns and pronouns

6.1 Word classes

Tudor and Stuart schoolboys would have been quite familiar with the grammatical concepts to be discussed in this chapter. As evidenced by Greaves's exercise in Chapter 2, parts of speech are the most enduring categories in Western grammatical thinking. In this chapter the traditional term *part of speech* will be used interchangeably with *word class* to stress structural reasons alongside semantic ones for setting up categories of words. Instead of simply saying that a noun is 'the name of a person, place or thing', as traditional grammar defines it, a structurally oriented approach also refers to the *inflectional* endings attached to nouns, and the relations nouns have with other word classes in sentences.

As opposed to derivational endings discussed in Chapter 5, which form new words from existing ones (create *lexemes*), inflectional endings mark grammatical distinctions in lexemes (create *word-forms*). English nouns, for example, take inflections that indicate a *number* contrast between the singular (*cat*) and the plural (*cats*), as well as a *case* contrast between the common case (*dog*) and the genitive (*dog's*). Inflections are similarly used to mark person, number, tense, aspect and mood contrasts in verbs. In the following we will see how the major word classes were constructed in Early Modern English, what long-term trends they showed, and how they differed from Present-day English. This chapter is concerned with nouns and pronouns, and Chapter 7 with verbs, adjectives and adverbs.

When talking about word classes, however, morphology makes up only part of the story. In order to understand the work they do we also need to know how they combine into larger constructions. These arrangements of words in sentences belong to the province of *syntax*, to be discussed in Chapter 8.

6.2 Nouns

The Early Modern English system of noun inflections is essentially that of Present-day English, and the same regular forms are found in number and case endings. The Old English four-case system has been reduced to two, the genitive and the common case, which appears in both subject and object positions in the sentence. Some more variability, however, exists in Early Modern number and case marking than in Standard English today.

6.2.1 Number

In Early Modern English, the plural of nouns was regularly formed with the -(e)s ending. There were a few exceptions, most of them the same as now such as *men, women, children, oxen, feet, mice* and *sheep*. But there were also forms no longer in current use such as *eyen* ('eyes'), *shoon* ('shoes'), *chicken*, often used as the plural of *chick*, and *kine*, the plural of *cow*. *Kine* is still more frequent than *cows* in texts in the first half of the seventeenth century; see examples (1) and (2).

(1) Touching the gentlenesse of **kine**, it is a vertue as fit to be expected as any other; for if she bee not affable to the maide, gentle, and willing to come to the paile... shee is vtterly vnfitte for the Dayrie. (HC, Gervase Markham, *Countrey Contentments*, 1615: 107)

(2) Wee lost in the service and prey about 100 serviceable **horse**, yᵉ draught **oxen**, and 130 **cowes**; I lost an horseman and my best horse. (CEEC, John Jones, 1651: JONES, 181)

Example (2) also illustrates the form *horse* after a numeral. It may be a sign of the noun being treated collectively (cf. *a hundred **pound***), or the unchanged relic plural of the word. It occurs in Shakespeare, for instance, together with other similar cases such as *year* and *winter*.

6.2.2 Case

The only case ending in Early Modern English nouns is the genitive -*s*, which is added to words in the singular (*child's*) and to irregular plurals (*children's*). In writing, the apostrophe was introduced to the singular form before -*s* in the latter half of the seventeenth century, and after the regular plural -*s* only in the eighteenth century (although text editors can add them even to original-spelling editions as a matter of punctuation). So no distinction was usually made in Early Modern English between the common-case plural (*kings*), the genitive singular (*king's*) or the genitive plural (*kings'*): all three were spelled *kings* and pronounced alike.

Although the historical unstressed vowel of the genitive ending -*es* had been dropped in most contexts in Late Middle English, it continued to be pronounced in nouns ending in sibilants ('s'-sounds), where the ending was /ɪz/ – the same as today. This genitive suffix was also sometimes replaced by the possessive pronoun *his* in Late Middle and Early Modern English texts. The writers of these texts may have felt that the regular -(*e*)*s* ending was an abbreviation of *his*, and indicated this in spelling by the use of *his*, particularly with masculine nouns ending in a sibilant sound (i.e. /s/, /z/, /ʃ/, /ʒ/). This variation is reflected in (3), where Henry Oxinden has -*s* in both *Mr Trusser's bond* and *Mr. Dickenson's bond* but resorts to a *his*-genitive in *Mr Crux his bond*.

(3) **Mr. Trusser's bond** and **Mr. Dickenson's bond** I intend, God willing, to pay tomorrow being Mooneday; if I see Mr. Twiman I intend to pay him what is due to Him; and if **Mr. Crux his bond** be sent up, I intend to pay that, so that I shall not be troubled with their summons any further. (CEEC, Henry Oxinden, 1663/5: OXINDEN, 292)

This use of *his* may also reflect a more general tendency in Late Middle and Early Modern English to mark syntactic relations by analytic means for the sake of clarity. By analogy, *her* was occasionally used with female possessors, as in the verse passage in (4) referring to the Greek goddess Pallas Athena.

(4) The which he did with duetifull regaird
   According to **heighe pallas her command**
   For loe that sacred altar vp he raird . . .
   (LION, Patrick Gordon, *The First Booke of Penardo and Laissa*, 1615, VIII: 1769–72)

Even with sibilant-final singular nouns the *his*-genitive was, however, less common than the regular -*s* genitive, or the plain base form of the noun (Altenberg 1982: 43). The suffixless or *zero genitive* was typically found with names ending in -*s*, as in example (5) from George Fox's autobiography. It also occurred with native English nouns especially in the north of the country throughout the Early Modern period. The two illustrations in (6) come from Frances Basire's letters to her husband.

(5) And att last there came two or three women to **Tho: Atkins wife** into her shoppe pretendinge to by somethinge of her . . . (HC, George Fox, *Autobiography*, 1694: 153)

(6) I ham sory for **your deare frend deth.** Thoue you are not plesed to nam him, yet I thinke I know him – **Ser John Gudrike brother.** (CEEC, Frances Basire, 1651: BASIRE, 108)

Although it is customary to call the English genitive a case ending, this is not quite accurate because it can attach not only to a noun (*king's*) but also to a noun phrase (*king of Denmark's*). The example in (7) illustrates this *group genitive*, which was well established in Early Modern English. It was also recognised by the contemporary grammarian John Wallis in his *Grammatica Linguae Anglicanae* (1653).

(7) great endeavrs are acted by Sweden to take of that Crowne from theire allyance with the States to w*ch* purpose that King desires **the King of Denmarkes sister** in Marriage . . . (ICAME, *Newdigate Newsletters*, 1674: 117)

One of the broad trends in the history of English is a tendency to level inflections to zero endings or to replace them by alternative (*periphrastic*) expressions. The genitive, the sole surviving nominal case ending, also has zero representation with regular plural nouns in -*s* (the apostrophe is only a spelling device!). In many cases the genitive is replaced by an *of*-construction. In (8) *y**f forces of y**f King of Denmark* could in principle have been *y**f King of Denmark's forces* (cf. (7)).

(8) ye Citty of Hamburg has Writt to y*e* Elector of Brandenburg that they are very much allarmd at y*e* march of **y*e* forces of ye King of Denmark** w*ch* will in all lykelyhood fall upon them . . . (ICAME, *Newdigate Newsletters*, 1674: 51)

The *of*-construction gained ground in Middle English as many functions of the Old English genitive were taken over by this prepositional phrase. The genitive case came to be confined largely to personal nouns, and the *of*-construction to non-personal nouns. In a large database of seventeenth-century possessive constructions, the genitive occurred in two out of three animate nouns (persons, animals), but only in one in ten inanimate nouns; the genitive was also much more frequent in informal than formal prose (Altenberg 1982: 147, 254). These differences may reflect the subject matter – focusing on people – and the stylistic preferences of informal prose, which favour the use of the genitive rather than the *of*-construction.

6.3 Pronouns

Pronouns can basically assume the same functions in sentences as nouns and phrases made up of nouns. But unlike nouns, pronouns are *closed-class* items as their number cannot be increased freely. Only one personal pronoun form was introduced into Early Modern English, the possessive *its*. It was motivated by animacy, the distinction between personal and non-personal reference, which also largely lay behind the division of labour between the *-s* genitive and the *of*-construction.

6.3.1 Personal pronouns

Personal pronouns are used to indicate the speaker (*I*) and the addressee (*you*) or others involved in the text or discourse context (*he/she/it, they*). English personal pronouns show number (singular v. plural) and case, but mark personal as opposed to non-personal reference only in the third-person singular (*he/she* v. *it*). Apart from the possessive, the case system distinguishes between forms used as subjects and those used as objects in the sentence. Possessive forms are used either as independent pronouns (*it's **ours***) or, more often, as determiners of nouns, that is, alongside *a(n)* and *the* (*it's **our cat***, cf. *it's **a cat***, for determiners, see Chapter 8, section 2). Table 6.1 provides an outline of the Early Modern English

Table 6.1 Early Modern English personal pronouns

Person/ Number	Subjective case	Objective case	Possessive, determiner	Possessive, independent
1st sing.	*I*	*me*	*my/mine → my*	*mine*
1st pl.	*we*	*us*	*our*	*ours*
2nd sing.	*thou ~ ye → you*	*thee ~ you*	*thy/thine → thy ~ your*	*thine ~ yours*
2nd pl.	*ye → you*	*you*	*your*	*yours*
3rd sing. personal	*he, she*	*him, her*	*his, her*	*his, hers*
3rd sing. non-personal	*(h)it → it*	*him, (h)it → it*	*his (thereof) → its (of it)*	*(his → its)*
3rd pl.	*they*	*them ('em)*	*their*	*theirs*

system and the changes it underwent; the major changes are indicated in boldface.

The overall trend in the General dialect is towards less variation in the personal pronoun system, but the system itself has forms of both southern and northern origin. Let us begin by looking at the third-person plural. In Late Middle English the southern subject and possessive pronouns with *h-* had largely been replaced by the northern *they* and *their(s)* even in the south. This process was completed in the fifteenth century when the northern third-person plural object form *them* replaced the southern *hem*. The southern form can occasionally be found in writing in the early sixteenth century. The change would perhaps have been harder to detect in speech, because the unstressed forms of *hem* and *them* could have identical realisations, often rendered by *'em* in writing imitating speech. The example in (9) comes from Aphra Behn's *Oroonoko*.

> (9) They knew he and *Clemene* were scarce an hour in a day from my lodg-
>   ings; that they eat with me, and that I oblig'd **'em** in all things I was
>   capable of. I entertained **them** with the loves of the *Romans*, and great
>   men . . . (HC, Aphra Behn, *Oroonoko*, 1688: 192)

Another change of northern origin affected the first and second-person singular possessives when the long determiner forms with *-n*, *mine* and *thine*, went out of common use by the early seventeenth century. These long forms had been employed before words beginning with a vowel (*mine uncle*, cf. *an uncle*), and the short ones elsewhere (*my friend*, cf. *a friend*). The loss of *-n* occurred earlier in the north than in the south. In the course of the sixteenth century the short forms *my* and *thy* spread to most contexts and the long ones were retained only in poetic language and fixed expressions (*mine own, thine eyes*).

A notable asymmetry arose in the personal pronoun system when the singular *thou* (*thee, thy, thine*) retreated from the General dialect and, with the generalisation of the originally plural *you* (*ye, you, your, yours*), the number distinction between the second-person singular and plural was lost. This gradual process started in Middle English, when the plural *you* spread as the polite form in addressing one person (cf. French *vous*, German *Sie*). Social inferiors addressed their superiors by using *you*, and in the upper ranks *you* came to be established as the norm even among equals. *Thou* retreated to the private sphere, but could surface in public discourse when emotions ran high. Around 1600, *thou* is found in fiction, drama and poetry and in religious contexts of all kinds, especially with reference to God, as well as in trial records. The passage in (10) shows how *you* and *thou* varied in Sir Walter Raleigh's trial in 1603, where Sir

Edward Coke, the Attorney General, combined *thou* with terms of abuse, and even used it as a verb. By the early eighteenth century *thou* gradually disappeared from most kinds of writing, including trial records.

(10) *Raleigh.* I do not hear yet, that **you** have spoken one word against me; here is no Treason of mine done: If my Lord *Cobham* be a Traitor, what is that to me?

Attorney. All that he did was by **thy** Instigation, **thou** Viper; for I thou **thee, thou** Traitor.

Raleigh. It becometh not a Man of Quality and Virtue, to call me so: But I take comfort in it, it is all **you** can do.

Attorney. Have I anger'd **you**?
(HC, *The Trial of Sir Walter Raleigh*, 1603: 209)

Throughout the Early Modern period *you* vastly outnumbers *thou* in personal letters, which reflect everyday language use. The contexts where *thou* typically occurs in seventeenth-century correspondence include a mother writing to her child, or spouses expressing their mutual affection. Even these writers alternate between the two pronouns within one and the same letter. The excerpt in (11) is from Lady Katherine Paston's letter to her young son, a student in Cambridge, and the one in (12) from Henry Oxinden's letter to his beloved wife. Both writers come from rural areas, Katherine Paston from Norfolk and Henry Oxinden from Kent. The use of *thou* continues in regional dialects until the present day especially in the north and west of England (Trudgill 1999: 92–3).

(11) My good Child the *Lord* blese **the** ever more in all **thy** goinges ovtt and **thy** Cominges in. euen in all **thy** ways works and words, for his mercy sake: I was very glad to heer by **your** first letter that **you** wer so saffly arriued at **your** wished portt. (HC, Katherine Paston, c. 1624: 65)

(12) I read **thy** Letters over and over and over, for in them I see **thee** as well as I can. I am **thine** as much as possibly. I hope our Children are well. My service to all **you** think fitting to speake it to. (HC, Henry Oxinden, 1662: 274)

Thou is regularly included in the personal-pronoun paradigm by Early Modern English grammarians, but John Wallis (1653) notes that using the singular form in addressing someone usually implies disrespect or close familiarity (Kemp 1972: 323). In his *Short Introduction to English*

Grammar (1762: vi), Robert Lowth remarks that *thou* is disused even in the familiar style.

Another change that simplified the Early Modern English second-person pronoun system was the loss of the subject form *ye* when the object form *you* was generalised in the subject position in the General dialect. This levelling of case forms took place in the sixteenth century, spreading from informal contexts to more formal ones. It never made it to the King James Bible, however, which retained the traditional subject form *ye*.[1] Among the early adopters of *you* was King Henry VIII, who consistently used it in the subject function in his personal correspondence; see (13).

(13) Myne awne good Cardinall, I recomande me unto you with all my hart, and thanke yow for the grette payne and labour that **yow** do dayly take in my bysynes and maters, desyryng yow (that wen **yow** have well establyshyd them) to take summe pastyme and comfort, to the intent **yow** may the longer endure to serve us; (CEEC, King Henry VIII, 1520s: ORIGINAL 1, 269)

By contrast, the third-person singular non-personal pronoun generalised its weak subject form *it* to both subject and object functions, so losing its strong variant *hit* and the old neuter objective case form *him*. This change was completed in the course of the sixteenth century. One reason for it must have been the potential confusion of the non-personal *him* with the masculine form *him*. The example in (14) shows a typical late use of non-personal *him* in that it refers to an artery, part of the human body, which might be thought of as personified by the writer.

(14) The other Arterye that hath two cotes, is called *vena Arterialis*, or the great Artery that ascendeth and dissendeth; and of **him** springeth al the other Arteirs that spreade to euery member of the body, for by **him** is vnified and quickneth al the members of the body. (HC, Thomas Vicary, *The Anatomie of the Bodie of Man*, 1548: 59)

This transfer of *it* to the objective case went part of the way to solving a conflict created by forms going back to the earlier *grammatical gender* system at a time when English had already gone over to *notional gender*. In Old English all nouns were assigned a grammatical gender, just as in French or German today. Grammatical gender is semantically arbitrary: there is no inherent reason why *soleil* ('sun') in Modern French should be masculine but its German equivalent, *Sonne*, feminine. These distinctions are used to express grammatical relationships between words and word groups in sentences, and pronoun choices are determined by the grammatical gender of the word. Notional (or *natural*) gender, by contrast, is semantically motivated in that it encodes real-life distinctions such as the animacy and sex of the entities referred to. These are indicated in English by the third-person singular personal pronouns (*he*, *she*, *it*) and *reflexive pronouns* (*himself* (often *hisself* in Early Modern English), *herself*, *itself*).

Now, the problem that Early Modern English speakers had even after the levelling of the object forms of *it* was the non-personal possessive *his*, which coincided with the masculine possessive *his*. This form, illustrated by the passage from Thomas Blundeville's treatise on geometry in (15), was common at the turn of the seventeenth century.

(15) WHICH IS THE ARCTIQUE CIRCLE, AND WHY IS IT SO CALLED?
The Arctique Circle is that which is next to the North Pole, and hath **his** name of this worde *Arctos*, which is the great Beare or Charles wayne . . . (HC, Thomas Blundeville, *The Tables of the Three Speciall Right Lines Belonging to a Circle*, 1597: 156r)

This clash between personal and non-personal gender was resolved by the introduction of the new possessive form *its*, presumably by analogy with the genitive suffix -*s*. The excerpt in (16) from John Taylor's *Pennyles Pilgrimage* spells the new form with an apostrophe.

(16) I was faine to wade ouer the Riuer of *Annan* in *Scotland*, from which Riuer the County of *Annandale*, hath **it's** name. (HC, John Taylor, *Pennyles Pilgrimage*, 1630: 128)

Its is first found in John Florio's Italian–English dictionary, *A Worlde of Wordes* (1598). The traditional form persisted in the 1611 Bible, as in *if the salt haue lost **his** savour, wherewith shall it be salted?* (Matthew 5: 13). The new variant *its* spread to the determiner function in the first half of the seventeenth century, becoming the norm in the second half of the century. Unlike the determiner, the independent possessive pronoun *its* is marginal even today (Quirk et al. 1985: 346).

Notional gender, however, is subject to cultural conventions as well. Although a word like *earth* takes the non-personal possessive *its* in the seventeenth century, it can also be assigned the feminine pronoun. The same optionality applies to *church*, *city*, *month*, *moon*, *sun* and similar words, which may take a personal pronoun besides a non-personal one. A change of perspective can take place even within one sentence as in (17), where the Mother Earth begins as a neuter (*its*) but changes to feminine (*her*) after the mention of the Sun, which takes the masculine. Cases such as this are not simple instances of *personification*, but are also textually motivated: the use of *it*(*s*) across the board would have obscured the internal reference relations in the paragraph.

> (17) But as **the Earth**, the Mother of all Creatures here below, sends up all
> **its** Vapours and proper emissions at the command of **the Sun**, and yet
> requires them again to refresh **her** own Needs, and they are deposited
> between them both in the bosome of a Cloud as a common receptacle,
> that they may cool **his** Flames, and yet descend to make **her** Fruitful:
> So are the proprieties of a Wife to be dispos'd of by her Lord; (HC,
> Jeremy Taylor, *The Marriage Ring*, 1673: 19)

The rise of *its* was not a straightforward case of substituting one form for another but involved other morphological options, notably *thereof* and *of it*. They link it up with the choice of the *of*-construction instead of the genitive with inanimate nouns. *Thereof* was a frequent alternative in Late Middle English, but became rare in most registers in the second half of the seventeenth century. Blundeville uses it in a chapter heading in (18). By contrast, *of it* has continued as an option until the present day. It is illustrated in (19) by the description of a flea from Robert Hooke's *Micrographia*, which draws a parallel between *its* and *of it*.

> (18) OF THE MERIDIAN, AND OF THE VSES **THEREOF**.
> (HC, Thomas Blundeville, *The Tables of the Three Speciall Right Lines*,
> 1597: 153v)

> (19) The strength and beauty of this small creature, had it no other rela-
> tion at all to man, would deserve a description. For **its** strength, the
> *Microscope* is able to make no greater discoveries of it then the naked
> eye, but onely the curious contrivance of **its** leggs . . . But, as for the
> beauty **of it**, the *Microscope* manifests it to be all over adorn'd with a
> curiously polish'd suit of *sable* Armour . . . (HC, Robert Hooke,
> *Micrographia*, 1665: 210)

Notional gender distinctions also emerge in the Early Modern English *relative pronouns*, which will be discussed below in 6.3.2.

The *generic* use of personal pronouns does not appear to have undergone any major changes in Early Modern English. When the sex of the referent was undetermined, the traditional masculine *he* was used throughout the period, but we often also find the plural pronoun *they*, which in this use goes back to Middle English. Generic *he* is found in (20), which comes in George Colville's *Boethius* translation (*whosoeuer . . . he*). Generic *they* occurs in (21a), in Lucy Russell's letter to her friend Jane Cornwallis (*nonne of yours . . . them*), and in (21b), Arabella Stuart's letter to her grandmother Elizabeth Talbot (*one . . . they, theyr*).

(20) For when euerye one of them is the selfe same, and lyke the other, **whosoeuer** seketh to get any one of them w'out the others, certes **he** hath not that **he** desyrethe. (HC, George Colville (transl.), *Boethius*, 1556: 70)

(21a) be confident that ther is **nonne of yours** to whom I will be more wanting in any thing I may do for **them** then I wold have binn to my owne if God had continued me a mother . . . (CEEC, Lucy Russell, 1619: Cornwallis, 62)

(21b) He taught me by the example of Samuell that **one** might pretend on errand and deliver an other with a safe conscience. By the example of Sampson that **one** might and (if **they** be not too foolish to live in this world) must speake riddles to **theyr** frends and try the truth of offred love . . . (CEEC, Arabella Stuart, 1603: Stuart, 130)

Early Modern legal language also displays the double form *him or her*, illustrated in (22a). That this use is motivated by the need to provide for all eventualities rather than to avoid a gender bias can be seen in cases like (22b), where the plural *them* is singled out separately.

(22a) Then **everie person** soe offendinge shall forfeyte and lose fower tymes the value of everie suche Cable so by **him or her** made or cause to be made as ys aforesaide . . . (HC, *The Statutes of the Realm*, 1592–3: 857)

(22b) Provided always neverthelesse That this Act shall not extend to any **Person or Persons** in Execution for any Fine on **him her or them** imposed for any Offence by **him her or them** committed. (HC, *The Statutes of the Realm*, 1695–6: 76)

It is worth noting, however, that the avoidance of a gender bias may be reflected in *indefinite pronouns*, whose referents are not specified. The generic use of *man* declined in the compounds *some man, any man, no man* and *every man* during the Early Modern English period, as *-one* and *-body* compounds gained ground (cf. the relic use of *man* in *no man's land*).

6.3.2 Relative pronouns

Relative pronouns introduce relative clauses, which modify nouns and noun phrases. English has three basic relativisation strategies: *wh-*, *th-* and *zero* (*a person who(m)/ that/* [0]/ *I know*). *Wh-* pronouns distinguish personal from non-personal referents (*who* v. *which*), but do not show number contrast (*a person/ persons who; a thing/ things which*), and only *who* inflects for case (subjective, objective and possessive). *That* has the same functions as *wh-* relative pronouns in the subjective and objective case, but it is uninflected and does not distinguish between personal and non-personal referents or number (*a person/ things that I know*). The *zero* strategy is found in cases where the relative clause does not have an overt relative marker (*a person/ things* [0] *I know*). Table 6.2 shows the Early Modern English system, which is quite similar to the one we have today.

A formal distinction between subjective and objective case becomes part of the relative pronoun system in Early Modern English, when the subject pronoun *who* is consolidated in the language. As *who* gradually replaces *which* with human referents, it also strengthens the animacy distinction. This is yet another case where notional gender appears to be the driving force behind linguistic change in Early Modern English.

The relative *who* is first attested as a subject relative pronoun in the early fifteenth century in closing formulae of letters and prayers with reference to God (. . . *that knoweth* **God**, **who** *have you in his blessed kepyng*, from the Stonor letters; Rydén 1983: 127). *Who* began to diffuse from divine to human reference towards the end of the fifteenth century. Because of its origins, it was first used in relative clauses that provided new information about the referent (*non-restrictive relative clauses*) but were not required to identify it (as is the case in *restrictive relative clauses*). Example (23) is typical of the sixteenth-century usage. The convention of separating a non-restrictive relative clause by commas is of later date.

Table 6.2 Early Modern English relativisers

Gender	Subjective case	Objective case	Possessive, determiner	Determiner
personal	*which* → *who*	*whom*	*whose*	*which*
	that	*that*		
	(zero)	zero		
non-personal	*which*	*which*	*whose*	*which*
	that	*that*	(*whereof*)	
	(zero)	zero	(*of which*)	

(23) All this I shewed to G. Nonne **who** semeth very lothe that Dobbes
shuld have yt becawse he thynketh he will deale streyghtlye with the
tenantes ... (CEEC, Francis Wyndham, 1577: BACON, 249)

In the sixteenth century the relative pronoun *which* could be used
with personal and non-personal referents and in restrictive and non-
restrictive functions; *that* occurred in both but with a preference for the
restrictive function; and the zero relative was confined to the restrictive
function alone. In (24) *which* introduces a restrictive clause which iden-
tifies the particular messenger talked about, and in (25) the relative
clause headed by a zero relative is similarly used to describe the generic
no man.

(24) The messenger **which** had my last letters was reternyd back by
whether ageyn ... (CEEC, Robert Dudley, 1586: LEYCESTER, 134)

(25) There is no man here [0] dealethe more honorably and faythefully
towardes your lordship then this bearers master ... (CEEC, Francis
Walsingham, 1586: BACON 273)

In the course of the Early Modern English period, the zero strategy
lost ground in the subject position and *who* was established especially in
the written language. *Who* could also appear in the object position
instead of *whom*, although this was less common with the relative *who*
than with the corresponding *interrogative* pronoun. The two alternative
forms of the relative *who* in (26) come from *Richard III.*

(26a) Hath she forgot alreadie that braue Prince,
Edward, her Lord, **whom** I (some three monthes since)
Stab'd in my angry mood, at Tewkesbury?
(William Shakespeare, *Richard III*, 1623: I.ii. 255–7)

(26b) *Clarence*, **who** I indeede haue cast in darknesse,
I do beweepe to many simple Gulles ...
(William Shakespeare, *Richard III*, 1623: I.iii. 335–6)

Whose continued to function as a possessive determiner with personal
as well as non-personal referents, as in (27). This is the case even today
in written language. But parallel to *thereof*, the synthetic relative *whereof*
could be used with non-personal referents (28). The analytic alternative,
of which, parallel to the *of*-construction found with nouns and personal
pronouns, also gained ground with non-personal referents especially in
the seventeenth century (Schneider 1992). It is illustrated in (29).

(27) So is it by me also wel approoued, this plaister called *Oxicroceum*, **whose** composition is not far to be sought for. (HC, William Clowes, *Treatise for the Artificiall Cure of Struma*, 1602: 15)

(28) Besides he spake of Plots and Invasions; of the Particulars **whereof** he could give no Account, tho *Raleigh* and he had conferred of them. (HC, *The Trial of Sir Walter Raleigh*, 1603: 209)

(29) most of the white branchings disappear'd, and most also of the redness or sucked blood in the guts, the *peristaltick* motion **of which** was scarce discernable; (HC, Robert Hooke, *Micrographia*, 1665: 213)

In Middle English the relative pronoun *which* had a longer variant, *the which*, but the plain *which* largely replaced it in the General dialect in the course of the sixteenth century (see Chapter 10, section 4).

The determiner *which* is used with personal and non-personal referents particularly in formal registers. The case in (30) from Francis Bacon's *Aduancement of Learning* is typical of relative clause use in written Early Modern English in that it illustrates a *continuative relative clause*.

(30) For it is one thing to set forth what ground lyeth vnmanured; and another thing to correct ill husbandry in that which is manured.
    In the handling & vndertaking of **which** worke, I am not ignorant, what it is, that I doe now mooue and attempt, nor insensible of mine own weakenes, to susteine my purpose . . . (HC, Francis Bacon, *Aduancement of Learning*, 1605: 6v)

Modelled on Latin, continuative relative clauses could begin a sentence, or even a new paragraph as in (30), and were intended to improve the cohesion of the text. They are very frequent especially in the sixteenth century. *Demonstrative* pronouns and determiners (*this, these, that, those*) could be used for similar purposes.

6.4 Summary

Apart from the zero and *his*-genitives, the number and case marking of Early Modern English nouns does not basically differ from Present-day English. More changes took place in pronouns. The number distinction began to erode in the second-person pronouns when *you* became common for singular as well as plural addressees; the process was completed when *thou* went out of use in the General dialect in Early Modern English. The case contrast between the subjective *ye* and objective *you* was similarly lost with the generalisation of *you* in both functions.

One of the few additions to the pronoun system of the language was the introduction of the inflectional possessive pronoun *its* at the end of the sixteenth century. Like the subject relative *who*, another latecomer to the system, *its* is unambiguous between personal and non-personal reference. Marking this semantic distinction is expedient in a language with notional gender, and there is a clear trend towards animacy and personal gender being marked in Early Modern English pronouns. This is also apparent in the 'dehumanisation' of the relative pronoun *which*, and in the variation between the genitive and the *of*-construction in nouns.

Note

1. This second-person plural form *ye* should not be confused with the <ye> spelling of the definite article *the* found in many editions of Early Modern English texts; see, for instance, example (4) in Chapter 2. This spelling of *the* normally appears in manuscripts in an abbreviated form (*yᵉ*), which goes back to an earlier spelling with the letter thorn <þ>. The spelling of the pronoun *ye* reflects its pronunciation with /j/; it is also occasionally spelled with the letter yogh <ȝ> in the sixteenth century.

Exercises

1. In *The English Grammar*, published in Oxford in 1633, Charles Butler writes about the plural of nouns formed in -*en* (Butler's special characters have been replaced with their standard equivalents, for example, <ð> with <th>):

> The Plural number is likewise made of the Singular, by adding *en*: as of *ox oxen, chick chicken, marg margen, brother brotheren*, and contracte[d] *brethren*, of *childe* (*r* put betweene) *children*, of *man mannen*... which wee contract into *men*, of *hous housen*, though most usually *houses*, of *hose, peas, hosen peasen*: but in these two the singular is most used for the plural: as a pair of *hose*, a pek of *peas*, though the Londoners seeme to make it a regular plural, calling a *peas* a *pea*. (Butler 1633: 34)

Using the OED, comment on (a) these plural forms and (b) the criteria Butler introduces to account for the choice of forms.

2. Discuss the *periphrastic* (circumlocutory) means of expressing (a) the genitive case in nouns and (b) the possessive case in personal and relative pronouns in Early Modern English. What semantic motives could be suggested for the use of the periphrastic forms?

3. Hope (1993: 97) argues that the use of second-person pronouns in drama may not correspond to that in real life in Early Modern England. Compare the passage from Middleton's comedy (3) and the personal letter (4) in Appendix 2. How consistent is the use of *you* and *thou* in these texts?

4. Discuss the ambiguities that notional gender created in third-person singular pronouns at the beginning of the Early Modern period. How were they resolved?

Further reading

Basic definitions of the grammatical terms used in this chapter (and in Chapters 7 and 8), such as *case*, *number* and *grammatical gender* can be found, for example, in David Crystal's *A Dictionary of Linguistics and Phonetics* (2003) or in the glossary appended to the same author's *The Cambridge Encyclopedia of the English Language* (1995; 2nd edn 2003).

For a recent discussion of the history of grammatical and notional gender in English, see Curzan (2003). Altenberg (1982) provides a corpus-based description of the variation between the genitive and the *of*-construction in the seventeenth century. The second-person pronouns *you* and *thou* are analysed in all the works referred to in Chapter 1; Busse's monograph on the topic (2002) focuses on Shakespeare. For the generalisation of *you*, the rise of *its*, and loss of *man* compounds, see Nevalainen and Raumolin-Brunberg (2003), and for relative pronouns, Rydén (1966) and Romaine (1982), who deals with Older Scots. For Present-day English, see Quirk et al. (1985), Chapter 5 on nouns and Chapter 6 on pronouns. Biber et al. (1999) adopt a register-oriented approach to the grammatical categories of English, and discuss nouns and pronouns in Chapter 4.

7 Verbs, adjectives and adverbs

7.1 Verbs

English verbs have changed more than nouns between the fifteenth century and the present day. With the loss of the second-person singular pronoun *thou, person* and *number* marking was reduced in verbs. The third-person present-tense singular suffix changed in the General dialect as -(*e*)*th* gave way to -(*e*)*s* by the middle of the Early Modern period. There was also a great deal of variation in the *tense* forms of irregular verbs, and new developments were under way in the *mood* and *aspect* systems.[1] Overall, the Early Modern English verb was less modern than the noun.

7.1.1 Person and number

Early Modern English verbs typically mark person and number contrast in the second (-(*e*)*st*) and third person singular (-(*e*)*th*/-*s*) as opposed to zero marking in the first person singular and the whole of the plural. But the third-person singular ending applies only in the present tense. As shown by Table 7.1, it is the recessive second-person singular *thou* which really justifies us talking about person marking in Early Modern English: the second-person singular suffix -(*e*)*st* also attaches to past-tense verbs. It is appended to lexical verbs when there is no auxiliary verb present, and to auxiliaries (*can/could, may/might, will/would, shall/should*, and so on), which occur with lexical verbs. *Thou wilt* and *thou shalt* are used with *will* and *shall*, and *thou art* and *thou hast* with *be* and *have*. Example (1) from Preston's *Boethius* illustrates some second-person past-tense forms.

(1) And also that thou **mightst** be satisfied that evil Men, who as thou **didst** complain went unpunished, do never indeed escape Punishment: And also that thou **mightst** learn that that Licence of doing Evil, which thou **prayedst** might soon end, is not long; (HC, Richard Preston (transl.), *Boethius*, 1695: 181)

Table 7.1 Early Modern English verbs

Person/ Number	Present tense	Past tense	Present/past perfective aspect	Present/past progressive aspect
1st sing.	*I pray*	*I prayed*	*I have/had prayed*	*I am/was praying*
1st pl.	*we pray*	*we prayed*	*we have/had prayed*	*we are/were praying*
2nd sing.	***thou pray(e)st*** ~	***thou prayedst*** ~	***thou hast/hadst prayed*** ~	***thou art/wert praying*** ~
2nd sing. and 2nd pl.	*you (ye) pray*	*you (ye) prayed*	*you (ye) have/had prayed*	*you (ye) are/were praying*
3rd sing.	*he/she prayeth → prays*	*he/she prayed*	*he/she **hath** → **has**/had prayed*	*he/she is/was praying*
3rd pl.	*they pray*	*they prayed*	*they have/had prayed*	*they are/were praying*

The verbs *be* and *have* distinguish the first, second and third person in the present tense in the singular (*am, art, is; have, hast, hath/has*), but not in the plural (*be/are, have*). The present-tense plural of *be* became distinct from the base form in the General dialect when the originally northern plural form *are* replaced the southern *be*-form (cf. *the powers that be* in the Tyndale Bible, 1534; see p. 38). *Have* and *be* are not only lexical verbs but, as shown by Table 7.1, also auxiliaries, *have* in the perfect and *be* in the progressive aspect, which gains ground in the course of the Early Modern period (see section 7.1.2).

The only person inflection that is found in Standard English today is the third-person singular present-tense suffix -(*e*)*s*. Of northern origin, -(*e*)*s* had largely replaced the southern -(*e*)*th* in the General dialect by the early seventeenth century, although -(*e*)*th* prevailed in some regional dialects and formal genres much longer. Example (2), which illustrates southern usage in the first half of the sixteenth century, contains the third-person singular -(*e*)*th* and the present-tense plural form *be* of the verb *be*.

(2) Barley and otes **be** moste commonly mowen, and a man or woman **folowythe** the mower with a hande-rake halfe a yarde longe, with .vii. or .viii. tethe, in the lyfte hande, and a syckle in the ryghte hande, and

with the rake he **gethereth** as moche as wyll make a shefe. (HC, Anthony Fitzherbert, *The Book of Husbandry*, 1534: 36)

The originally northern *are*-form replaced *be* in the plural in the course of the sixteenth century, but the southward diffusion of -(*e*)*s* took longer. At the end of the sixteenth century -(*e*)*th* and -(*e*)*s* can be found side by side in the same text, as in (3), an extract from one of Queen Elizabeth's letters to King James VI of Scotland.

(3) that a question may, upon allegeance, be demanded by yourselfe of the mastar Gray, whether he **knoweth** not the prise of my bloude, wiche shuld be spild by bloudy hande of a murtherar, wiche some of your nere-a-kin did graunt. A sore question, you may suppose, but no other act than suche as I am assured he **knowes**, and therfor I hope he wyl not dare deny you a truthe . . . (CEEC, Queen Elizabeth I, 1585: ROYAL 1, 11)

The three verbs *do*, *have* and *say* were slow to acquire the northern suffix in the General dialect. *Hath* and *doth* persisted well into the second half of the seventeenth century, when -(*e*)*s* was the regular ending with other verbs, as in Samuel Pepys's letter to his brother from 1670 in (4). This phenomenon is known as *lexical diffusion*: the incoming form does not spread to all contexts at once but some acquire it earlier than others.

(4) Brother. something **hath** offered it selfe which may prove of advantage to you, that **makes** it necessary for mee to have you here on Tuesday night next. (CEEC, Samuel Pepys, 1670: PEPYS, 16)

Phonological constraints were also involved in the diffusion of -(*e*)*s*: *-eth* was retained longer in verbs ending in the sibilants /s/ (*compasseth*), /z/ (*causeth*) and /ʃ/ (*diminisheth*), and sibilant-final affricates /tʃ/ (*catcheth*) and /dʒ/ (*changeth*). In these contexts the ending preserved its vowel, just as it does today. Elsewhere the vowel had been lost in ordinary speech in the course of the sixteenth century. The distinction appears in spelling in (5).

(5) his conscience **opposeth** his wisedome of Gouerment, and his Soueraignity **runs** a daunger. (HC, Edward Conway, 1623: 155)

Early Modern English also showed the tendency found in many present-day regional dialects to level person marking in the third-person singular. It was not a very prominent trend, but instances of it occur especially in private writings (2 per cent of all the instances of the third-person singular in the HC; Kytö 1993: 118). See example (6).

(6) My humble service to yᵉ Lady Thanet and my Lady Cicelea. Yʳ sister **disir** yᵉ same to you and to the Lᵃ Cicelea. (HC, Elizabeth Hatton, 1666: 50)

These occasional omissions of the third-person singular present-tense suffix fall in with a more general tendency towards levelling person and number marking in English verb morphology. Here the singular follows the model set by the plural. The southern plural suffix -(*e*)*th* had largely been lost by the beginning of the Early Modern period, as had the plural -(*e*)*s* in the North and -(*e*)*n* in the Midlands, which both used to vary with zero depending on the construction type. In the General dialect, zero plurals predominate in the present tense in the sixteenth century, although occasional plural marking still occurs. The passage in (7) from Vicary's treatise on anatomy (1548) marks the third co-ordinate verb *drinketh*.

(7) and in some places of the brayne the Veynes and the Arteirs **goo** foorth of him, and **enter** into the diuisions of the brayne, and there **drinketh** of the brayne substaunce into them, (HC, Thomas Vicary, *The Anatomie of the Bodie of Man*, 1548: 30)

7.1.2 Tense and aspect

Tense marking relates the action of the verb to the time of the utterance. The *present tense* is unmarked in Early Modern and Present-day English alike: verbs appear in their base forms in the present tense, and person and number are singled out only in the second- and third-person singular. But the *past tense* is marked (-*ed*), and so are the two aspectual categories (see Table 7.1). The auxiliary *have* followed by the past participle (*have* + -*ed*) expresses the *perfective aspect*, completed action, whereas action in progress, the *progressive aspect*, is expressed by the auxiliary *be* and the present participle (*be* + -*ing*). Besides the *regular* or *weak* forms in -*ed*, a number of verbs have *irregular* past-tense and past-participle forms.

The past-tense and past-participle forms of the great majority of verbs were formed by means of the regular -*ed* suffix in Early Modern English. The vowel sound in the suffix was usually deleted in colloquial language especially in the second half of the period, but in formal styles -*ed* was pronounced as a separate syllable until the end of the seventeenth century. In example (8), dating from 1670, John Milton indicates the omission of the vowel by an apostrophe. He also indicates how the consonant was pronounced: /d/ after a voiced sound (/v/ in *receav'd* and /n/ in *Crown'd*), but /t/ after a voiceless one (/s/ in *renounc't* and /ʃ/ in *banish't*). Note that the vowel is always retained, just as today, in verbs such as *sounded* and *enacted*, which end in /t/ or /d/.

(8) Canute having thus **sounded** the Nobility . . . **receav'd** thir Oath of fealty, they the pledge of his bare hand, and Oath from the *Danish* Nobles; whereupon the House of *Edmund* was **renounc't**, and *Canute* **Crown'd**. Then they **enacted**, that *Edwi* Brother of *Edmund*, a Prince of great hope, should be **banish't** the Realm. (HC, John Milton, *The History of Britain*, 1670: 275)

Throughout the Early Modern English period there was a great deal of variation in the past-tense and past-participle forms of irregular verbs. In some verbs the levelling of the past-tense singular and plural in Middle English increased the number of available forms. Many common verbs such as *bear, begin, break, get, give, help, run, speak, take* and *write* return more than one past-tense and at least two past-participle forms in the Early Modern English section of the *Helsinki Corpus* (Lass 1994: 97). The data in (9) illustrate the alternative past participles of *help*. In this case it was the regular -*ed* form that won the day in Late Modern English.

(9a) And so had god **holpen** them, yᵗ yᵉ mischief turned vpon them yᵗ wold haue done it. (HC, Thomas More, *The History of King Richard III*, 1514–18: 53)

(9b) Many be **holp** by this bathe from scabbes and aches. (HC, John Leland, *The Itinerary of John Leland*, 1535–43: 142)

(9c) Yff I had remayned with you, I wolde have **helped** him in this case; (CEEC, Edmund Grindall, 1579: HUTTON, 61)

The corpus shows that -*en* participles tended to be generalised with *break* (*broken*), *eat* (*eaten*), *get* (*gotten*), *speak* (*spoken*), *take* (*taken*) and *write* (*written*), but that they were far from being fixed by the end of the Early Modern period. *Gotten*, for instance, was retained in American English, while the shorter form *got* was generalised in British English.

Much more variation in the strong verbs was recorded in seventeenth-century school grammars than is recorded today. John Wallis recognises up to three possible past-tense and past-participle sets for verbs such as *abide* (*abode – abode; abidd – abidd; abided – abided*), *choose* (*chose – chose*; *chose – chosen; chosed – chosed*) and *thrive* (*throve – throve/ thriven; thrive – thrive; thrived – thrived*) (Wallis 1653: 107–8).

Variation is even allowed by the prescriptive grammarian Robert Lowth (1762), who admits the past-tense forms *bare* and *bore* for *bear*, *brake* and *broke* for *break*; *clang* and *clung* for *cling*, *gat* and *got* for *get*, *sank* and *sunk* for *sink*; *sang* and *sung* for *sing*, and *swam* and *swum* for *swim*, as well as the past participles *helped* and *holpen* for *help*, and *drunk* and *drunken* for *drink* (Lass 1994: 99, 107).

Despite the fluctuation in the form of individual verbs, the perfective structure was well established in Early Modern English. One difference between the Present-day and Early Modern English constructions is that Early Modern English normally preferred the auxiliary *be* with verbs of motion (for example, *arrive*, *come*, *depart*, *enter*, *fall*, *go*, *land*, *return*, *ride*, *run*, *sail*, *set*) and change of state (for example, *become*, *change*, *grow*, *melt*, *turn*, *wax* 'grow'). *Come* is illustrated in (10). The preference changed in the course of the Late Modern period, when *have* replaced *be*.

(10) Al thes **are come** (sayde he,) to see yow suffer deathe; there ys some here that **ys come** as farre as Lyengkecon [Lincoln], but I truste ther commynge shal be yn vayne. (HC, Thomas Mowntayne, *Narratives of the Days of the Reformation* 1553: 203)

The simple past could sometimes be used where the speaker of modern standard British English (but not necessarily of American English) would expect the perfective. This is particularly the case when the action of the sentence is limited by a time adverbial such as *never*. Compare the three cases from Raleigh's trial in (11).

(11) *Attorn.* The King's Safety and your Clearing cannot agree. I protest before God, I **never knew** a clearer Treason.

Raleigh. I **never had** Intelligence with *Cobham* **since I came to the Tower**.

Attorn. Go to, I will lay thee upon thy Back, for the confidentest Traitor that **ever came** at a Bar. (HC, *The Trial of Sir Walter Raleigh*, 1603: 216)

The progressive *be* plus *-ing* construction was only consolidated in the Early Modern period. That it might be related to an earlier verbal noun is suggested by an alternative structure with a remnant of a preposition preceding *-ing* in cases like (12) ('on playing'). But overall, the simple verbal *be* plus *-ing* construction was more common in Early Modern English, and steadily gained ground in the course of the period (Elsness 1994: 11–13). The two cases in (13) come from *The Merry Wives*.

(12) As I **was a playing** at cardes, one seeing I wonne all I playd for, would needes haue the knaue from mee, (HC, Robert Armin, *A Nest of Ninnies*, 1608: 8)

(13) *Mis Ford. Mistris Page*, trust me, I **was going** to your house.

Mis Page. And trust me, I **was comming** to you: (HC, William Shakespeare, *The Merry Wives of Windsor*, 1623: 43.C2)

The use of the progressive aspect has expanded and multiplied since the Early Modern period, where the simple present could also often assume a progressive meaning, as in Polonius's question cited above in Chapter 4: *What do you read, my Lord?* When *be* plus *-ing* became fully productive as a progressive construction, it also acquired the passive form. In Early Modern English the active form was still typically used with a passive sense. The case in (14) could be paraphrased 'is being made'.

(14) my french hood is bought already, and my silke gowne **is a making**, likewise the Goldsmith hath brought home my chayne and bracelets: (HC, Thomas Deloney, *Jack of Newbury*, 1619: 70)

In the latter half of the seventeenth century, the progressive construction *be going to* developed a special meaning indicating *future time*. Unlike in (13), no physical action of going is implied in example (15), but only the future fulfilment of Sir John Walter's present intention is being referred to (cf. Quirk et al. 1985: 214). The new construction is an instance of *grammaticalisation*, a process in which lexical material comes to be fixed in a given grammatical function. This is a way of creating grammatical 'short-cuts' from existing lexical resources. In Present-day English *going to* has grammaticalised even further and been reduced to *gonna* (*we're gonna go there*).

(15) Sr John Walter **is going to** be marryed to my Lady Stoel, wch will be very happy for him. (HC, Anne Hatton, 1695: 214)

Other typical ways of expressing future time in Early Modern English are illustrated by the examples in (16). Futurity was generally expressed by means of the auxiliaries *shall* (16a) and *will*, with *will* gaining ground in the first person in the Early Modern period (16b). The quasi-auxiliary *be to* was also available (16c). And, as today, the simple present could be used to express future time when the future event was associated with a high degree of certainty (16d).

(16a) Neither do I thincke yt is any newes to you, that your cousen Carleton bishop of Chichester **shall marrie** the Lady Nevill Sir Henries widow. (CEEC, John Chamberlain, 1619: CHAMBERLAIN, 270)

(16b) *Nurse*. . . . if you shou'd be married now, what **will** you do when Sir *Tunbelly* calls for you to be wedd?

   Miss. Why then we **will be married** again. (HC, John Vanbrugh, *The Relapse or Virtue in Danger*, 1697: 64)

(16c) Next week Lady Ann Churchill **is to be married** to Lord Spencer. (HC, Alice Hatton, 1699: 242)

(16d) Yesterday the Quene feasted all that gave presents to her last bride, and on Shrove-Sonday she **marries** another of her maides, (one of the Lady Southwells daughters,) to Radney a man of goode living in Somerset-shire. (CEEC, John Chamberlain, 1614: CHAMBERLAIN, 512)

7.1.3 Mood

The mood system records the distinction between real and hypothetical verbal activity. It can be signalled inflectionally by a contrast between the *indicative* and the *subjunctive*, the indicative being the default value. In Modern English the present subjunctive is indicated by the base form of the verb, and the past subjunctive by the past-tense form. Inflectional mood marking is therefore neutralised except in the second- and third-person singular, or if the verb is *be*. So in the third-person singular the suffixed verb form represents the indicative mood (*he goes*), and the base form the subjunctive (*they insist that he go*). The uninflected *be* functions as the present subjunctive of *be*, and *were* as its past form in all persons.

The subjunctive had a more significant role to play in the Early Modern English verbal system than it has now especially in British English, where the indicative mood and *modal auxiliaries* have taken over many of its former contexts of use (*they insist that he goes/ that he should go*). The subjunctive continues on a firmer footing in American English (*they insist that he go*). In Early Modern English it was routinely triggered by certain hypothetical, conjectural and volitional contexts. These include nominal *that*-clauses in demands and suggestions, intentions and wishes, as well as in expressions of possibility, (non-)desirability and surprise. Some of these are illustrated with the subjunctive *be* in (17).

(17a) After that a childe is come to seuen yeres of age, I holde it expedient that he **be** taken from the company of women: (HC, Thomas Elyot, *The Boke Named the Gouernour*, 1531: 23)

(17b) I beseche you, my Lord that the said Prior may be so entreated by your help, that he **be** not sory, (HC, Thomas Bedyll, 1537: 77)

(17c) Now for his hey you shall see that it **be** hie short vplandish hey, and so it **be** sweet, respect not how course or rough it is; (HC, Gervase Markham, *Countrey Contentments*, 1615: 77)

The subjunctive also occurred in wishes and exhortations in main clauses. Some such collocations became fixed phrases (*as help me God; how be it; heaven/ God forbid*). Frequent use reduced *God be with you* to *goodbye*.

The subjunctive was also used to mark hypothetical or unreal meaning in clauses indicating condition, concession and time. Even hypothetical main clauses could take a subjunctive in Early Modern English, although it was more typical of subordinate clauses beginning with *(al)though, as though, before, except* ('unless'), *if, lest, provided, till, unless, until* and *whether* (for example, *if I were*). The subjunctive *were* occurs in a hypothetical main clause in (18), and *were* and *be* in the subordinate clauses in (19).

(18) *Dan.* Because the hogges and the Cow died, are you sure the Cat did kil them, might they not die of some naturall causes as you see both men and beasts are well, and die suddainlie?

Sam. That **were** strange, if they should die of naturall causes, and fall out so fit at the time after he was sent? (HC, George Gifford, *A Dialogue Concerning Witches and Witchcraftes*, 1593: E2r)

(19) Lastly, it maketh his will to be no will, **as though** his goods **were** not his owne: for nothing is ours but that which wee haue rightlie got: and therefore wee say, It is mine by right, **as though** it **were** not ours, **vnles** it **be** ours by right. (HC, Henry Smith, *Of Usurie*, 1591: D7v)

The subjunctive has never been the only way of signalling hypothetical verbal activity in English. Periphrastic modal expressions date back to Old English. Just like today, modal auxiliaries were the typical means of conveying these various semantic notions in main and subordinate clauses in Early Modern English. In (20), hypothetical condition is expressed by periphrastic (*should, would*) and inflectional means (*were*); see also example (18), above (*if they should die*).

(20) That is all one. **If** any body **should** ask me ... I **should** say, I heard so; and it **would** be very good Evidence, **unless** some one else **were** produc'd. (HC, *The Trial of Titus Oates*, 1685: 75)

7.2 Adjectives and adverbs

7.2.1 Adjectives

English adjectives have four characteristics. They can modify nouns (*a happy day*), and complement the subject (*the day was happy*) and the object of the sentence (*it made me happy*). Adjectives can be modified by adverbs like *very* (*very happy*), and they can be compared (*she was happier, she was the happiest of them all*).

Adjectives are only inflected for comparison, and have forms for the comparative (*-er*) and superlative degrees (*-est*). Early Modern English also makes full use of the periphrastic system of comparison by means of *more* and *most* established in Late Middle English (*more beautiful, most beautiful*). This is yet another instance of the rivalry between traditional inflectional endings and more transparent, analytic forms.

The same basic principle holds for Present-day and Early Modern English alike that short, mono- and disyllabic adjectives are usually compared by means of inflectional endings, and longer ones periphrastically with *more* and *most*. Both these means of comparison are illustrated by comparative forms in (21) and (22). Some native irregular forms such as (*good*) *better, best* and (*bad*) *worse, worst* are still in use.

(21) those meates and drinkes that are of **grosser** substance and **hoter** than others be, cause and breede the stone rather than other meates and drinkes that are **thinner, finer** and of a **colder** complexion, but both French, Clared and Gascone Clared wine are of **grosser** and **thicker** substaunce, and **hoter** of complexion than white Rhennish wine and white french wines be of. (HC, William Turner, *A New Boke of the Natures and Properties of All Wines*, 1568: B7v–8r)

(22) but for as much as those tables be not altogether truely Printed, and for that they haue beene lately corrected, and made **more perfect** by *Clauius*, who doth set downe the saide Tables in quarto and not in folio, whereby they are the **more portable**, and the **more commodious**, as well for that they are more truely Printed, (HC, Thomas Blundeville, *The Tables of the Three Speciall Right Lines*, 1597: 51r)

The periphrasis is preferred in literary genres such as philosophical and religious treatises in Early Modern English. By contrast, inflectional forms are favoured in texts reflecting the spoken language, where even long adjectives can take inflectional endings (cf. *confidentest* in example (11), above). This pattern of distribution is parallel to the analytic *of-*

construction being more common than the -s genitive in formal kinds of writing in Early Modern English (see 6.2.2).

Overall, periphrastic forms, especially comparatives, are somewhat more common in Early Modern English than today, and they are also found with disyllabic adjectives (Kytö and Romaine 1997). The passage in (23) contains both means of comparison.

(23) This is holden the **surer** and **more easie** way: But this at your owne judgement. (HC, John Brinsley, *Ludus Literarius*, 1612: 16)

However, double comparatives and double superlatives (that is, combining an inflectional form with a periphrastic one) are less common than is sometimes assumed. In the Early Modern English part of the *Helsinki Corpus*, the frequency of double comparatives is 1 per cent of all comparatives, and 2 per cent of the superlatives, and none is found after 1640 (Kytö and Romaine 1997: 337). The double superlative *the **most** hyghest God* in the Tyndale Old Testament (1530), for instance, becomes *the **most** high* God in the King James Bible (1611). Double comparatives and superlatives are illustrated by examples (24) and (25).

(24) Furthermore, ye shal vnderstand that the brayne is a member colde and moyst of complexion . . . Also, why he is moyst, is, that it should be the **more indifferenter and abler** to euery thing that shoulde be reserued or gotten into him: (HC, Thomas Vicary, *The Anatomie of the Bodie of Man*, 1548: 33)

(25) And bycause that shepe in myne opynyon is **the mooste profytablest** cattell that any man can haue, therfore I pourpose to speake fyrst of shepe. (HC, Anthony Fitzherbert, *The Book of Husbandry*, 1534: 42)

7.2.2 Adverbs

As noted above, one of the functions of *adverbs* is to modify adjectives (*very smooth*). They can also modify other adverbs (*very smoothly*), and most importantly, they can complement or modify verbs (*his life has not been running smoothly*). The regular way of forming an adverb in Early Modern English is to add the suffix *-ly* to an adjective. Zero derivation resulting in suffixless adverbs is no longer as productive in the General dialect as it had been in Middle English, although suffixless adverbs are more frequent than in Present-day Standard English (cf. *The course of true loue neuer did run smooth*, from *A Midsummer Night's Dream*, I. i. 134). However, many suffixless adverbs common in Early Modern English texts such as *even, long, right, still* and *very* go back to earlier times and continue in frequent use today (Nevalainen 1997).

Early Modern English *-ly* adverbs are normally compared by means of *more* and *most*. See the illustrations from Turner in (26). As today, old suffixless adverbs such as *late, long* and *soon* retain their inflectional comparatives and superlatives, as in (27).

(26) Yelow wines that are grossest in substance are conueyed into the bodie **more slowlie** tha*n* these be, howbeit they are more piercing then all soure and binding wines, but these redish yellowe wines againe doe nourish more than thin wines, and correct fautie iuices, of all other wines **most speedily** engendring a good bloud. (HC, William Turner *A New Boke of the Natures and Properies of All Wines*, 1568: C8r)

(27) And doubtless as of Sea-fish the *Herring* dies **soonest** out of the water, and of fresh-water-fish the *Trout*, so (except the *Eel*) the *Carp* endures most hardness, and lives **longest** out of his own proper Element. (HC, Izaac Walton, *The Compleat Angler*, 1676: 292)

However, as there are always exceptions to generalisations, it is possible to come across inflectional forms even with *-ly* adverbs. The two cases in (28) come from the diary of the young King Edward VI.

(28) Removing to Westmister, bicaus it was thought this matter might **easlier** and **surelier** be dispachid there, and likewise al other. (HC, Edward VI, *The Diary of Edward VI*, 1550–2: 354)

7.3 Summary

Both linguistic and external factors contributed to changes in the Early Modern English verb. An external factor was dialect contact producing variable regional input into the mainstream variety preserved in writing. With its distinct southern bias, the General dialect became more mixed dialectally with time as it assimilated many features of northern origin. These included the third-person present-tense singular suffix *-(e)s* and the present plural form *are* of the verb *be*.

Verbal inflections marking person and number have been greatly reduced in English in the course of time. In Early Modern English, this process continued with the loss of the second-person pronoun *thou*. In the mood system, the subjunctive was losing ground as many of its functions were taken over by modal auxiliaries. New periphrastic systems also evolved as a result of grammaticalisation, including the progressive aspect (*be* + *-ing*) and *be going to* as an indicator of future time.

Early Modern English adjectives and adverbs have both periphrastic and inflectional forms. The choice between them largely depends on linguistic factors but register variation also plays a role. The length of the adjective is relevant in adjective comparison, with polysyllabic adjectives taking periphrastic forms in *more* and *most*. Periphrasis is similarly the usual option for *-ly* adverbs in comparatives and superlatives. Here little has changed between Early Modern English and the present day.

Note

1. The term *irregular* comprises both *strong* verbs, that is, those showing vowel gradation, as in *ride – rode – ridden*, and other irregular verbs such as *be*, which are hard to classify. Both are contrasted with *weak* or *regular* verbs such as *love* or *pray*, which show no such alternation.

Exercises

1. Discuss the use of the third-person singular present-tense endings -(*e*)*s* and -(*e*)*th* in Early Modern English. Compare either (a) texts representing the three time periods in Appendix 1 (for example, A3, A5; B1, B5; and C1, C5), or (b) the official letter by Cecil and Harley's private letter in Appendix 2. How systematic is the use of these endings in each text? What factors might have motivated the choice between the two forms?

2. Lass (1994) found the following past-participle forms for *get* in Early Modern English in the HC: *got, gotten, getten*; for *help*: *helped, holpen, holp*; for *speak*: *spoken, spoke, spake*; and for *write*: *written, writ, wrote*. Using either *The Harvard Concordance* (Spevack 1973) or electronic Shakespeare, identify the past-participle forms of these verbs found in Shakespeare's plays. Which variant is the most frequent for each verb?

3. Some auxiliary verbs such as *can* and *will* could still be used as full lexical verbs in Early Modern English. The example below from a treatise on witchcraft illustrates *will* as a full verb. Compare its auxiliary use in (16b), and discuss the syntactic differences between the full verb and the auxiliary. To find out how the two are historically related, see the OED entry for *will*, v.[1], under B, significations and uses.

> My wife hath had fiue or sixe hennes euen of late dead. Some of my neighbours wishe me to burne some thing aliue, as a henne or a hogge. Others **will** me in time to seeke helpe at the handes of some cunning man, before I haue any further harme. (HC, George Gifford, *A Dialogue Concerning Witches and Witchcraftes*, 1593: B1r)

4. Görlach (1991: 113) argues that '[b]efore 1650 the frequency of the subjunctive varied from one author to the next; no regular distribution according to type of text or style can be determined.' Examine his statement by identifying the subjunctive uses of *be* and *do* in texts 1 (Cecil) and 2 (Bacon) in Appendix 2.

Further reading

Practically all textbooks look at the variation between the third-person endings -(*e*)*s* and -(*e*)*th* (see the works listed at the end of Chapter 1); corpus-based studies include, e.g., Kytö (1993) and Nevalainen and Raumolin-Brunberg (2003: 67–8, 177–80). Lass (1994) compares past-tense (= preterite) and past-participle forms of strong verbs in the *Helsinki Corpus* and contemporary Early Modern English grammars; and their standardisation between 1680 and 1790 is traced by Gustafsson (2002). Rydén and Brorström (1987) and Kytö (1997) study the choice of the auxiliary (*be* v. *have*) in perfective constructions, and Elsness (1994) explores the Early Modern progressive. The subjunctive mood in Middle English is discussed by Mustanoja (1960: 451–78), and Moessner (2002) analyses its users in the seventeenth century. Kytö (1991) gives a detailed account of the development of the auxiliaries *can, may, shall* and *will* in Early Modern British and American English. Adjective comparison from Late Middle English on is discussed by Kytö and Romaine (1997), and patterns of Late Middle and Early Modern English adverb formation by Nevalainen (1997). For Present-day English, see Quirk et al. (1985), Chapters 3 and 4 on verbs, and Chapter 7 on adjectives and adverbs; Biber et al. (1999) discuss verbs in Chapters 5 and 6, and adjectives and adverbs in Chapter 7.

8 Syntactic structures

8.1 Larger structures

The previous chapters have examined the properties of *words* and *word classes* in Early Modern English. To find out how they were used, we will now turn to larger structures. The main principle is that words are packaged into *phrases*, which assume various functions in the sentence. Although the same basic phrasal categories and functions apply from Old to Present-day English, major changes have occurred in their internal make-up and the rules governing their position in the sentence.

The most important phrasal categories are the *noun phrase* (NP) and the *verb phrase* (VP). The key element or *head* of a noun phrase is a noun or a pronoun, and the head of a verb phrase is a verb. The verb in the VP is the hub of the sentence on which the other core elements depend.[1] These typically consist of or contain noun phrases. Noun phrases can assume multiple grammatical functions such as those of the subject and the object of the sentence. Phrases combine into larger constructions, *clauses* and *sentences*. So the title *Love's Labour's Lost* forms a simple sentence (that is, one made up of a single clause) consisting of the NP *love's labour* and the VP [*i*]*s lost*; see Figure 8.1. The subject NP determines the number of the verb: *love's labours* in the plural changes the VP into *are lost*.

Syntactically Early Modern English resembles Present-day English more than Middle English both in terms of phrase structure and *word-order*. (A more appropriate term would perhaps be *element order*, as the sentence elements considered under word-order usually refer to phrasal units). The focus of this chapter falls on the properties of noun and verb phrases and word-order developments in Early Modern English. Special attention will be paid to syntactic innovations such as the rise of the auxiliary *do*.

Figure 8.1 Sentence structure

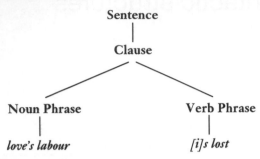

8.2 Noun phrases

English noun phrases usually consist of a pattern where a *determiner* and one or more optional adjective *modifiers* precede a noun: *a* (*brave, new*) *world*. The noun is the head of this construction, that is, the key element that decides the choice of determiners, and how the phrase can be used in a sentence. Determiners and modifiers supply more information about the noun. As noun phrases and pronouns assume the same syntactic functions (*the world is new/ it is new*), pronouns also constitute noun phrases. The basic NP structure is the same for Early Modern and Present-day English.

8.2.1 Determiners

Determiners consist of several subclasses including the articles (*a/an, the*), and possessive (*my, his, her, its, our, your, their*) and demonstrative determiners (*this/these, that/those*). A genitive form can also in principle serve as a determiner (cf. *love's labour*). Determiners mark the noun as definite or indefinite: *the cat* or *his cat* is a cat known to the speaker, but *a cat* may be any cat.

Except for a few formal and distributional differences, the Early Modern determiner system was like the Present-day one. In the sixteenth century, the long possessive forms *mine* and *thine* could still appear as determiners (see 6.3.1). It was also possible for two definite determiners, a possessive and a demonstrative, to precede the noun, as in the two cases in (1).

(1a) And, I do not meene, by all **this my** taulke, that yong Ientlemen, should alwaies be poring on a booke ... (HC, Roger Ascham, *The Scholemaster*, 1570: 216)

(1b) My Case doth differ, I graunt, but specially bicause I haue not suche a Judge: yet there is another cause to restraine **these your** strange and extraordinarie Constructions . . . (HC, *The Trial of Sir Nicholas Throckmorton*, 1554: 75)

As the period wore on, this option became increasingly infrequent, and came to be replaced by the *of*-construction, which had previously existed as a minority alternative. See example (2).

(2) Dear Nurse, **this** goodness **of yours** shan't go unrewarded . . . (HC, John Vanbrugh, *The Relapse or Virtue in Danger*, 1697: 64)

This development brings the usage in line with the article system. As in Present-day English, an *of*-phrase was obligatory when the noun took an article but was also specified by a possessive pronoun. This pattern is shown in (3).

(3) **A** neighbour **ot mine** had his childe taken lame, a girle of ten yeares olde . . . (HC, George Gifford, *A Dialogue Concerning Witches and Witchcraftes*. 1593: B1r)

8.2.2 Heads and modifiers

It has always been possible in English to use adjectives with reference to people in general, as in (4). These cases can be analysed as noun phrases with noun heads formed from adjectives by means of the word-formation process of conversion (see 5.1.3). Alternatively, they may be understood as noun phrases with adjective heads.

(4) *Ph.* Have we not granted already that **the Good** are happy, and **the Impious** miserable? (HC, Richard Preston (transl.), *Boethius*, 1695: 179)

This noun-like use of adjectives was more widespread in earlier English. In Middle and Early Modern English we also find cases such as those in (5), where the noun head is left unexpressed even if it is in the singular.

(5a) For as **an excellenter** than my self sayde: 'A good man, his vertues doo inhabite him.' (HC, Elizabeth I (transl.), *Boethius*, 1593: 94).

(5b) And it is so great within, that it was told me that a Childe was once gotten there: but I, to make tryall crept into it, lying on my backe, and

> I am sure there was roome enough and spare for **a greater** then my selfe. (HC, John Taylor, *Pennyles Pilgrimage*, 1630: 129)

Cases like this were becoming fewer as the Early Modern English period advanced, and the phrasal head began to be supplied by structural means by the prop-word *one* (pl. *ones*). There was a notable increase in the use of the prop-word in the course of the seventeenth century. The examples in (6) illustrate the range of contexts in which *one* is found.

(6a) *Ka.* Must I dance too.

> *Jo.* Ay **pretty one**, every body will strive to dance with the Bride. (HC, *Penny Merriments*, 1684–5: 118)

(6b) There might bee some other schoole in the towne, for **these little ones** to enter them. (HC, John Brinsley, *Ludus Literarius*, 1612: 14)

(6c) So that if, as before I have demonstrated, there be a certain imperfect Felicity, a fading Good, there must also be, without doubt, **a solid and perfect one**. (HC, Richard Preston (transl.), *Boethius*, 1695: 134)

The usual order of the noun head and the adjective modifying it was the same as today: the adjective normally preceded the head. There are fixed collocations such as *letters patent*, where the order is reversed, but even here variation can be found: *God Almighty/Almighty God*. The Latinate pattern of the adjective following the noun is found in legal language, as in (7), and also in poetry.

(7) Of all whiche Treasons, to proue mee guiltie, the Queenes learned Counsayle hath giuen in Euidence **these Pointes materiall**: that is to saye, for the compassing or imagining the Queenes Death, and the Destruction of hir Royal Person . . . (HC, *The Trial of Sir Nicholas Throckmorton*, 1554: 70–71)

In a corpus of writings by the sixteenth-century humanist Sir Thomas More, only 2 per cent of one-word adjective modifiers deviated from the adjective + noun order. The split pattern found in Middle English of one adjective preceding the head and another following it had similarly almost disappeared by the early sixteenth century. It can occasionally be found in More, as in (8) (Raumolin-Brunberg 1991: 267, 274).

(8) And said it was **a goodly cry and a ioyfull** to here, euery man with one voice no manne sayeng nay. (HC, Thomas More, *The History of King Richard III*, 1514–18: 76)

In complex noun phrases, nouns and pronouns can be postmodified by *relative clauses* (for the pronouns introducing relative clauses, see 6.3.2). In colloquial language, relative pronouns are more frequent as subjects and objects than in other syntactic functions. The typical relativiser in Early Modern English informal registers is *that*, capable of functioning as a subject (*all's well **that** ends well*) as well as an object (*all **that** I know*).

When *that* is associated with a preposition, the preposition is left stranded at the end of the relative clause. The case in (9) (*that . . . of*) comes from Thomas More's letter to his daughter (Raumolin-Brunberg 1991: 234). In parallel but more formal contexts we would expect to find a *wh*-pronoun preceded by a preposition, as in (10) from the King James Bible.

> (9) I like speciall well Dorithe Coly, I praye you be good vnto her. I woulde wytte whether this be she **that** yow wrote me **of**. (HC, Thomas More, 1534: 564)

> (10) We haue found him **of whom** Moses in the Law, and the Prophets did write, Iesus of Nazareth the sonne of Ioseph. (HC, *The Authorised Version*, 1611: 40)

Formal registers typically employ *wh*-relatives in all syntactic functions, including complex relative clauses with possessive relatives, and relative pronouns functioning as objects of comparison. The latter construction is found in texts or phrases modelled on Latin. Example (11) illustrates both the use of the subject relative *which* (modifying *nothing*) and a complex comparative construction with *than whom* (modifying *Him*, that is, 'him . . . better than whom nothing can be').

> (11) For since nothing can be found out **which** is better than God, who will deny Him to be good, **than whom** nothing can be **better**? (HC, Richard Preston (transl.), *Boethius*, 1695: 134)

8.3 Verb phrases

The head of a verb phrase is a lexical verb. In VPs, auxiliary verbs have functions that parallel the work done by determiners in NPs. As we saw in section 7.1, above, auxiliaries such as *have*, *be*, *can/could*, *may/might*, *shall/should* and *will/would* are used to express temporal, aspectual and modal meanings in the verb phrase. Auxiliaries also have structural functions in the VP. *Do* comes to be fixed as an obligatory element in certain sentence types in Early Modern English. The auxiliary *be* and the past participle (*-ed*) are used to form *passive* constructions (*they **are** used*). The

passive goes back to earlier English but it spread to new uses in Early
Modern English.

8.3.1 Auxiliary do

Unlike the rest of the auxiliaries, *do* is regularly introduced into the VP
in certain contexts in Present-day Standard English when there is no
other auxiliary present. It is triggered by *not*-negation (*they **did** not see it*),
by inversion especially in questions (***did** they see it?*), and by emphasis (*they
DID see it*). It is also used as a prop-word in reduced clauses (*they saw it,
and we **did** too*). All these uses of *do* are generalised in the Early Modern
period. But there is also an interesting development of *do* being used in
affirmative sentences which are not necessarily emphatic.

Although there is some earlier evidence from the capital region, East
Anglia, and the west of the country on the use of *do* as an auxiliary verb,
this *periphrastic do* only gathers momentum in the sixteenth century.
During the Early Modern period, *do* first spreads to negative questions,
then to affirmative questions and most negative statements as well as, to
a certain extent, to affirmative statements (Ellegård 1953: 162).

The following examples from (12) to (15) illustrate the use and non-
use of *do* in negative and affirmative questions in the sixteenth century.
It is noteworthy that one and the same text may contain instances of
both, as suggested by the affirmative questions in (14) from Sir Nicholas
Throckmorton's trial.

(12) Why **do ye not knowe** my speache? Even because ye cannot abyde the
hearynge of my wordes. (HC, William Tyndale (transl.), *The New
Testament*, 1534: VIII, 20)

(13) **Seest thou not** his eyes, how they bee fylled with blood and bytter
teares? (HC, John Fisher, *Sermons*, 1521: 400)

(14a) **Do you bring** me hither to trie mee by the Lawe, and will not shewe
me the Lawe? (HC, *The Trial of Sir Nicholas Throckmorton*, 1554: 71)

(14b) **Come you** hither to checke us *Throckmorton*, we will not be so used, no,
no. (HC, *The Trial of Sir Nicholas Throckmorton*, 1554: 64)

(15) But al that is good, **grauntest thou** to be good [by] perticipation
or partakyng, or not? (HC, George Colville (transl.), *Boethius*, 1556:
78)

In questions, and especially in negative interrogatives, *do* became the rule
by the end of the seventeenth century. In 1593 Queen Elizabeth trans-

lates the *do*-less question in Colville's *Boethius* (***grauntest thou** to be good?*) with *do*: *dost thou suppose it good?*

In negative statements the process was slower, reaching the frequency of about 60 per cent of the cases at the end of the seventeenth century in most verbs. There were certain verbs that took even longer to accept *do*, such as *know, doubt, mistake, trow* ('trust') and *wot* ('know'). Thus the spread of *do* to negative statements proceeded by *lexical diffusion*. The examples in (16) illustrate variation with *know* in the sixteenth century, when *do*-less forms predominated with most verbs in negative statements.

(16a)   I **knowe not** wether ye be aparaphryser or not, yf ye be lerned in that syence yt ys possyble ye may of one worde make ahole sentence . . . (CEEC, Catherine Parr, 1547: ORIGINAL 2, 152)

(16b)   and how your Lordship can of right denie this moch vnto hym, I **do not know**. (CEEC, Thomas Wilson, 1572: PARKHURST, 107)

Although *do* also occurs in affirmative statements in Present-day English, it is not required by a rule of grammar in the same way as in the other sentence types discussed above. It is used for emphasis or contrast, and it is prosodically prominent. In the sixteenth century affirmative *do* enjoyed much greater popularity, and it was quite common both in emphatic and non-emphatic contexts of use. In the HC, Nicholas Throckmorton's trial returns clusters of *do* such as the one in (17). Although the first instance of *do* might be thought of as emphatic, confirming the accusation that Throckmorton had resented Queen Mary's marriage to Philip II of Spain, it is more difficult to attribute this function to all the instances of *do* in the passage.[2]

(17)   I confess I **did** mislike the Queenes Mariage with *Spain*, and also the comming of the *Spanyards* hither: and then me thought I had reason to doe so, for I **did** learne the Reasons of my misliking of you M. *Hare*, M. *Southwell*, and others in the Parliament House; there I **did** see the whole Consent of the Realm against it; and I a Hearer, but no Speaker, **did** learne my misliking of those Matters, confirmed by many sundry Reasons amongst you: (HC, *The Trial of Sir Nicholas Throckmorton*, 1554: 66)

A striking feature in (17) is that there are so few clauses like *I confess*, in which the lexical main verb immediately follows the subject. Evidence like this suggests that there may have been a tendency in the sixteenth century to generalise *do* in all VPs when there was no other auxiliary present. If this tendency had become a grammatical rule, the result would have been a fully regular verb-phrase structure: the English VP would have had an auxiliary even in the present and past tenses, with no need to inflect the main verb. But this did not happen. What had looked like a steady increase in the use of affirmative *do* took a decisive downward turn in the middle of the Early Modern period. Dialect contact has been proposed as one possible reason why this happened (see 10.5).

8.3.2 Passives

The passive construction involves both the verb phrase and the sentence in which it appears. When the active sentence *everyone admires you* is turned into the passive *you are admired by everyone*, the object of the active (*you*) becomes the subject of the passive and the subject (*everyone*) goes into an *agent phrase* headed by the preposition *by*. By foregrounding the object, the passive construction functions as a device for rearranging the information conveyed by the subject and the object. The *passive voice*, as it is traditionally called, can be traced back to Old English, but it spread to new constructions in later periods, and the agent preposition changed from *of* to *by*.

In the sixteenth century, one in five agent phrases had *of* instead of *by* in the HC (Peitsara 1992: 384). *Of* was often used with abstract and mental activity verbs, and *by* with verbs referring to more concrete actions and events. But there were also verbs that could take both. The two instances of *receive* in (18) come from the diary of the young King Edward VI.

(18a)   The marquis du Means, conte d'Anguien, and the constable's son **wer received** at Blakheth **by** my lord of Rutland, my lord Gray of Wilton, my lord Bray, my lord Lisle, and divers gentlemen ... (HC, Edward VI, *The Diary of Edward VI*, 1550–2: 264)

(18b)   The lord Cobham, the secretary Petre, and sir Jhon Mason cam to the French king to Amyens, going on his journey, wher thei **were received of** al the nobles, and so brought to thear loginges ... (HC, Edward VI, *The Diary of Edward VI*, 1550–2: 268)

Present-day English can passivise (a) *direct* and (b) *indirect objects* (*we gave money to them:* (a) *money was given to them* ~ (b) *they were given money* [*by us*]). The Early Modern English passive was rarely used to promote indirect objects to the subject position. As Barbara Strang notes: 'though we understand them, we would hardly now produce such passive structures as Shakespeare's *attorneys are deny'd me* or *it was told me* (1970: 151). However, indirect passives became more frequent towards the end of the Early Modern period; see (19) (Denison 1993: 103–23).

> (19) There is so slow a progress made in ordering the dismal ceremony of the Queens funeral, that I cant ges when it will be finishd. **I was told** this day that the heralds had yet a quarter of their work to do ... (HC, Anne Hatton, 1695: 212)

Early Modern English also marked the early stages of the *get*-passive now common in colloquial language: *the thief got caught*. Only sporadic instances of this construction appeared in the Early Modern period, but the pseudo-passive with *get* did occur (as in *get cured, get dressed, get rid of*). It resembles the *get*-passive but cannot be expanded by an agent. Example (20) shows the pseudo-passive (*having got fudled* 'intoxicated') as well as the regular *be*-passive (*was seizd & carry'd*).

> (20) M*r* of y*e* Company **having got fudled** afronted y*e* D*r* ... calling him Rogue sev*ll* times upon w*ch* he **was seizd** & **carry'd** before y*e* L*d* Mayre who b*d* him over to y*e* sessions. (ICAME, *Newdigate Newsletters*, 1684: 980)

8.4 Changing syntactic patterns

8.4.1 Negation

As we saw above, one of the syntactic contexts into which the auxiliary *do* was introduced was verb phrases containing the negator *not*. Another process completed in the Early Modern English period was marking the negative polarity of the sentence by placing the negator *not* close to the auxiliary, and even fusing the two as in *don't, can't, shan't* and *won't*. But perhaps the major change affecting the patterning of negation was the disappearance from the General dialect of *multiple negation*, also known as *negative concord* (*you haven't seen nothing like it*).

In Old English *ne* was the principal sentential negator, which could co-occur with other negative elements. In Middle English it was frequently reinforced with *not* (a reduced form going back to *nought*). This two-part negator could be accompanied by other negative elements (*ne ... not ... never*, and so on). In the fourteenth century *not* progressively replaced *ne* as the sentential negator. In the course of the Early Modern period, the other negative forms accompanying *not* (*not ... never/nothing*) were replaced by *non-assertive forms* (*not . . . ever/anything*), especially in the written language.

Two Boethius translations from different periods illustrate these developments. In (21a) we have Geoffrey Chaucer's fourteenth-century version of a passage that is rendered into seventeenth-century English by Richard Preston in (21b). *Ne* and *not* co-occur with *no* (*manere*) in the same clause in Chaucer; *ne* is also used as a conjunction meaning 'nor'. Preston articulates the same subject matter slightly differently. He, too, uses a negative co-ordinating conjunction (*neither . . . nor*), but it is followed by the non-assertive form *any*, not by another negative element.

(21a)   Thanne is sovereyn good the somme and the cause of al that oughte ben desired; forwhy thilke thing that withholdeth **no** good in itselve, **ne** semblance of good, it **ne** mai **not** wel in **no** manere be desired **ne** requerid. (HC, Geoffrey Chaucer (transl.), *Boethius*, 1380s: 433.C2)

(21b)   Good then, is the Cause why all things are desired; for that which **neither** in Reality **nor** Shew doth retain **any** thing of Good, is by **no** means to be desired: (HC, Richard Preston (transl.), *Boethius*, 1695: 139)

The negator *ne* had largely gone out of use by the beginning of the Early Modern English period, but some instances of the conjunction *ne* 'nor' could be found in the early part of the sixteenth century, as in (22). As in the Chaucer example in (21a), the negative co-ordinating conjunction *ne* was followed by other negative elements.

(22)   the last precept concerning benefites or rewardes is, to take good hede that he contende **nat** agayne equitie, **ne** that he upholde **none** iniurie. (HC, Thomas Elyot, *The Boke Named the Gouernour*, 1531: 148)

In the General dialect, multiple negatives persisted longest in coordinate and additive constructions (*nor/not . . . neither*). In other contexts they gave way to single negation followed by non-assertive forms, which is the norm of Standard English today. The vast majority of the writers in the *Corpus of Early English Correspondence* (CEEC) used the incoming pattern by about 1600. Shakespeare's use of it is illustrated in (23).

(23)   and the Boy **neuer** neede to vnderstand **any** thing; for 'tis **not** good that children should know **any** wickednes . . . (HC, Shakespeare, *The Merry Wives of Windsor*, 1623: 46.C1)

The disappearance of multiple negation was, however, socially strati-
fied: those who used multiple negation most in the Early Modern period
came from social ranks below the gentry and professions. Women also
used it more than men throughout the period. The additive construction
with *not . . . neither* in (24) comes from Dorothy Osborne (see 10.2).

(24) I am not of her opinion at all but I doe **not** wonder **neither** that she is
of it. (CEEC, Dorothy Osborne, 1653: OSBORNE, 104)

8.4.2 Word-order

Word-order developments went hand in hand with the loss of inflectional
endings in English over time. As case endings were no longer available to
mark syntactic functions except in certain pronouns, it became necessary
to signal these relations by means of word-order. The pattern established
in declarative sentences was verb-medial: subject–verb–object (SVO).

The placement of the core elements in the sentence became more
fixed during the Early Modern period. The major developments took
place in declarative sentences. The Elyot passage cited in (22) continues:
*Nowe will I procede seriously and in a due forme to speke more particulerly of these
thre vertues.* The modern reader will notice the inverted word-order after
now, the auxiliary *will* preceding the subject form *I*. In the sixteenth
century, inversion often took place after initial adverbial elements such
as *here, now, then, therefore, thus* and *yet.* It was particularly common when
the verb phrase consisted of an auxiliary and a main verb, as in (25) (but
cf. also the heavy subject in *then followeth feebleness of the wittes . . .*).

(25) the Brayne is eyther too drye or too moyst, **then can it** not worke his
kinde: for **then is the body** made colde: **then are the spirites of lyfe**
melted and resoluted away: and **then foloweth feebleness of the
wittes, and of al other members of the body, and at the laste death**.
(HC, Thomas Vicary, *The Anatomie of the Bodie of Man*, 1548: 33–4)

This pattern of inversion triggered by sentence-initial adverbials
largely disappeared in the Early Modern English period. It has been generalised only in focusing constructions such as *here comes/is NN.*

In Old and Middle English, subject/verb inversion has been attributed
to the grammatical *verb-second constraint*, which is still found in Germanic
languages such as Dutch and German. The constraint stipulates that, in
a declarative main clause, the inflected (*finite*) verb comes second after
any element that begins the clause. When this first element is not the
subject, the order of the verb and the subject is automatically inverted.

In a corpus of Early Modern English consisting of half a dozen genres, the inversion rate fell from the average of one inverted declarative main clause in five in 1500 to one in ten in 1700 (Bækken 1998: 60). In Present-day English, subject/verb inversion after a non-negative fronted element is governed by text and discourse factors rather than a syntactic rule, and its average rate is even lower.

Bækken's figures suggest that inversion was quite common in English between 1500 and 1600. This was particularly the case in religious prose, while the rate of inversion was considerably lower in letters, documents, histories and geography, which were among the genres studied. The cases in (26) to (28) present the various sentence-initial grammatical elements triggering inversion. *Adverbials* typically occupy this position, as in (26). *Direct objects* are a good deal rarer but also possible (27), as are *subject complements* (28) (the adjective phrase *universal* ascribing that property to the subject of the sentence, *mourning*). Inverted word-order in cases like these may be seen as the last remnant of the verb-second constraint. At the same time, it could be argued that the lifting of the syntactic rule licensed some re-use of inversion for text and discourse purposes.

(26)   And **in this penaunce lyued Robert** vii yeres or there aboute . . . (*Robert the Deuyll*, c. 1500: 192 (Bækken 1998: 62))

(27)   **These words spake Jesus** in the treasury. (*The Gospel according to St John*, 1611: 152 (Bækken 1998: 63))

(28)   **Universal was the mourning** for him, and the eulogies on him . . . (*The Diary of John Evelyn*, 1680–2: 148 (Bækken 1998: 65))

The lifting of the verb-second rule also licensed another, more restricted rule of inversion in Early Modern English: inversion after clause-initial negative elements. The new rule gained ground rapidly, and became fully established in the seventeenth century. The development was particularly noticeable with simple negative elements such as *never, neither* and *nor*. Examples (29) and (30) illustrate the recessive and the incoming pattern, respectively. Note the parallel use of the incoming negative pattern *not . . . anie* in (30).

(29)   but bycause we be not gouerned by that Law, **neither I haue** my Trial by it, it shal be superfluous to trouble you therewith . . . (HC, *The Trial of Sir Nicholas Throckmorton*, 1554: 68)

(30)   I have **not** hard **anie** thing of you or M^r. Cheke touching that matter, **nether wyll I** beleave yt yf yt shold be reported, knoweng you bothe so well as I doe. (CEEC, John Whitgift, 1583: HUTTON, 72)

Despite this rule of introducing inversion after initial negative elements, the overall frequency of inversion in declarative sentences with a fronted element dropped in the Early Modern period.

In the Middle and Early Modern English periods many 'light' one-word adverbials increasingly came to be placed either before the finite main verb or between the main verb and the auxiliary. This was typically the case of adverbial modifiers of time (for example, *always, once, now, soon*), place (*here, there*), degree (*greatly, much*), and mood (*certainly, indeed, simply*, and so on). Some of them are illustrated in (31) and (32).

(31) havyng but Yorke, wych ys **now** decayd by viijC.[li] by the yeere I can **nat** tell how to lyve and kepe the poore nombyr of folks wych I **nowe** have ... (CEEC, Thomas Wolsey, 1520s: ORIGINAL LETTERS II, 7)

(32) she **sharply** reply'd, have a care then Sir, you do **not** meet you Wife, for then you will **certainly** break your neck. (HC, *Penny Merriments*, 1684–5: 161)

The negator *not* also followed this pattern. When *do* was established in negative declaratives, *not* fell between the auxiliary and the main verb. The preverbal position similarly came to be favoured by the adverb *only* even where the sentence element it focused on came after the verb, as in (33). This preverbal position of *only* was later condemned as illogical by Robert Lowth and his fellow eighteenth-century grammarians. Despite continued prescriptive censure, it still predominates in speech.

(33) What may be my fortune herafter I know not, for it is **onli** known **to Him which is the disposer of all things** ... (CEEC, Jane Cornwallis, 1613: CORNWALLIS, 1)

These changes reflect the establishment of the subject–verb–object order in English. Intervening elements are not easily allowed to break the close bond between the main verb and the object following it. Adverbials will therefore have to go either at the beginning or the end of the sentence or, in the case of those closely attached to the verb, before the main verb.

8.5 Summary

The subject–verb–object order was firmly established as the basic word-order type in Early Modern English. Despite the relative commonness of subject/verb inversion in many sixteenth-century genres, and the new pattern of negative inversion, the verb typically followed the subject in Early Modern English declarative sentences. At the same time, the use of the passive to rearrange the information conveyed by the subject and the object gained ground in new constructions.

The regulation of word-order supported the rise of periphrastic *do*: in interrogatives, the presence of an auxiliary prevented the inversion of the subject and the main verb, and in negatives it maintained the verb–object order. The introduction of *do* and other auxiliaries into the verb phrase formed part of the analytic tendency of English to mark such verb-phrase features as tense, mood and polarity in the auxiliary. The frequency of *do* in affirmative statements in Early Modern English could be linked with this tendency.

Analytic developments were also at work in the noun phrase. The prop-word *one* was introduced to mark the head of NPs which consisted of a determiner followed by an adjective but did not have an explicit noun head. Where two definite determiners preceded the head (*this my N*) they were redistributed into pre- and post-head elements utilising the *of*-phrase strategy familiar from other possessive constructions (*this N of mine*).

Multiple negation to a large extent disappeared from the General dialect in the Early Modern period. In this process the syntactic use of negative determiners, pronouns and adverbs was replaced by the corresponding non-assertive forms.

Notes

1. Grammars have varying approaches to the VP and the notion of *head*. The approach adopted here is common in descriptive studies of English (for example, Biber et al. 1999). Besides NPs and VPs, phrasal categories include the *prepositional phrase*, which consists of a noun phrase preceded by a preposition (*they are **in a hurry***), the *adjective phrase* (*they are **slow***), and the *adverb phrase* (*they move **slowly***).

2. Various views have been proposed to account for the spread of *do* to affirmative statements, ranging from avoiding ambiguity with certain verb forms to marking the discourse topic (Denison 1993: 457–69; Rissanen 1999: 240–3).

Exercises

1. Identify the first ten noun phrases (NPs) with noun heads in any text in Appendix 1. Describe the various patterns that you find, analysing

their determiners (present v. absent) and modifiers (none v. adjective/ relative clause(s)/ both, and so on). Did you come across any patterns that deviate from Present-day usage?

(Note that an NP can also consist of two (or more) NPs co-ordinated by means of the conjunction *and*; it is treated as one NP because it functions as one syntactic unit. Some complex NPs may also have other NPs embedded in them.)

2. Compare the use and non-use of the auxiliary *do* (a) in interrogative and negative clauses and (b) in affirmative statements in any two texts in Appendix 2. Can the time of writing (earlier, later) be used to account for any of the differences you found?

3. Discuss syntactic developments that affected negation in Early Modern English. The relevant issues include (a) *do*-periphrasis, (b) loss of multiple negation, and (c) negative inversion.

4. Identify the one-word adverbs ending in -*ly* that appear in text 1 (Cecil) in Appendix 2 and describe variation in their placement in the sentence (before the subject; after the subject but before the verb; after the verb). Which patterns predominate?

Further reading

Miller (2002) gives a linguistic introduction to the structure of Present-day English; for a compact overview, see, for example, Crystal (1995: 214–33). The standard reference grammars of Huddleston and Pullum (2002), Biber et al. (1999), and Quirk et al. (1985) offer comprehensive coverage of Present-day English. Old and Middle English are discussed by Hogg (2002) and Horobin and Smith (2002), respectively. Rissanen (1999) is a comprehensive survey of Early Modern English syntax, including phrase structures and word-order. Raumolin-Brunberg (1991) discusses the noun phrase in sixteenth-century English, and Denison (1993) traces the major historical developments of the English verb phrase.

For the history of the auxiliary *do*, see Ellegård's classic work (1953), and Nurmi's historical sociolinguistic study of affirmative and negative *do* (1999). The history of English negation is outlined by Mazzon (2004); and Nevalainen and Raumolin-Brunberg (2003) trace the disappearance of multiple negation and the rise of negative inversion in sociolinguistic terms. Bækken (1998) provides a detailed description of English word-order patterns from 1475 to 1725. On preverbal adverbs in Middle and Early Modern English, see Jacobson (1981). Nevalainen (1991) studies focusing adverbs such as *only* and *just* between 1500 and 1900.

9 Changing pronunciation

9.1 Surprising and confusing?

It is much easier to describe the grammar of Early Modern English than to account for its pronounciation. Although there are fewer contrasting speech sounds (*phonemes*) in English than there are function words, for instance, historical phonology has to make do with mixed evidence and the range of interpretations it is open to. Suggesting that Early Modern English speech would not make much sense to a modern listener, Roger Lass writes about the Elizabethan pronunciation of Shakespeare:

> (1) A modern listener would find the (probably rather small) part of the language that was comprehensible at all both surprising and rather confusing. The impression would be something like a cross between Irish and Scots and West Yorkshire, with touches of American. (Lass 2001: 257)

Part of Lass's evidence comes from verse data such as the following (2), where a modern speaker with a standard British English accent (*Received Pronunciation*, RP) would not be able to rhyme a single couplet.

> (2) Through the Forrest haue I **gone**,
> But *Athenian* finde I **none**,
> One whose eyes I might **approue**
> This flowers force in stirring **loue**.
> Night and silence: who is **heere**?
> Weedes of *Athens* he doth **weare**:
> This is he (my master **said**)
> Despised the *Athenian* **maide**:
> (W. Shakespeare, *A Midsummer Night's Dream*, 1623: 2.2.65–72)

On the other hand, the passage from *Gammer Gurton's Needle* cited in Chapter 2 could be used to challenge Lass's view: it is not hard to find instances where a modern reader could rhyme all couplets in a similar passage. This evidence would rather support James Milroy, who argues that Elizabethan English 'would sound like a somewhat archaic dialect of English' (2002: 22).

Apart from the evidence of rhyming poetry, the Early Modern period offers contemporary descriptions of how English was pronounced at the time. They include lists and dictionaries of rhyming words, among the earliest Peter Levins's *Manipulus Vocabulorum* (1570). The work of early orthoepists and phoneticians was discussed in Chapter 3, where John Hart's reformed spelling was considered. Taken together, these various sources enable us to trace the phonological underpinnings of the mainstream accents of the period although their exact phonetic details may fall beyond our reach. Early Modern English pronunciation clearly had many stable features but also underwent a series of sound changes.

9.2 Some general features

Standards of pronunciation are not fixed like orthographic standards but continue to change with time. An accomplished phonetician, John Hart gives us a general idea of what the metropolitan speech norm was like in the mid-sixteenth century. Just like other varieties of English at the time, it was *rhotic*: /r/ was regularly pronounced after the vowel in words such as *car* and *door*. In the Shakespeare quotation in (2) *heere* ('here') and *weare* ('wear') both ended in /r/. There was also no qualitative difference between the vowels in words like *trap* and *path*. In these respects, the southern Early Modern English speech norm resembled modern General American more than the current norms of RP, Australian, New Zealand and South African English.

No difference was made in the sixteenth century between the vowels in words like *put* and *cut* (pronounced with an /u/ as in northern dialects in England today). In (2), both *approue* ('approve') and *loue* ('love') were pronounced with an /u/ sound and hence rhymed (cf. the colloquial and dialectal respelling *luv*). On the other hand, the vowels in *meet* and *meat*, *piece* and *peace*, *see* and *sea*, and similar word pairs were kept distinct. Their vowels only merged into /iː/ in the south at the close of the Early Modern period; their spelling reflects a pronunciation distinction which goes back to Middle English.

The southern variety that Hart describes contains an /o/ sound in *long* and *strong*, whereas contemporary northern English dialects often pronounced these words with an unrounded vowel, *lang* and *strang*. Hart's metropolitan norm differed from the western dialects, especially West Midland, in that it had the unrounded vowel /a/ in words such as *hand*, *land* and *man* as opposed to the rounded one common in the west (*hond, lond, mon*).

The General dialect also differed from regional dialects further south. A case in point is the voicing of initial fricatives, as in *zeven* ('seven') and *vour* ('four'), which appeared in the southern and south-western dialects from Kent to Devon. It was one of the stock features stigmatised on the London stage. However, although regional pronunciations like this were generally ruled out from the future pronunciation standard, some of them found a place in Standard English vocabulary. Southern initial fricative voicing is retained, for instance, in the form *vixen* ('female fox'), which corresponds to the voiceless initial fricative in *fox*; in *vat*, the southern form for *fat* ('a large vessel for holding liquid'); and in *vane* for *fane*, as in *weather-vane* ('weathercock').

9.3 Developments in the vowel system

Vowels changed a good deal more than consonants in Early Modern English, especially in the southern dialects. The following sections will introduce the major vowel changes found in stressed syllables, and illustrate the sets of words in which they appeared (*lexical sets*).

9.3.1 Raising long vowels

One of the phonological developments that obliterated earlier sound–spelling correspondences were changes in *long vowels* known as the *Great Vowel Shift* (GVS). It was a series of events which began in the fifteenth century and came to completion in the eighteenth century with the bulk of the changes working their way through the sound system in the Early Modern period. It was not, however, a uniform process leading to the standard RP system, but rather a series of local developments that only looks like an orderly *chain shift* when approached at a higher level of abstraction. Similar chain shifts, in which one sound affects the next, are currently under way, for instance, in North American English (the Northern Cities Shift; cf. Labov 1995: 31, 145–54, 184).

The Great Vowel Shift was local in three respects. First, it never ran its course in all regional dialects: in the northern dialects it affected the front vowels but not all back vowels. Secondly, it did not proceed uniformly across the lexicon as one might expect a fully regular sound change to do, that is, it did not affect all the words that contained a sound that qualified for a given change. Finally, there are some developments in words containing long vowels with outcomes that could not have been predicted from their Middle English forms. Some of these 'irregularities' in the southern mainstream variety may be attributed to dialect contact.

Putting these reservations aside, however, we can say that the changes covered by the GVS profoundly altered the way English words were pronounced between 1500 and 1700. The chain of changes moved all long vowels to a higher position in the vowel space.[1] The process that probably set the shift in motion was the diphthongisation of the high vowels /iː/ and /uː/, for which there is good spelling evidence from the late fifteenth century onwards. In this process the high front vowel /iː/ acquired the quality of /ei/, and the high back vowel /uː/ the quality of /ou/. As a result, words like /liːf/ (*life*) and /tiːm/ (*time*) were pronounced as /leif/ and /teim/, and /huːs/ (*house*) and /uːt/ (*out*) as /hous/ and /out/.

Writing the Lord's Prayer in his phonemic alphabet John Hart spells *thy name* /ðei naːm/ (1570). Evidence like this suggests that a diphthongised form of /iː/ had become acceptable by Hart's time. In the early phases of the shift, /ei/ and /ou/ probably had a centralised first element, something like [əi] in *time* and [əu] in *house*. At the end of our period they sounded much the same as today, /taɪm/ and /haʊs/.

There are some writers with little formal education whose spelling can be taken as indicative of completed or ongoing sound changes. The example in (3) comes from a letter written by William Fawnte around 1600 to Edward Alleyn, an actor and organiser of animal displays in London. Fawnte's regular <ey> spellings in words like *my*, *by*, *desire*, *buy* and *time* suggest that the diphthong must have been the norm for him.

> (3) Mʳ. Allin **mey** Loue remembered I vnderstoode **bey** a man which came with too Beares from the gardeyne that you haue a **deseyre** to **beȳ** one of **mey** Boles. I haue three westerne boles at this **teyme** . . .
> (CEEC, William Fawnte, 1600s: HENSLOWE, f.83)

The diphthongisation of high vowels in words like *time* and *house* left the space for high vowels unoccupied. It was filled by the high-mid vowels /eː/ and /oː/, which raised becoming /iː/ and /uː/, respectively. As a result, words such as /meːt/ (*meet*) and /seː/ (*see*) were systematically changed to /miːt/ and /siː/, and words like /loːs/ (*loose*) and /moːn/ (*moon*) came to be pronounced /luːs/ and /muːn/ in the south.

The raising of /eː/ and /oː/ began in the fifteenth century, almost parallel to the diphthongisation of /iː/ and /uː/. In fact scholars continue to argue which of the two was earlier, and whether the shift involved a *pull chain* (diphthongisation first, as described above) or a *push chain* (raising first, 'pushing' the high vowels /iː/ and /uː/ out of the way, forcing them to diphthongise). The textual evidence available points to both lexical and regional variation. The chicken-or-egg question aside, raised variants of /eː/ and /oː/ are systematically preferred by John Hart in the mid-sixteenth century.

The shift continued, as low-mid vowels were raised to the space of high-mid vowels, which was vacated by the raising of /eː/ and /oː/. The front vowel /ɛː/ in words like /mɛːt/ (*meat*) and /sɛː/ (*sea*) became /eː/, and the back vowel /ɔː/ in words such as /bɔːt/ (*boat*) and /hɔːm/ (*home*) became /oː/. Finally, the low /aː/ vowel in /maːk/ (*make*) and /naːm/ (*name*) and other similar words was raised to a low-mid /ɛː/, resulting in /mɛːk/ and /nɛːm/. These shifts in the long vowel system are summarised in (4).

(4) The Great Vowel Shift

Late ME			EModE		Examples
high	iː	→	diphthong	ei	*mile, ripe, side, time, write*
high	uː	→	diphthong	ou	*house, mouth, out, south, thou*
high-mid	eː	→	high	iː	*meet, piece, see, sweet, tree*
high-mid	oː	→	high	uː	*do, loose, moon, move, tooth*
low-mid	ɛː	→	high-mid	eː	*meat, please, sea, speak, tea*
low-mid	ɔː	→	high-mid	oː	*boat, home, rose, soap, stone*
low	aː	→	low-mid	ɛː	*case, late, make, name, take*

Looking at the outcome of the Great Vowel Shift in (4) we can see that words like *meet* and *meat* had distinct qualities in Early Modern English. Their vowels only merged around 1700 as the high-mid vowel /eː/ was raised to /iː/ in southern dialects. This vowel coalescence is often called the *meet* and *meat* merger. It increased the number of /iː/ words, including *please* and *speak* listed in (4), and created *homophones* such as *meet* and *meat*, *piece* and *peace*, *see* and *sea*, *tea* and *tee*.

But in the latter half of the seventeenth century John Dryden could also rhyme *speak* and *make*. The low-mid /ɛː/ in *make* and similar words had become higher, and could coincide with /eː/ words such as *meat, sea* and *speak*, which had not yet been raised to /iː/ at the time. Rhymes like this did not persist, however, as the high-mid /eː/ in the *make*-words did not continue to raise. It gave way to /ei/ in the southern mainstream dialect at the end of the eighteenth century. A parallel process of diphthongisation was undergone by /oː/ in words like *boat* and *home*, which in the south became /bəʊt/ and /həʊm/ in Late Modern English.

9.3.2 Long vowels from diphthongs

Early Modern English diphthongs also underwent a series of changes which masked their earlier sound–spelling correspondences. Almost all these changes were processes of monophthongisation, as a diphthong (a vowel with a changing quality) was reduced to a pure long vowel. Only two Middle English diphthongs retained their diphthongal quality in the southern dialects, /ɔɪ/ (*joy*) and /ʊɪ/ (*join*); they were both often realised as [ɔɪ]. The table in (5) summarises the major changes in Early Modern English diphthongs.

(5) Monophthonging of diphthongs

Late ME		EModE	Examples
iu	→	juː	*chew, due, hue, June, new, true*
eu	→	juː	*beauty, dew, few, hew, newt*
aʊ	→	ɒː	*all, cause, chalk, law, taught*
ɔʊ	→	oː	*bowl, flow, know, low, soul*
aɪ	→	eː	*bait, day, may, day, tail, way*

Two Middle English diphthongs, /iu/ and /eu/, coalesced in Early Modern English and became /juː/. Most /iu/ words such as *due, hue, new* and *true* acquired the pronunciation /juː/ in the early seventeenth century. The /eu/ diphthong (in *dew, few, hew,* and so on) first moved to the position of /iu/, and then joined its development becoming /juː/. In the early eighteenth century the initial /j/ in /juː/ began to be lost and the sound was reduced to /uː/ in many words such as *brew, chew, crew* and *threw*. The change from /juː/ to /uː/ (*yod dropping*) has not been completed yet, and there is a good deal of regional variation. Words such as *dew, few, new* and *tune* retain the /j/ in RP, but, except for *few*, not in General American. East Anglian accents have gone even futher and extended yod dropping to most environments, including *few, music* and *beautiful* ('bootiful').

The two Middle English diphthongs ending in an /ʊ/ glide, /aʊ/ and /ɔʊ/, became monophthongs in Early Modern English. They resulted in the low back vowel /ɒː/ and the high-mid back vowel /oː/, respectively. The Late Middle English /aʊ/ in words like *all, cause, chalk, law, salt* and *taught* retracted and monophthongised in the first half of the seventeenth century becoming a low /ɒː/. Later it raised to a low-mid /ɔː/. The high-mid back vowel /oː/ emerged in words like *bowl, flow* and *soul* as the diphthong /ɔʊ/ first monophthongised into /ɔː/, and then raised to /oː/. It joined the development of the Middle English long /ɔː/ in words belonging to the *boat* and *home* set, which the GVS had raised to /oː/ by about 1600. Both these categories of /oː/ words became centring diphthongs (/əʊ/) in the south in Late Modern English.

The Middle English /aɪ/ diphthong occurred in words like *day, bait, eight, may, tail* and *way*. In certain Early Modern varieties it was first raised to /ɛi/, which gave way to the monophthong /ɛː/, later /eː/. So it fell in with what had been /aː/ in Middle English, which the GVS had raised to /ɛː/. This coalescence created many word pairs identical in pronunciation (for example, *days/daze, bait/bate, hail/hale, raise/raze, tail/tale* and *waive/wave*). In Late Modern English, /ɛː/ words underwent a process of diphthongisation. Spelling differences often reflect their earlier pronunciation, /aɪ/ or /aː/.

John Hart is among the early adopters of the monophthong pronunciation for the /aɪ/ diphthong. He spells words like *day, may, pray, say* and *way* with a long <e> symbol in his orthoepic works from the mid-sixteenth century onwards. Hart would have rhymed **said** and **maide** as /sɛːd/ and /mɛːd/ in the Shakespeare quotation in (2). Whether this was common in the City of London in Shakespeare's time is another matter. Alexander Gil, for one, conservatively transcribes Middle English /aɪ/ words with the diphthong <ai>.

In *Logonomia Anglica* Gil criticises Hart's monophthong realisation of the diphthong associating it with the affected pronunciation of upper-rank women he calls *Mopsae*. Gil maintains that '[t]hese are not our words but Mopsey inventions' (1619 [1972: 87]). Some other contemporary writers look upon this realisation as an affectation influenced by French, but as there is also regional evidence for the monophthong, its history remains controversial.

9.3.3 Short vowel shifts and splits

The Middle English high vowel /i/ in *bit* and *ship* was typically realised as [ɪ] in Early Modern English, the same as today – but /ɛ/ and /a/ were raised. The low-mid /ɛ/ (*bed, set*) moved up leaving room for /a/ to raise to /æ/ by the mid-seventeenth century. This is when words like *hat, man* and *trap* gained the pronunciation they have today.

The number of words included in this /æ/ set was, however, much larger in the Early Modern period than in RP and southern British English dialects today. It contained *bath, castle, glass, last, master, pass, path* and many other words with similar sound patterns. The set split when the vowel in these words was lengthened in the south in the course of the seventeenth century and backed to /ɑː/ in Late Modern English. There was fluctuation in various subgroups but most of these changes did not take place in the north of England or in American English, which have retained the front vowel in both *trap* and *path* words.

In the back vowel series, the low-mid /ɔ/ was lowered in the course of the Early Modern period. Its lexical set includes words such as *dog, hot, lot* and *pot*. This vowel continued to change in American dialects, where it was unrounded to /ɑ/ probably in the late seventeenth or early eighteenth century.

Another change that divided southern and northern English dialects (but not southern British, Scottish and American English) was the split of the Middle English vowel /u/ into a rounded and unrounded variant in the south by the middle of the seventeenth century. The rounded vowel /ʊ/ continued to be pronounced in words like *bull, bush, full, put* and *wolf,* but was lowered and unrounded yielding [ʌ] in *cup, cut, dull, fun, luck, mud* and similar words. The split came about in the south when the /uː/ created from earlier /oː/ in words such as *book, foot, good* and *look* had become [ʊ] in such contexts, yielding minimal pairs such as *book* and *buck, look* and *luck.*

There is spelling-book evidence to suggest that the split had not taken place before 1600. In *The English Schoole-Maister,* Edmund Coote (1596: 28) remarks that '[s]ometime we pronounce (o) before (m) or (n) as (u) as in *come, nomber, custome, some, sonne, &c'.* Although the spelling of most words had been fixed in print by the mid-seventeenth century, even educated writers could deviate from these conventions in their private letters. Sir Thomas Wentworth, a northerner by birth, spells <sum> for *some* and <cum> for *come,* suggesting that his pronunciation contained the /ʊ/ sound in these words. Example (6) comes from a letter written in the 1630s.

(6) I will with all diligence and perseverance treade the stepps which may leade me to **sum** happy issue, which may **becum** in **sum** degree acceptable unto you ... (CEEC, Thomas Wentworth, 1632: WᴇSᴀ, 2)

At the beginning of the Early Modern period, words like *bird, verb* and *turn* were pronounced with vowels corresponding to their Middle English forms: /bɪrd/, /vɛrb/ and /tʊrn/. These forms are also found in Hart in the middle of the sixteenth century. But 100 years later, commentators suggest that /ɪ/, /ɛ/ and /ʊ/ were no longer distinct when followed by /r/ in a word-final position or before another consonant. They had centred and merged as a mid central vowel /ə/. Having started in northern and eastern dialects in the fifteenth century, the merger had reached the capital by the seventeenth century.

A number of /ɛr/ words such as *clerk, mercy, person* and *serve* did not always follow this pattern in Early Modern English, but had been lowered to /ar/ in Late Middle English. Queen Elizabeth, for instance, spells these four words with <ar>. Similar phonemic spellings occur in the letters of Robert Dudley, the Earl of Leicester, as in (7).

> (7) And, besydes the good which you shall doe unto them, which I am sure they will indebvor themselves by **sarvice** to **desarve**, I shall also take yt very freendlye ... (CEEC, Robert Dudley, 1586: LEYCESTER, 148)

This development was in keeping with the Late Middle English pattern which had produced the /ar/ pronunciations (and spellings) of such earlier /ɛr/ words as *dark, far, harvest, heart* and *star*.

9.4 Developments in the consonant system

The changes in the Early Modern English consonant system are minor in comparison with those undergone by the vowel system. The following sections discuss consonantal developments which were either in progress or completed in the mainstream southern dialect during this period. Most of these changes were to do with the weakening and loss of consonant phonemes, and the simplification of initial consonant clusters. With two minor additions, the consonant phoneme inventory itself remained the same throughout the period, and indeed remains the same today.

As pointed out in section 9.2, Early Modern English was /r/-pronouncing. A few early instances of /r/-deletion can be found in southern England in the fifteenth century, where occasional spelling such as *passell* ('parcel') and *mosselle* ('morsel') are reported; more appear in sixteenth-century private writings, for instance, *skasely* ('scarcely'), *posshene* ('portion') and *Dasset* ('Dorset') (Wyld 1936: 298). Observations of the phonetic weakening of postvocalic /r/ are reported in the seventeenth century but there is no systematic orthoepic or textbook evidence for its loss before the eighteenth century.

By contrast, /h/-dropping is well documented from Early Middle English onwards. It was common in words beginning with /h/ in weakly stressed positions and gave rise, for instance, to the generalisation of the /h/-less variant *it* of the neuter pronoun *hit* in all positions. Another category that varied in Early Modern English was French loan words with an initial /h/. In Middle English the /h/ was not pronounced in *habit, heritage, history, honour, host* and similar words, and it could be omitted in spelling, but in most cases it was subsequently reintroduced on etymological grounds. A third category of /h/-dropping involves /h/-initial

Germanic words (*hand*, *heart*), which are normally stressed in speech. These cases occur variably from Early Middle English onwards especially in eastern and southern dialects, as do additions of unhistorical /h/ to words such as *halle* ('all'), *helde* (for *elde* 'age') and *hunkinde* ('unkind') (Milroy 1992: 141–2).

The situation remains variable in Early Modern English. Shakespeare continues to draw on it, for instance, in puns involving *air*, *hair* and *heir*. The examples in (8) illustrate the various categories of /h/-dropping and /h/-insertion in the diary of Henry Machyn, a merchant-tailor living and writing in mid-sixteenth-century London. Many features in Machyn's language, however, suggest that he was a native of Yorkshire (Britton 2000). Machyn frequently deletes the initial /h/ in unstressed *his*, as in (8a), and occasionally in *have*. in (8b) *had* varies with *ad*. The case in (8c) has /h/ deletion in the native adverb *hard*. The example also contains an instance of /h/-insertion before -*ing* in *plahyng* ('playing'). In (8d) Machyn inserts an unetymological /h/ to the Romance loan verb *ordain*.

(8a) and at **ys** gatt the corse [corpse] was putt in-to a wagon with iiij welles, all covered with blake, and ower the corsse **ys** pyctur mad with **ys** myter on **ys** hed ... (HC, Henry Machyn, *Diary*, 1553–9: 196)

(8b) [if] my lord mer and my lord Cortenay **ad** not ben ther, ther **had** bene grett myscheyff done. (HC, Henry Machyn, *Diary*, 1553–9: 41)

(8c) The sam nyght abowtt viij of the cloke at nyght the Quen['s] grace toke her barge at Whyt hall ... and so crost over to London syd with drumes and trumpetes **playhyng ard** be-syd, and so to Whyt hall agayne to her palles. (HC, Henry Machyn, *Diary*, 1553–9: 201)

(8d) and the gentyll-woman had **hordenyd** a grett tabull of bankett, dyssys of spyssys and frut ... (HC, Henry Machyn, *Diary*, 1553–9: 100)

The illustrations in (8) show the range of variation in both /h/-deletion and /h/-insertion in one of earliest private diaries that have been preserved from the Early Modern period. Although the use of /h/ in cases like (8d) in an official document might have suggested the writer's lack of formal education, there was no general stigma attached to /h/-dropping in Early Modern English. The omission of /h/ became stigmatised only towards the end of the eighteenth century, when it assumed a prominent role in the Late Modern English prescriptive tradition.

In Early Modern English a systematic change took place in the southern dialects concerning the realisation of /h/ in word-final position and

before /t/. Just as in German today, in Middle English the velar variant
[x] had occurred after back vowels (as in *bough, thought, through*) and the
palatal variant [ç] before front vowels (*eight, high, light*). Both were either
lost or, in some dialects, the velar variant was replaced by /f/ (*cough,
laugh, rough*). In Middle English all these words were commonly spelled
with <gh>. Although the spelling prevailed, Late Middle English occasional <hie> spellings for *high*, for instance, suggest that the change was
well under way before the Early Modern period. The loss of the final
fricative typically had an effect on the preceding vowel, which was
lengthened. So [lıçt] 'light' became [li:t], and this long /i:/ diphthongised in the course of the Great Vowel Shift.

In most Early Modern English dialects word pairs like *wine* and *whine*,
witch and *which* were not pronounced in the same way. Although there is
evidence to suggest that the distinction was not always made in Middle
English, word pairs like this only became homophones in the precursor
of RP in the eighteenth century. The difference consists of an opposition between /hw/ and /w/. The fricative /h/ (or its velar variant [x])
precedes the approximant /w/ in *which* /hwɪtʃ/ but *witch* /wɪtʃ/ begins
with the plain approximant. This change was the last in the line of /h/-
deletions in initial consonant clusters; /hl/, /hn/, and /hr/ had already
simplified in Middle English. The process increased the number of
homophones in those dialects where it occurred.

Some word-initial consonant clusters consisting of stops and nasals
were also simplified in Late Middle and Early Modern English. They
involved the sequence /gn/ in words like *gnash, gnat* and *gnaw* and /kn/
in *knee, knit* and *know*, which lost the initial stop, and were ultimately
reduced to /n/. The reduction was earlier in /gn/ than in /kn/, and it
was completed in the south in the eighteenth century. A parallel process
of reduction took place with the initial /wr/ cluster, where the approximant /w/ was lost in words like *write, wrist* and *wrong* in the southern
dialects in the fifteenth and sixteenth centuries.

As a result of simplification of consonant clusters, Early Modern
English also gained a consonant phoneme. Until about 1600, the final
cluster in words like *rang* and *sing* consisted of a combination of the velar
nasal [ŋ] and voiced velar stop [g] ([raŋg], [sɪŋg]), paralleling the clusters ending in the voiceless stop [k] in *rank* and *sink* ([raŋk], [sɪŋk]).
While the clusters in *rank* and *sink* have been preserved until the present
day, those in *rang* and *sing* were reduced to the velar nasal. The velar
nasal before /g/ and /k/ is a contextual variant of /n/, and hence predictable. When the stop /g/ is deleted and the cluster reduced to /ŋ/,
however, we have a new phoneme that can be used to distinguish
minimal pairs such as *rang* and *ran*, *sing* and *sin*. The change began in

word-final position, and spread to derived nouns (*sing-er*) in the seventeenth century. But it does not apply to comparative forms of adjectives (*strong-er*) and non-derived words (*finger, Bangor*), where the cluster [ŋg] prevails (Lass 1999: 120).

A process of assimilation produced the other new consonant in Early Modern English, namely the sibilant /ʒ/. It arose from the coalescence of the sequence /zj/ in words ending in -*sion* (*division, occasion, vision*) in the seventeenth century. So /vizjən/ became /viʒən/. It is phonologically a natural change in that it supplies a voiced counterpart for the voiceless sibilant /ʃ/, which has the same place of articulation. The distribution of the new phoneme was at first limited to the word-medial position but it was extended to word-final use in French loans in -(*a*)*ge* in Late Modern English (*entourage, garage, sabotage, beige, rouge*, and so on).

9.5 Stress and prosody

John Hart is the first to describe a number of features to do with Modern English prosody, including *phonological units*, sequences of unstressed and stressed elements, 'which we ought to sound as though they were writen together' (Hart 1551 [1955: 155]. His examples include phrasal combinations of lexical and function words, prepositions, articles, pronouns and auxiliaries (Hart's links are here replaced with plus signs): *of+an+apple, tu+a+frind, at+the+but, from+the+Citie, the+rich men, a+noble man, a+Duke,* or *an+Erle, may moch help the+poore, thow+ dost+rune, he+doth+rune, thow+runst, he+runth, thow+rannest,* and *he+ranne*.

Early Modern English was like Present-day English in that vowels in unstressed syllables were commonly reduced to a central vowel in ordinary speech. This vowel had developed from other short vowels in unstressed positions in the Middle English period, and could be spelled with most vowel letters and their combinations. In Early Modern English the vowel probably varied more in quality than in Present-day English, but it may nevertheless be identified as a *schwa* sound /ə/.

In connected speech, unstressed syllables can also be dropped. In Early Modern and Present-day English alike, function words have contracted variants such as *they're, we'll* and *won't*. The form of some of them has, however, changed in the course of time. Whereas Standard English today attaches an auxiliary enclitically to the pronoun *it* (*it's, it'll*), until the end of the seventeenth century it was typically the pronoun that was clipped in the General dialect (*'tis, 'twas, 'twill*). *It's* and *'tis* appear side by side in (9). The passage from Vanbrugh's comedy also contains other contractions characteristic of spoken English.

(9) **It's** well I have a Husband a coming, or Icod, **I'd** marry the Baker, I wou'd so. No body can knock at the Gate, but presently I must be lockt up; and **here's** the young Greyhound Bitch can run loose about the House all the day long, she can; 'tis very well. (HC, John Vanbrugh, *The Relapse or Virtue in Danger*, 1697: 59)

The vowel developments discussed in 9.3 referred to vowel qualities in stressed syllables. In native words the primary stress is predictable and normally falls on the first syllable of the word. In Early Modern English this also appears to be the case with many Latinate loans, especially in the speech of less educated people. In his rhyming dictionary, *Manipulus Vocabulorum* (1570), Peter Levins places the primary stress on the first syllable, for instance, in *cóntribute, cónuenient, défectiue, délectable, dístribute, éxcusable, míschance, óbseruance, pérspectiue, próclamation* and *súggestion* (Lass 1999: 128).

This is explained by the relative prominence of the secondary stress in words consisting of three or more syllables. When the secondary stress weakened or was lost altogether in the following centuries, the primary stress could move away from the first syllable. The secondary stress has often survived in words longer than three syllables in American English (for example, *témporàry*; Dobson 1968: 446–9).

It was, however, also common for Latinate loans to continue to follow the Romance stress pattern, where the primary stress falls on the first heavy syllable counting from the end of the word. Non-initial primary stress is well documented by Levins in polysyllabic words with certain suffixes (as in *ceremóniall, domésticall, matrimóniall; accélerate, accómmodate, apóstate, partícipate, antíquitie, calámitie, fidélitie*). Just as today, stress placement already had a phonemic function in Early Modern English as it could distinguish nouns from verbs. Levins includes the minimal pairs (*a*) *députe* and (*to*) *depúte* and (*a*) *súrname* and (*to*) *surnáme*.

Early Modern English grammarians also note that contrasting two words (*contrastive stress*) can move the primary stress away from its normal position. Charles Butler describes the various patterns in *The English Grammar* (1633) as follows (his special characters have been rendered in conventional orthography):

(10) In all Polisyllables, the difference of like woords draweth the Accent: as *Cómmend it, or ámend it*, the Accent beeing properly in the last. So, *You shoolde not díscoorage, but éncoorage a learner*, the Accent being beeing properly in the forelast. Likewise, *Every cómmoditi hath his díscommodity* . . . the Accent being properly in the foreforelast. (Butler 1633: 57)

Phonologists continue to argue about the number of *intonation types* or *tones* there are in English. The minimum often suggested is two, falling and rising. Butler (1633: 58–61) also proposes this traditional minimum for Early Modern English. The falling tone is the default, and the rising tone is used in questions when there is no question word – just as today.

9.6 Summary

The Early Modern English consonant system remained relatively stable. The General dialect gained two new consonants, the nasal /ŋ/ and the sibilant /ʒ/, and lost the palatal and velar realisations of /h/ in words like *light* and *thought*. In short vowels, a new contrast was created when /u/ split into /ʊ/ (*put*) and /ʌ/ (*cut*). The most radical changes occurred in the long vowel system as a result of the Great Vowel Shift. While no new vowel contrasts were created, their values were redistributed across the lexicon. The high vowels /iː/ and /uː/ diphthongised, and the rest moved up one step in the vowel space. Long vowels also emerged from Middle English diphthongs, most of which monophthongised. These processes resulted in vowel mergers, and many word pairs became homophones.

Early Modern English word stress remained basically Germanic, falling on the first syllable of lexical words. At the same time, intense borrowing strengthened the position of Romance stress patterns, which had become a permanent, although variable, part of English lexical phonology.

Note

1. The abstract notion of a *vowel space* may be roughly equated with the vowel quadrilateral and the *position of the tongue* in vowel production: as close as possible to the roof of the mouth in the *high* vowels [i] and [u], and as far away from it as possible in the *low* vowels [a] and [ɑ]. Note that *phonetic* transcriptions are traditionally placed within square brackets [a], the *phonemes* of a language within oblique lines /a/, and *orthographic* variants within angle brackets <a>.

Exercises

1. James Milroy (2002: 22) challenges Lass's view that 'the likelihood that Shakespeare ... would have been auditorily intelligible to a modern English speaker is vanishingly small.' Milroy argues that 'it is quite likely that Elizabethan English, if it survived today, would sound like a

somewhat archaic dialect of English and would be largely intelligible – more intelligible to mainstream speakers than an unadulterated rural dialect of present-day Lowland Scots, for example.'

Make your own contribution to the controversy. Select any rhyming passage from *A Midsummer Night's Dream* and, by studying words in line-final position, assess the extent to which a modern reader can rely on rhymes as evidence for words that must have sounded alike around 1600.

2. Here are the first four lines of Andrew Marvell's poem 'To His Coy Mistress' transcribed in Barber (1997: 139). The poem was published in 1681 but perhaps written a couple of decades earlier.

> hæd wiː bʌt wərld ɪ'nʌf ənd taɪm
> ðɪs 'kɔɪnɪs 'leːdɪ weːr noː kraɪm
> wiː wʊd sɪt daʊn ənd θɪŋk hwɪtʃ weː
> tʊ woːk ænd pas aʊr lɒŋ lʌvz deː

Make a list of the sounds that indicate that the text comes from the late seventeenth century and not, for instance, from the sixteenth. Seeing the passage as it was published may be helpful in analysing it:

> Had we but World enough, and Time,
> This coyness Lady were no crime.
> We would sit down, and think which way
> To walk, and pass our long Loves Day.

3. Discuss the sound changes that increased *homophony* in Early Modern English.

4. Using the information on vowel changes discussed in this chapter and your knowledge of Present-day English, establish those Early Modern English changes that today divide (a) the southern and northern dialects of British English and (b) RP and General American.

Further reading

This chapter assumes some basic knowledge of how speech sounds are classified. A good overview is included in McMahon's *An Introduction to English Phonology* (2002). Crystal's *The Cambridge Encyclopedia of the English Language* (1995; 2nd edn 2003) supplies the basics of the English sound system, and glosses the terms involved; fuller definitions are found in *A Dictionary of Linguistics and Phonetics* (2003) by the same author.

A great deal has been written on Early Modern English sound changes, the Great Vowel Shift in particular. Standard reference works for the specialist include Dobson's two-volume *English Pronunciation*

1500–1700 (1968), Lass's phonology chapter in the third volume of *The Cambridge History of the English Language* (1999), and the first volume of Wells's *Accents of English* (1982). These sources also discuss the prosody of Early Modern English to some extent. Barber (1997) provides a solid basic description of the changing Early Modern English system of pronunciation, and Cruttenden (1994, Chapter 6) a brief overview of it.

10 Language in the community

A period which began with a single conventional image of the social world, a single dominant construction of reality, ended with ambivalence. (Wrightson 1991: 52)

10.1 Widening perspectives

This book began by discussing linguistic motives for setting up an Early Modern English period. We will now return to the topic by surveying the external factors that characterised the language community during this period of 200 years. They include issues to do with literacy and the social world, migration and urbanisation, and technological advances such as the introduction of the printing press. The following sections will illustrate the effects of these factors on linguistic variation and change. The aim is to put the linguistic developments in the General dialect in a broader social and regional perspective.

10.2 Printing and literacy

10.2.1 Language maintenance in print

Linguistic changes always result from speaker activity in the language community. Historical linguists therefore often connect the periods of a language with the historical developments affecting its speakers: political, social and cultural changes such as wars, migrations and technological innovations usually have their linguistic consequences. A comprehensive reference work, *The Cambridge History of the English Language*, focuses on technological change by beginning its Early Modern English volume at 1476, the year when William Caxton introduced the art of printing to England by setting up his printing press in London at Westminster, where the Royal Court was. Being able to reproduce any number of identical copies of a text is a powerful means of spreading linguistic norms within the language community.

London became the capital of the English book trade with some 98 per cent of the books published in England between 1500 and 1700 being printed there. However, the impact of printing was not immediate: the number of titles published for the decade 1520–9, for instance, was 550, rising to 1,040 for the period 1550–9. During the last two decades of the reign of Queen Elizabeth I, between 1580 and 1603, as many as 4,370 titles were published. A large proportion of them, some 40 per cent, were religious texts; literature accounted for about one quarter, and the rest consisted of political tracts and the law, history, geography, travel and news, scientific writings, books on commerce, economics, education, guides to conduct, and so on (Bennett 1989, vol. 1: 194; vol. 2: 269–70). The *London Gazette*, the first official newspaper, and the *Philosophical Transactions*, the first English scientific periodical, both made their inaugural appearances in 1665.

Printing often serves as a medium for *language maintenance*. What is printed is closely connected with the kind of language that is preserved from generation to generation. The large number of religious texts that appeared in print in the Early Modern period was of direct relevance to the preservation of the language of religion. We only need to think of the King James Bible and the Book of Common Prayer, which had larger print runs than any other books in the period. They inherited a large part of their morphology from the sixteenth century and were to preserve it for centuries to come. These forms include the second-person pronoun *thou*, the subject *ye*, and the third-person singular verbal ending -(*e*)*th*. They became part of what was considered to be religious language. It is noteworthy, however, that they also continued to be used in English regional dialects, many without a written history. All three are recorded in the *Survey of English Dialects*, which was carried out in the 1950s and 1960s (Orton 1962).

10.2.2 Education and literacy

Printing had a positive effect on reading ability. There were always more people who could read at least the printed word than those who could write. Around 1500 the proportion of English speakers who could *both* read *and* write was not large. On the basis of the number of people who could sign their names, the social historian David Cressy (1980: 141–77) estimates that full literacy amounted to 10 per cent of the male, and 1 per cent of the female population at this time when the total population was no more than two million. Full literacy was higher in London than elsewhere. By 1640 it included an estimated average level of 30 per cent of the male population in the entire country, but some 60 per cent of the male population of London. The social divide between the gentry and the non-gentry surfaces in literacy figures: women's overall literacy rate was much lower than men's in the seventeenth century, but we may assume that all members of the gentry could both read and write at the time.

Women's lower overall literacy figures are connected with the different educational opportunities of the sexes even in the highest social ranks. Classical education was largely a male prerogative in the Early Modern period, and very few women knew Latin. Moreover, it is telling of the social practice of publishing that less than 2 per cent of the published texts in the Early Modern period were written by women. It is not until towards the end of the period that women playwrights and poets begin to appear in print, among them Aphra Behn and Margaret Cavendish (see Crawford 1985). Fortunately, there are private records such as personal letters and diaries that provide material for studying gender differences in Early Modern English. The proportion of female letter writers in the *Corpus of Early English Correspondence* (CEEC) is about 20 per cent throughout the period (Nevalainen and Raumolin-Brunberg 2003: 46–7).

One of the gender differences that emerges from the CEEC data is that women were more often than men the leaders of linguistic changes that became part of the General dialect. They include the replacement of the subject pronoun *ye* by the object form *you*. The mid-sixteenth century extracts in (1) come from an exchange of letters between the merchant John Johnson and his wife Sabine Johnson. John continued to use the traditional form *ye* while Sabine had adopted the incoming form *you*. (Their spelling is original but modern punctuation has been added by Barbara Winchester, the editor of these letters.)

(1a) that **ye** may knowe the trewthe, and then **ye** maie kepe and put from you whome **ye** thincke good, and that **ye** perseave to be fawlte. (CEEC, John Johnson, 1545: Johnson, 250)

(1b) Mr. Douse is nowe at London for the same mater: if **you** spake with hym, **you** shall knowe all. (CEEC, Sabine Johnson, 1545: Johnson, 245)

The opposite picture emerges, however, with changes that go back to educated or professional use such as the decline of multiple negation (see 8.4.1). Sabine Johnson retains multiple negation (2a), while

John usually has the incoming form even in letters addressed to his wife (2b).

> (2a) Har answar was that she wold **not** set har myend to **no** man tell she was delyvered and choirched ... (CEEC, Sabine Johnson, 1545: JOHNSON, 396)

> (2b) trusting ye will take it in no yll parte, for in good faithe I promes youe I had **no** joye of **annything**. (CEEC, John Johnson, 1551: JOHNSON, 1250)

10.3 Social variation

As suggested above, in social terms Early Modern England was divided into the gentry, those who owned land, and the non-gentry, those who had to do manual work for a living. In a famous passage in 'The description of England' (1577) William Harrison gives an account of how people moved up the social ladder:

> (3) Who soeuer studieth the lawes of the realme, who so abideth in the vniversitie giuing his mind to his booke, or professeth physicke and the liberall sciences, or beside his seruice in the roome of a captaine in the warres, or good counsell giuen at home, whereby his common-wealth is benefited, can liue without manuell labour, and thereto is able and will beare the port, charge, and countenance of a gentleman, he shall for monie haue a cote and armes bestowed vpon him by heralds ... and therevnto being made so good cheape be called master, which is the title that men giue to esquires and gentlemen, and reputed for a gentleman euer after. (*Holinshed's Chronicles; England, Scotland and Ireland*, 1577; vol. I: 273)

The division into the gentry and the non-gentry had further subdivisions, which were reflected in the use of titles. Table 10.1 shows that *Lord* and *Lady* were reserved for the titled nobility, and the highest orders of the clergy. *Sir* and *Dame* were used in addressing a knight or a baronet and his wife, while those who belonged to the lowest land-owning rank, gentlemen and gentlewomen, were accorded the titles *Master* (*Mr*) and *Mistress* (*Mrs*). Among the non-gentry, who made up the majority of the people, only the ranks of yeoman and husbandman had titles, *Goodman* and *Goodwife* (Nevalainen and Raumolin-Brunberg 2003: 36).

Professional people occupied an intermediate position in this hierarchy. Most of them did not own land, but neither did they earn their living

Table 10.1 Titles and social status in Tudor and Stuart England

GENTRY		
Nobility	duke, archbishop marquess, earl, viscount baron, bishop	*Lord, Lady*
Gentry (proper)	baronet, knight esquire, gentleman	*Sir, Dame* *Mr, Mrs*

Professions: army officer (*Captain*, etc.), government official (*Secretary of State*, etc.), lawyer, medical doctor (*Doctor*), merchant, clergyman, teacher

NON-GENTRY		
	yeoman, husbandman, merchant craftsman, tradesman, artificer journeyman, cottager labourer, servant	*Goodman, Goodwife* (*Carpenter*, etc.)

by manual labour. Those who could afford to purchase property in the countryside often qualified as gentlemen.

In the course of the sixteenth and seventeenth centuries, upward social mobility, social indeterminacy and politeness in discourse led to the generalisation of titles. *Goodman* and *Goodwife* (*Goody*) disappeared, and *Master* and *Mistress* came to apply to people whose social standing was not based on land-ownership. So Shakespeare's First Folio (1623), for instance, bears the title *Mr William Shakespeares Comedies, Histories & Tragedies*. Shakespeare's father, who had started out as a glover, had accumulated considerable wealth, acquiring a coat of arms and the use of the title *Master*, which was here extended to his son.

In the early sixteenth century this liberal use of *Master* and *Mistress* may not always have been deemed fitting even by merchants who practised foreign trade and owned a country estate. In (4a) the wool merchant John Johnson addresses his wife as *Mistress*; in her half-serious reply in (4b) Sabine Johnson is probably playing with the polysemy of these terms.

(4a) Jhesus anno 1545, the 15 in November, at Calles.

Mistris Sabyne,
I hertely comend me unto you, praing you I maie be the same to all our freindes when ye be, etc. Your lettre of the 8 of this present moneth I have receavid, and will according to your counsaill kepe myself for your sake the best I can … (CEEC, John Johnson 1545: JOHNSON, 481)

(4b) Jhesus anno 1545, the 28 in November, at Glapthorne.

> In moest loving wise, **welbeloved husbond** (**master** I shold saye, because yet doyth becom me baetter to call you **master** than you to call me **mystres**), your letter of 15 of this present I have receyved this day, for the which I thancke you, trustyng that you well kepe yoursellf well, as you wryt you well do for [my] sacke, and even so well I for your saike ... (CEEC, Sabine Johnson 1545: JOHNSON, 515)

John usually addresses Sabine as *welbeloved wife* or simply as *wife*, but regularly uses *Mistress* when writing to two women merchants in Calais, Mistress Bainham and Mistress Fayrey.

In the course of the seventeenth century *Mr* and *Mrs* percolated further down the social scale. The status name *lady* also spread to lower ranks, and gentlewomen were commonly referred to as *ladies* (cf. the case of Alice Lisle in 5.2). Although *Miss* appeared as a title of young unmarried women, *Mrs* continued to be the abbreviated form used of both single and married women until the end of the seventeenth century.

Apart from lexical variation of this kind, it is not easy to tell how social status variation was reflected in Early Modern English usage because we have direct access only to those who could write, and they mostly came from the higher social ranks. Stereotypical features of social and regional varieties appear in plays, comedies in particular, but they are not useful in tracking actual processes of linguistic change. Some valuable information is, however, available in the letters and other records left by those lower-ranking writers, typically lesser merchants, tradesmen and servants, who needed literacy and numeracy skills in their trade.

Although the upper ranks and professional people were instrumental in spreading new linguistic forms into the General dialect, many of these originated from below the gentry. Looking at male writers, the use of *you* as a subject form was more common among the middle ranks than either in the upper or lower ranks in the fifteenth century, when this innovation began to diffuse. But it rapidly spread across the social spectrum in the first half of the next century. King Henry VIII used the incoming form in his private correspondence, as in the letter to Anne Boleyn in (5). Also, as noted above, women in general promoted the use of *you*.

> (5) Whyche browght to pas, as I trust by theyre dylygence it shall be shortly, **yow** and I shall have oure desyryd ende, whyche shulde bee more to my hartes ease and more quiettnes to my mynd than any other thyng in thys worlde ... (CEEC, Henry VIII, 1528: HENRY 8, 112)

The generalisation of the third-person singular -(*e*)*s* has a more complex history. Originally a northern form, it is first attested in the south among London merchants in the late fifteenth century. Some of them were first-generation immigrants from the north. The form occurs quite frequently in letters written by lower-ranking men at the beginning of the sixteenth century but, unlike subject *you*, it is rare among the middle or uppermost ranks. The non-gentry writers in the CEEC increasingly used -(*e*)*s* in the south as the sixteenth century wore on. The illustration in (6) comes from Richard Preston's letter to his master, John Johnson in 1551.

> (6) Ellis thaer is nothyng to selle at Lenn. As for the yron thaer is none at Yaxlay nor Owndelle unesold, as Thomas **says**.
>
> As for youre deytes, I shalle doey that I can. Mr. Ottwelle **hays** resavyd of Fransis Bold at London xx *li* as he **wrytes** me. (CEEC, Richard Preston, 1551: JOHNSON, 1204–5)

The third-person -(*e*)*s* found its way into the personal correspondence of the nobility and the gentry in the last quarter of the sixteenth century. King Henry VIII had used -(*e*)*th* even in his love letters to Anne Boleyn in the 1520s, but their daughter Elizabeth I was already a frequent user of the incoming form, and women generally accepted it more readily than men (see 7.1.1).

10.4 Urbanisation and dialect levelling

Cultural historians often associate dialect levelling and standardisation with other phenomena compounded under 'modernity'. These modernity indicators include the population's high degree of urban as opposed to rural residence as well as geographical mobility and contact with mass media. In these respects London emerges as the hub of activity in Early Modern England.

In 1500 only 10 per cent of the English population is estimated to have lived in towns but the situation changed through the large-scale processes of internal migration which began in the fifteenth century. People moved from densely populated farming regions to undeveloped land, and from the countryside to London and other cities. Table 10.2 shows the tenfold population growth which took place in London between 1500 and 1700 (Boulton 1987: 3; Wrigley and Schofield 1981: 208–9, 252).

These figures are all the more remarkable if we think that more people probably died in London than were born there at this age of

Table 10.2 Population growth, 1500–1700

Year	1500	1600	1700
London	50,000	200,000	575,000
England and Wales	2,000,000	4,110,000	5,060,000

recurrent epidemic and endemic diseases. The bubonic plague – often simply called *the sickness* – was particularly feared, as appears from contemporary accounts. The extract in (7) comes from a letter by Philip Henslowe, the London theatre manager, writing at the end of the sixteenth century.

(7) I eand praysinge god that it doth pleass hime of his mersey to slacke his hand frome visietinge vs & the sittie of london for ther hath abated this last two weacke of the sycknes iiij hundreth thurtie and five & hath died in all betwexte a leven and twealle hundred this laste weack w^{cb} I hoop In the lord yt will contenew in seasynge euery weacke ... (CEEC, Philip Henslowe, 1594. HENSLOWE, 281)

The magnetism of London, however, outweighed these health hazards. Young men in particular migrated to London in search of employment, to be, for example, apprenticed to a trade, or study at the Inns of Court. People visited the capital both on business and for pleasure, to seek legal advice, settle their disputes in court, attend the sessions of the Parliament, to do business and go shopping, and to participate in social events.

The rapid growth and urbanisation of Early Modern London made it a linguistic melting pot: coming together from various parts of the country, London residents were exposed to a whole range of varieties of English. Although regional dialects were not necessarily localisable on the basis of spelling at the time, they had their distinct phonological and grammatical properties. In circumstances like this speakers often accommodate to each other by modifying their speech in order to be better understood and approved by others. These London encounters were therefore apt to lead to dialect levelling and, in many cases, to changes in the General dialect taking shape at the time.

Most of the grammatical changes discussed above spread from or via the capital to other parts of the country. The subject use of *you* advanced at the same pace in the City of London and the Royal Court at Westminster, and it was the capital, the City and Court alike, that checked the spread of affirmative *do* in the early seventeenth century (see 8.3.1). Sometimes the usage was divided between the Court and the

City. This was the case with three features with northern origins, the third-person -(e)s, the plural form *are* of the verb *be*, and the short determiners *my* and *thy*, which replaced *mine* and *thine*. All three spread to the City before they reached the Court. The traditional long forms *mine* and *thine*, for instance, were preferred by Sir Thomas More, King Henry VIII's First Secretary and Lord Chancellor (8a), but the short ones predominate in More's biography, written by his son-in-law William Roper, a London lawyer (8b).

(8a) if I might find those causes by any man in such wyse answered, as I might thinke **mine owne** conscience satisfied, I wolde after that with all **mine hart** swere the principall oth, to. (CEEC, Thomas More, 1534: MORE, 505)

(8b) In good faithe, master Riche, I am soryer for your periurye then for **my owne** perill. And yow shall vnderstand that neyther I, nor no man els to **my knowledge**, ever tooke you to be a man of such creditt . . . (HC, William Roper, *The Lyfe of Sir Thomas Moore*, 1556: 88)

For a change diffusing into the General dialect it was important sooner or later to be adopted by the Royal Court. Some forms appear to have been promoted by the Court circles in the first place. This was the case with the relative *which*, which in the early sixteenth century got the upper hand of the originally northern form *the which* common in the City. Thomas Cromwell wrote the letter excerpted in (9a) to Cardinal Thomas Wolsey, whose secretary he was at the time. King Henry VIII's similar preference for *which* is shown in (5), above.

(9a) It may therfore please your grace that your pleasure may be knowen whether this vacacion your counsaile shall farther commune withe hym and other **whiche** haue auctoritie in that behalf, or not, **whiche** in myn opynyon shulde be well done . . . (CEEC, Thomas Cromwell, 1528: CROMWELL, 322)

(9b) I do thanke your Grace for your kynd Letter, and for youer rych and goodly present, **the whyche** I shall never be able to desarve wyth owt your gret helpe, of **the whyche** I have hetherto hade so grete plente that . . . (CEEC, Anne Boleyn, 1528: ORIGINAL 1, 305)

However, as is typical of changes in progress, people living under similar social circumstances do not always behave alike. The relative pronoun *the which* was common in women's use regardless of status differences. Anne Boleyn used it when writing to Cardinal Wolsey at Court in 1528 in (9b), as did Sabine Johnson in her letter to her wool-merchant husband in (4b) (*for the which I thancke you*).

10.5 Expansion of English

In the Early Modern period English was spoken not only in England but also in Wales and Ireland, and Scots-English was spoken in Scotland. However, the indigenous Celtic languages (Welsh, Irish and Scottish Gaelic) still predominated outside England. As the Early Modern period advanced, English strengthened its position throughout the British Isles, and was enforced by legal measures, for instance, in Wales. In the early seventeenth century, English was also transported to North America.

10.5.1 Wales and Ireland

English became the official language of Wales as a result of the Act of Union in 1536. Although this Statute of Wales passed by King Henry VIII imposed English on speakers of Welsh, their native language was preserved as a literary medium, partly thanks to the foundations provided by the religious and linguistic works published in Welsh in the sixteenth century. The Welsh translations of the New Testament and the Prayer Book appeared in 1567, and the whole Bible in 1588.

The first Anglo-Norman settlements in Ireland go back to the twelfth century. In the sixteenth century Tudor monarchs began to extend their authority in Ireland. By the end of the seventeenth century large parts of Ireland had come into the possession of the English and Scots through the British rulers' plantation policy. These actions gave rise to Irish-English, but Irish Gaelic nevertheless continued to be spoken by the majority of the population until the nineteenth century.

10.5.2 Anglicisation of Scots-English

Throughout the late Middle Ages, Scotland was an independent country with two major languages, Scots-English (Scots) and Scottish Gaelic. The situation changed with the Union of the Crowns in 1603, when King James VI of Scotland (and I of England) succeeded Queen Elizabeth I to the throne of England. The parliaments of the two countries were united by the Act of Union in 1707. These political, economic and cultural ties led to the Anglicisation of Scots-English. Southern influence was soon reflected in book production: before 1580 the vast majority of the books printed in Edinburgh were in Scots-English, but after 1603 a decline set in, and in only a few decades literary Scots gradually merged with the written *Sudron* ('southern English') (Görlach 1991: 18–23).

Many southern English forms and spellings came to be part of Scots-English between the late sixteenth and the first half of the seventeenth centuries. Amy Devitt (1989) has studied this process in the five Scottish features listed in (10), which gave way to their southern equivalents in about 100 years.

(10) • *quh-* in relative clauses becoming *wh-* (*quhilk salbe ... defeased* > *which shall be defeased*)
      • preterite *-it* becoming *-ed* (*efter the proces be intendit* > *after the process be intended*)
      • indefinite *ane* becoming *a(n)* (*ane missive, ane oathe* > *a missive, an oath*)
      • negative particles *na* and *nocht* becoming *no* and *not* (*na man, he is nocht* > *no man, he is not*)
      • past participle *-and* becoming *-ing* (*all landis pertenand to him* > *all lands pertening to him*)

Figure 10.1 shows the rapid diffusion of the Anglo-English forms (based on Devitt 1989: 17, 87), which largely replaced the Scots-English forms by about 1650. The diagram depicts the combined frequencies of Anglo-English forms of the totals in Devitt's material, consisting of public and private writings. Spelling variation naturally prevailed especially in the private texts, but the features themselves moved 'toward increased use of variants that conformed to Anglo-English usage' (1989: 71).

Even the third-person singular present-tense suffix *-(e)th* found its way into written Scots-English. There were no instances of the southern

Figure 10.1 Anglicisation of five Scots-English forms by date.

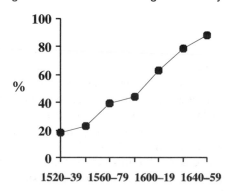

form in the *Helsinki Corpus of Older Scots* (HCOS) before 1500 and just a few before 1570. But there was a sharp increase in the use of -*(e)th* in the next seventy-year period, 1570–1640, and the form persisted even in the latter half of the seventeenth century (Meurman-Solin 1993: 250–2).

The text excerpt in (11) comes from a sermon Robert Bruce preached in Edinburgh in 1589, and it shows a mix of -*(e)th* and -*(e)s*. The -*(e)s* forms conform to Scots and northern English usage, including a plural in -*es* (*the eyes of God lookes*). The -*(e)th* forms cluster in and around biblical references. This may be partly explained by the fact that there was no printed Bible in Scots in the sixteenth century.

(11) The Lorde **hes** placed this feeling in the hart; quhy? becaus the eyes of God **lookes** not sa mekill vpon the outward countenance and exteriour behauiour, as vpon the inward hart. For he **saith** to SAMVEL, in his first book, 16. 7. verse, The Lord **behaldes** the hart. Siclike 1 CHRON. 28. 9. hee **saieth** to SALOMON: The Lord **searcheth** all harts, & **vnderstandes** al imaginations of thoughts. Also IEREMIE, 11. 20. **says**, the Lorde **tryes** the reines and the hart. (HCOS, Robert Bruce, *Upon the Preparation of the Lordis Supper*, 1590: 4–5)

A similar process of Anglicisation took place in syntax when the auxiliary *do* was generalised in Scots-English. Literary evidence suggests that *do*-periphrasis was established in Scots later than in southern English in all sentence types. With some dialectal exceptions, modern Scots follows general English usage (McClure 1994: 72).

Scots-English may, however, also have influenced the southern General dialect. The CEEC data suggest that the decline of affirmative *do* began in the London region in the first decade of the seventeenth century. We may only speculate as to what brought it about. One suggestion is dialect contact: the impact of the arrival of the Scottish court in London at the succession of King James in 1603. Affirmative *do* was rare in Scots-English at the time, and its sudden decline in the capital might therefore have been a sign of the linguistic influence wielded by these prestigious immigrants (Nurmi 1999: 179).

A latecomer in Scots-English, auxiliary *do* had only begun to gain ground in affirmative statements in the late sixteenth century. But by the second half of the seventeenth century it had already reached the same average level of use in Scotland as in southern England. In the late seventeenth century it could be found, for instance, in Scottish trials and educational treatises (Meurman-Solin 1993: 262–3). The clustering of *do* in (12), a passage drawn from the trial of Standsfield (1688), parallels the cluster in the southern Throckmorton trial over 100 years earlier (see 8.3.1).

(12) ... he **did** attempt to assassinat, and offered violence to his fathers person, and **did** chase and pursue him upon the King's high way at *Lothian-burn*, and **did** fire Pistols upon his father. And likewayes upon one or other of the dayes, of one or other of the moneth of one or other of the years of God above specified, he **did** attempt to assassinat his father for his life, at *Culterallors*, and **did** fire Pistols upon him ... (HCOS, *Tryal of Standsfield*, 1688: 4–5)

10.5.3 The rise of American English

The expansion of English reached global proportions in the seventeenth century when it was transported to the Caribbean and North America by about 400,000 immigrants from different parts of the kingdom. There were three large waves of immigration: Puritans from East Anglia settled in the Massachusetts Bay; gentry and their servants from the south of England moved to Virginia (named after Queen Elizabeth I); and Quakers from the North Midlands migrated to the Delaware Valley. In the fourth and last wave in the eighteenth century, common people from the north of England, northern Ireland and Scotland moved to the Appalachians (Fischer 1989: 16, 226–7, 421, 608–9). A political separation of the colonies from Great Britain was sealed by the American Declaration of Independence in 1776. Growing linguistic differences between the old country and the new eventually led to, in George Bernard Shaw's famous words, 'two nations separated by a common language'.

In the previous chapters we have seen that many forms that are typical of American English today were common variants in Early Modern English. They range from lexis (*autumn* and *fall*) and morphology (*got* and *gotten*) to pronunciation, as many features of Modern American English can be found in the Early Modern General dialect, including postvocalic /r/ and a front vowel in words like *last* and *path*.

With ongoing language changes it is often argued that colonies follow the linguistic developments of the mother country with some delay because of the geographical distance. This conservatism is called *colonial lag*. In the case of American English it is witnessed, for instance, in changes that took place in the modal auxiliaries *can* and *may*. *Can* gained ground in uses previously associated with *may* earlier and more rapidly in England than in the American colonies (Kytö 1991).

Colonial lag is not, however, in evidence with all linguistic changes. In the case of third-person singular present-tense suffixes, for instance, no such tendency can be observed. When personal letters are compared, the first American settlers show roughly the same level of -(*e*)*s* use as their contemporaries in England. Except with *have* and *do*, they use it in four cases out of five. This is understandable because the settlers grew up in England. But this is also the case with the first American-born genera tion and their English peers in the second half of the seventeenth century: -(*e*)*th* hardly ever occurs in the letters of either community (Kytö 1993: 124). To understand the workings of colonial lag better, we would need more research to show how linguistic changes travel long distances.

10.6 Summary

One way to delimit the Early Modern English period could be to follow its 'modernity indicators' not only linguistically, as we did in Chapter 1, but also on extralinguistic grounds. In the early sixteenth century the vast majority of the population in England, about 90 per cent, lived in the countryside and London was a town of merely 50,000 inhabitants. The social order was relatively fixed, and the impact of the printing press was not felt strongly at this early stage. The proportion of people who could both read and write was low, as was the number of printed publications: there are no more than fifty-four titles recorded for the year 1500. But as the period advanced, the Early Modern English language community became more urban, mobile and literate, and also socially more fluid.

Towards the end of the seventeenth century, 10 per cent of the English population lived in London alone, which had grown to be the largest city in the western world. People were highly mobile: on average one in six had some experience of London life at the time. England and Scotland had been united under one crown, and speakers of English had spread throughout the British Isles and to North America. With the rise of what contemporaries called the 'middling sort' of people, the old social order had grown increasingly fluid, and the titles of the gentry had become the property of the better part of the population.

By the end of the Early Modern period, a substantial number of English people were fully literate, not only the gentry and professionals but also many coming from the lower social ranks. The annual volume of book production had multiplied, and new forms of mass media such as the newspaper had emerged. One of the consequences of this rise of the written record was the standardisation of spelling. The printed medium also became the vehicle for the codification of English vocabulary and, especially in the eighteenth century, of all aspects of the language from grammar and pronunciation to 'good usage'.

Exercises

1. Discuss the idea, mooted in Chapter 1, that Early Modern English could be equated with the language of Shakespeare.

2. Discuss and illustrate the role the speakers' gender and social status played in processes of language change in Early Modern England.

3. Compare the sociolinguistic circumstances (a) in Scotland, and (b) in North America in the seventeenth century. How do Scots and American English change in the course of time in relation to the General dialect?

Further reading

For more information about the social circumstances in Early Modern England, see Wrightson (1982 and 2002), and Sharpe (1990). The language of the Bible is discussed by Partridge (1973), and the Book of Common Prayer by Brook (1965). Blank (1996) reviews language policies and regional dialects in Early Modern England, and Görlach (1999) considers the different sources of variation in Early Modern English. Nevalainen and Raumolin-Brunberg (2003) place Early Modern English in its sociohistorical context, and examine external factors such as social, regional and gender variation in relation to changes in the General dialect.

Surveys of the history and current status of the languages spoken in the British Isles, including the Celtic languages, Latin and French, are found in Price (2000); for Scots, see *The Edinburgh History of the Scots Language* (Jones 1997). Volume 6 of *The Cambridge History of the English Language* (Algeo 2001) introduces North American English. For a general introduction to the history and present-day developments of colonial Englishes, see also Bauer (2002).

Appendix 1 Mini-corpus of Early Modern English texts

A: 1500–70

(A1, Play). Nicholas Udall. [Ralph] Roister Doister, *1556, London: Hacket.*

> Actus. iij. Scæna.iiij.
>
> *Custance. Merygreeke. Roister Doister.*
>
> C. *Custāce.* What gaudyng and foolyng is this afore my doore?
>
> M. *Mery.* May not folks be honest, pray you, though they be pore?
>
> C. *Custāce.* As that thing may be true, so rich folks may be fooles,
>
> R. *Royster.* Hir talke is as fine as she had learned in schooles.
>
> M. *Mery.* Looke partly towarde hir, and drawe a little nere.
>
> C. *Custāce.* Get ye home idle folkes. *M. M.* Why may not we be here?
> Nay and ye will haze, haze: otherwise I tell you plaine,
> And ye will not haze, then giue vs our geare againe.

[ll. 7–8: *haze* = 'ha' 's', 'have us'; l. 8: *And* = 'if']

(A2, Letter). King Henry VIII. A Letter to Cardinal Wolsey, c. 1516.
(*Original Letters, Illustrative of English History* (1825), ed. Henry Ellis, vol. 1, London: Harding, Triphook, and Lepard, p. 126.)

> My Lord Cardinall I recommand vnto yow as hartely as I can, and I amme ryght glade to here of your good helthe, whyche I pray god may long contynv. So it is that I have resavyd your letters, to the whyche (by cause they aske long wrytyng) I have made answar by my Secretary. Tow thyyngs ther be whyche be so secrete that they cause me at thys tyme to wrytte to yow myselfe; the won is that I trust the quene my

wyffe be with chylde; the other is chefe cause why I am soo lothe to repayre to London ward, by cause aboght thys tyme is partly off her dangerus tymes and by cause off that I wolde remeve har as lyttyll as I may now.

(A3, Travelogue). John Leland. The Itinerary of John Leland in or about the Years 1535–43.
(Ed. Lucy Toulmin Smith, vol. 1, London: George Bell and Sons, 1907, p. 71.)

Ar I cam by a mile and more to Branspeth I passid by a ford over Were ryver. The village and castelle of Branspeth stondith on a rokky among hilles higher then it. On the southe west part of the castelle cummith doune a litle bek out o the rokkes and hilles not far of. The castelle of Branspeth is stronly set and buildid, and hath 2. courtes of high building. Ther is a litle mote that hemmith a great peice of the first court. In this court be 3. toures of logging, and 3. smaule *ad ornamentum*.

[l. 1: *Ar* = 'ere', 'before']

(A4, Educational Treatise). Thomas Elyot. The Boke Named the Gouernour, *1531, London: Berthelet, fol. 21v.*

In what wise musike may be to a noble man necessarie: and what modestie ought to be therin. Cap. vij.

The discretion of a tutor / consisteth in temperance: that is to saye / that he suffre nat the childe to be fatigate with continuall studie or lernyng: wherwith the delicate and tender witte may be dulled or oppressed: but that there may be there with entrelased and mixte / some pleasaunt lernynge / and exercise / as playenge on instruments of musike / whiche moderately vsed / and without diminution of honour / that is to say / without wanton countenance and dissolute gesture / is nat to be conténed.

[l.8: *conténed* = 'condemned']

(A5, Sermon). John Fisher. The Sermon of Iohñ the Bysshop of Rochester Made again ye P[er]nicious Doctryn of Martin Luther, *1527, London: Wynkyn de Worde, fol. B. iv.*

But now let vs retourne to our instruccyõ. Thus than ye vnderstãde how that in the vnyuersal chirche of chryste remayneth the spyryte of trouthe for euer. and yᵗ the heed of this chirch the pope is vnder chryſt.

Bi this breuely it maye appeere that the spiryte of christ is not in Martyn luther. The spyryte of euery naturall body gyueth lyfe noo forther. but to the members & partes of the same body. whiche be naturally ioyned vnto the heed. And so lykewyse it must be in the mystycall body of our mother holy chirche.

B: 1570–1640

(B1, Play). Thomas Middleton. A Chast Mayd in Cheape-side; A Pleasant Conceited Comedy, *1630, London: Constable, p. 2.* (Written c. 1611–12.)

> *Enter Yellow-hammer.*
>
> *Yell.* Now what's the din betwixt Mother and Daughter, ha?
>
> *Maudl.* Faith small, telling your Daughter *Mary* of her Errors.
>
> *Yell.* Errors, nay the Citie cannot hold you Wife, but you must needs fetch words from Westminster, I ha done. I faith, has no Atturneys Clarke beene here a late, and changed his Halfe-Crowne-peece his Mother sent him, or rather cozend you with a guilded Two-pence, to bring the word in fashion, for her faults or crackes, in dutie and obedience, terme em eeue so sweet Wife. As there is no Woman made without a Flaw, your purest Lawnes haue Frayes, and Cambrickes Brackes.
>
> *Maudl.* But 'tis a Husband sowders vp all Crackes.
>
> *Moll.* What is he come Sir?

[*Lawnes, Cambrickes* = (pieces of) fine linen]

(B2, Letter). King Charles I. A Letter to George Villiers, the Duke of Buckingham, 1626.
(*Original Letters, Illustrative of English History* (1825), ed. Henry Ellis, vol. 3, London: Harding, Triphook, and Lepard, p. 244.)

> Steenie
> I have receaved your Letter by Dic Greame, this is my Answer. I command you to send all the French away to morrow out of the Toune. If you can, by faire meanes (but stike not longe in disputing) otherways force them away, dryving them away lyke so manie wyld beastes untill ye have shipped them, and so the Devill goe with them. Lett me heare no answer bot of the performance of my command. So I rest

Your faithfull constant loving frend
Charles R.
Oaking, the 7th. of Agust 1626.

(B3, Travelogue). Robert Coverte. A True and Almost Incredible Report of an Englishman, 1612, London: Archer and Redmer, pp. 18–19.

The 21. day about ten of the Clock in the forenoone Riding there at twelue or thirteene fathome water, and a reasonable good harbour, we staied there vntill the first day of February, and then waighed Ancor, and departed. Here we refreshed our selues very well with fresh water, Coquonuts, fish, Palmitoes, and Doues, great plenty.

They first day of February, we set saile, and sailed with a faire winde vntill the 19. day, that wee passed the Equinoctiall line, and on the fifteenth day in the morning betime, we came within ken of land, which was the coast of *Melueidey* vpon the maine.

(B4, Educational Treatise). John Brinsley. Ludus Literarius: or, the Grammar Schoole, 1612, London: Man, pp. 8–9.

CHAP. II.When the Scholler should first be set to the Schoole . . .

Spoud. For the time of their entrance with vs, in our countrey schooles, it is commonly about seuen or eight yeeres old: sixe is very soone. If any beginne so early, they are rather sent to the schoole to keepe them from troubling the house at home, and from danger, and shrewd turnes, then for any great hope and desire their friends haue that they should learne any thing in effect.

Phil. I finde that therein first is a very great want generally; for that the child, if hee be of any ordinary towardnesse and capacitie, should begin at fiue yeere old at the vttermost, or sooner rather.

(B5, Sermon). Richard Hooker. Two Sermons vpon Part of S. Judes Epistle, 1614, Oxford: Barnes, p. 36.

Edifie your selues. The speech is borrowed frõ material builders, and must be spiritually vnderstood. It appeareth in the 6. of *S.Iohns* gospel by the Iewes, that their mouthes did water too much for bodilie food, *Our Fathers,* say they, *did eate Manna in the Desert, as it is written, He gaue them bread from heaven to eate; Lord, evermore giue vs of this bread.* Our Saviour, to turne their appetite another way, maketh thē this answere,

I am the bread of life, hee that cōmeth to me shall not hunger, and hee that beleeveth in mee, shall never thirst.

C: 1640–1700

(C1, Play). John Vanbrugh. The Relapse, 1697, London: Briscoe, p. 22.

Enter Loveless *and* Amand[a].

Love. How do you like these Lodgings, my Dear? For my part, I am so well pleas'd with 'em, I shall hardly remove whilst we stay in Town, if you are satisfy'd.

Aman. I am satisfy'd with every thing that pleases you; else I had not come to Town at all.

Lov. O, a little of the noise and bussle of the World, sweetens the Pleasures of Retreat: We shall find the Charms of our Retirement doubled, when we return to it.

Aman. That pleasing prospect will be my chiefest Entertainment, whilst (much against my Will) I am oblig'd to stand surrounded with these empty Pleasures, which 'tis so much the fashion to be fond of.

(C2, Letter). King Charles II. A letter to the Earl, afterwards Duke of Lauderdale, 1669.

(*Letters of the Council to Sir Thomas Lake* (1864), ed. Samuel Rawson Gardiner (Camden Miscellany 5, Camden First Series 87), London: Camden Society, pp. 21–2.)

Whithall, 2 Nouember 1669.

Though Robin Moray has by my derections answerd your letters, and tould you how well I am satisfied with your proceedings in Scotland, yett I cannot forbeare the repeating it to you my selfe, and withall to tell you the true sence I have of your industry and dexterity in the whole proceedings. I shall not say any thing particularly now concerning the vnion, because Robin has at large tould you my thoughts in order to what is to be done on your parts, which I thinke you will aproue of when you consider the length of our Parlament deliberations heere, and how inconvenient a long sessions there would be in all respects. I shall say no more to you now but to assure you of my kindnesse and constant frindship.

C. R.

(C3, Travelogue). John Fryer. A New Account of East India and Persia, *1698, London: Chiswell, p. 235.*

The rest of this day's Journy was between the Mountains, where we were encounter'd by strange Flashes of Lightning, the Foretellers of this Night's Rain, which we hardly escaped before we came to *Caurestan,* in all Twenty Miles: This *Caravan Ser Raw* is named from a Tree growing here, and a Village properly so called (of which it is a Composition in *Persian*), it being the first we met with whose Houses were fixed.

The following Day we continued going between two Chains of Dry and Burnt Hills, through a stony Valley, not without fear of suffocating, although it was near Evening e're we set out, and Yesterday's Showers had benignly distilled on the Fiery Drought, to cool the parched Earth:

(C4, Educational Treatise). John Locke. Some Thoughts concerning Education, *1693, London: Churchill, p. 33.*

§. 32. If what I have said in the beginning of this Discourse, be true, as I do not doubt but it is, *viz.* That the difference to be found in the Manners and Abilities of Men, is owing more to their *Education,* than to any thing else, we have reason to conclude, that great care is to be had of the forming Children's *Minds,* and giving them that seasoning early, which shall influence their Lives always after. For when they do well or ill, the Praise or Blame will be laid there; and when any thing is done untowardly, the common Saying will pass upon them, That it is suitable to their *Breeding.*

(C5, Sermon). John Tillotson. Several Discourses upon the Attributes of God, *1699, London: Chiswell, p. 52.*

And this is very agreeable to the language and sense of the holy Scriptures, which every where make the Practice of Religion to consist in our Conformity to God, and the Laws which he hath given us; which are nothing else but a transcript of his Nature. The great business of Religion is to do the Will of God, and *this is the Will of God, our sanctification;* and our sanctification is our conformity to the holiness of God; and this is the scope of the general Exhortations of Scripture, to perswade us to holiness, that is, to an imitation of the Moral *Perfections* of the Divine Nature.

Appendix 2 Four longer
Early Modern English texts

William Cecil, Lord Burghley: A letter to the University of
Cambridge, 1588.
(From: Henry Ellis (ed.) (1825), *Original Letters, Illustrative of English*
History, 2nd edn, vol. 3, London: Harding, Triphook, and Lepard, pp.
24–8.)

To my loving frend M^r. D^r. Legge Vicechancellor &c. and to the rest
of the Heads there.

Wheras the great excess and disorder of Apparell hath not only
impoverished the Realme, but hath bene a special cause of many other
vices and evil examples in all degrees; for the due reformation whereof
it is godly provided for in all persons and places, if due execution were
had accordingly: for want wherof, many have greatly exceeded the
prescription of Law, and left the ancient, grave, and comely apparell
generally used of all scholars in both Universities heretofore; whereby
they were known and reverenced, every man in his degree, both in the
University and withoute, in Court and City; by wearing of that
comely, decent, and wonted apparell; the due consideration whereof,
is referred by her Majesties Proclamation to the Chancellors of both
Universities, supposing that their commandement will work a perfect
reformation of all disorders in both the said Universities. Wherefore
these are straitly to charge and command you the Vicechancellor and
Hedds of the Colleges in the University of Cambridge, that the
Statutes and Orders made in your University for the special apparell
to be worne of all degrees of scholars, made sithens her Majestie's
most gracious raigne, be duely observed and kept, and that no hatt be
worne of any Graduate or Scholer within the University, except it be
when he shall journey out of the Town, the same Graduate or Scholar
having his name in any Table, or being in commons in any House of
Learning in the said University; except in the time of his sicknes. And
that all Scholers being Graduats upon the charges of any Howse, do

wear a square cap of clothe, and lykewise scholers of Howses that be no Graduats, and all other Scholers that have taken no degree of Scholers, and do lyve upon their own charges, do weare in the said University a round clothe cap. Saving that it may be lawful for the sons of Noblemen, or the sons and heirs of Knights, to wear round caps of velvet, but no hats. [. . .]

And that no Scholer do weare any longe locks of heare upon his hedd, but that he be notted, polled, or rounded after the accustomed manner of the gravest scholers of the said University, under the pain of six shillings and eight pence for everye tyme that any graduate Fellow, Scholer, Pensioner, or Sizer shall offende in any of the foresaid Orders. The forfeycture for every publique offence committed without the College to be collected, immediatelye after the offence done, by the bedells or other Officers therunto appoynted within the said University, and to be payd either to the Chancellor, or in his absence to the Vicechancellor of the said University, to th'onlye use of the same, and by him to be accompted for at his general accompts for his yeare.

And the punishments and forfeytures of all the aforesaid offences by any of the aforenamed Students within any of the Colleges or Halls in the said University, to be taken by the Hedds and Sub-Hedds of the said Colleges and Halls where such offence is committed, and to be converted to the use of the said College or Hall.

And thes Orders, together with all other good Orders heretofore taken for exercises of Learning within the aforesaid University, I require you and every of you duely to observe and precisely to kepe according to your Oath and duties, as you will retaine my favour and would have me to continue my careful government over you: which I assuer you I will cast off, yf I fynde not a due and spedye reformation of all disorders among you: for her Majesty looketh for the same, both at myne and your hands, and that forthwith. So I bid you hartelye farewell, from my House in the Strand, this 7th. of Maye 1588.
Your loving frend
W. Burghley.

Francis Bacon: The Twoo Bookes of the Proficience and Aduancement of Learning, London: Henrie Tomes, 1605.
(The Second Booke, pp. 17r–19r; EE 218.)

There be therfor chiefly three vanities in Studies, whereby learning hath been most traduced: For those things we do esteeme vaine, which are either false of friuolous, those which either haue no truth,

or no vse: & those persons we esteem vain, which are either credulous
or curious, & curiositie is either in mater or words; so that in reason,
as wel as in experence, there fal out to be these 3. distēpers (as I may
tearm thē) of learning; The first fantastical learning: The second con-
tentious learning, & the last delicate learning, vaine Imaginations,
vaine Altercations, & vain affectatiōs: & with the last I wil begin,
Martin Luther conducted (no doubt) by an higher prouidence, but in
discourse of reason, finding what a Prouince he had vndertaken
against the Bishop of *Rome*, and the degenerate traditions of the
Church, and finding his owne solitude, being no waies ayded by the
opinions of his owne time, was enforced to awake all Antiquitie, and to
call former times to his succors, to make a partie against the present
time: so that the ancient Authors, both in Diuinitie and in Humanitie,
which had long time slept in Libraries, began generally to be read and
reuolued. This by consequence, did draw on a necessitie of a more
exquisite trauaile in the languages originall, wherin those Authors did
write: For the better vnderstāding of those Authors, and the better
aduantage of pressing and applying their words: And thereof grew
againe, a delight in their manner of Stile and Phrase, and an admiration of that kinde of writing; which was much furthered & precipitated
by the enmity & opposition, that the propounders of those (primitiue,
but seeming new opinions) had against the Schoole-men: who were
generally of the contrarie part: and whose Writings were altogether in
a differing Stile and fourme, taking libertie to coyne, and frame new
tearms of Art, to expresse their own sence, and to auoide circuite of
speech, without regard to the purenesse, pleasantnesse, and (as I may
call it) lawfulnesse of the Phrase or word: And againe, because the
great labour that then was with the people (of whome the Pharisees
were wont to say: *Execrabilis ista turba quae non nouit legem*) for the
winning and perswading of them, there grewe of necessitie in cheefe
price, and request, eloquence and varietie of discourse, as the fittest
and forciblest accesse into the capasitie of the vulgar sort: so that these
foure causes concurring, the admiration of ancient Authors the hate of
the Schoole-men, the exact studie of Languages: and the efficacie of
Preaching did bring in an affectionate studie of eloquence, and copie
of speech, which then began to flourish. This grew speedily to an
excesse: for men began to hunt more after wordes, than matter, and
more after the choisenesse of the Phrase, and the round and cleane
composition of the sentence, and the sweet falling of the clauses, and
the varying and illustration of their workes with tropes and figures:
then after the weight of matter, worth of subiect, soundnesse of argument, life of inuention, or depth of iudgement. Then grew the flowing,

and watrie vaine of *Osorius* the Portugall Bishop, to be in price: then did *Sturmius* spend such infinite, and curious paines vpon *Cicero* the Orator, and *Hermogenes* the Rhetorican, besides his owne Bookes of Periods, and imitation, and the like: Then did *Car* of *Cambridge*, and *Ascham* with their Lectures and Writings, almost diefie *Cicero* and *Demosthenes*, and allure, all young men that were studious vnto that delicate and pollished kinde of learning. Then did *Erasmus* take occasion to make the scoffing Eccho; *Decem annos consumpsi in legendo Cicerone.* and the Eccho answered in Greeke, *Oue; Asine.* Then grew the learning of the Schoole-men to be vtterly despised as barbarous. In summe, the whole inclination and bent of those times, was rather towards copie, than weight.

Thomas Middleton: A Chast Mayd in Cheapeside. A Pleasant Conceited Comedy, 1630, London: Francis Constable, pp. 45–6. (Written c. 1611–12.)

Enter Maudline.

Maudl. Here's nothing but disputing all the day long with 'em.

Tut[or]. Sic disputas, stultus est homo sicut tu & ego sum homo est animal rationale, sicut stultus est animal rationale.

Maudl. Your reasons are both good what e're they be Pray giue them or'e, faith you'le tire your selues, What's the matter betweene you?

Tim. Nothing but reasoning about a Foole Mother.

Maudl. About a Foole Son, alas what need you trouble your heads about that, none of vs all but knowes what a Foole is.

Tim. Why what's a Foole Mother? I come to you now.

Maudl. Why one that's married before he has wit.

Tim. 'Tis prettie I faith, and well guest of a Woman neuer brought vp at the Vniuersitie: but bring forth what Foole you will Mother, I'le proue him to be as reasonable a Creature, as my selfe or my Tutor here.

Maudl. Fye 'tis impossible.

Tut. Nay he shall do't forsooth.

Tim. 'Tis the easiest thing to proue a Foole by Logicke, By Logicke I'le proue any thing.

Maudl. What thou wilt not?

Tim. I'le proue a Whore to be an honest Woman.

Maudl. Nay by my faith, she must proue that her selfe, or Logicke will neuer do't.

Tim. 'Twill do't I tell you.

Maudl. Some in this Street would giue a thousand pounds that you could proue their Wiues so.

Tim. Faith I can, and all their Daughters too, though they had three Bastards. When comes your Taylor hither?

Maudl. Why what of him?

Tim. By Logicke I'le proue him to be a Man, Let him come when he will.

Maudl. How hard at first was Learning to him? Truly Sir I thought he would neuer a tooke the Latine Tongue. How many Accidences doe you thinke he wore out e're he came to his Grammer?

Tut. Some three or foure.

Maudl. Beleeue me Sir some foure and thirtie.

Tim. Pish I made haberdins of 'em in Church porches.

Maudl. He was eight yeeres in his Grammer, and stucke horribly at a foolish place there call'd *Asse in presenti.*

Tim. Pox I haue it here now.

Maudl. He so sham'd me once before an honest Gentleman that knew me when I was a Mayd.

Tim. These women must haue all out.

Maudl. Quid est Gramatica? Sayes the Gentleman to him (I shall remember by a sweet sweet token) but nothing could he answer.

Tut. How now Pupill, ha, *Quid est Gramatica?*

Tim. Grammatica? Ha, ha, ha.

Maudl. Nay doe not laugh Sonne, but let me heare you say it now: There was one word went so prettily off the Gentlemans tongue, I shall remember it the longest day of my life.

Tut. Come, *Quid est Gramatica?*

Tim. Are you not asham'd Tutor, *Gramatica?* Why *Recte scribendi atque loquendi ars,* ser-reuerence of my Mother.

Maudl. That was it I faith: Why now Sonne I see you are a deepe Scholler:

Brilliana Harley: A letter to her husband, 1627.
(From: T.T. Lewis (ed.) (1854), *Letters of the Lady Brilliana Harley, Wife of Sir Robert Harley, of Brampton Bryan, Knight of the Bath* (Camden Society LVIII), London: Camden Society, pp. 3–4.)

[Addressed: To my deare husband Sr Robert Harley]
Deare S^r – Your two leters, on from Hearifort and the other from Gloster, weare uery wellcome to me: and if you knwe howe gladly I reseaue your leters, I beleeue you would neeuer let any opertunity pase. I hope your cloche did you saruis betwne Gloster and my brother Brays, for with vs it was a very rainy day, but this day has bine very dry and warme, and so I hope it was with you; and to-morowe I hope you will be well at your journis end, wheare I wisch my self to bide you wellcome home. You see howe my thoughts goo with you: and as you haue many of mine, so let me haue some of yours. Beleeue me, I thinke I neuer miste you more then nowe I doo, or ells I haue forgoot what is past. I thanke God, Ned and Robin are well; and Ned askes every day wheare you are, and he says you will come to-morowe. My father is well, but goos not abrode, becaus of his fiseke. I haue sent you vp a litell hamper, in which is the box with the ryteings and boouckes you bide me send vp, with the other things, sowed up in a clothe, in the botome of the hamper. I haue sent you a partriche pye, which has the two pea chikeins in it, and a litell runlet of meathe, that which I toold you I made for my father. I thinke within this muthe, it will be very good drinke. I sende it vp nowe becaus I thinke carage when it is ready to drincke dous it hurt; thearefore, and please you to let it rest and then taste it; if it be good, I pray you let my father haue it, because he spake to me for such meathe. I will nowe bide you god night, for it is past a leauen a cloke. I pray God presarue you and giue you good sugsess in all your biusnes, and a speady and happy meeting.

Your most faithfull affectinat wife, Brilliana Harley.
I must beeg your bllsing for Ned and Rob. and present you with Neds humbell duty.
(Bromton, the 5 of October, 1627.)

References

EL = *English Linguistics, 1500–1800*, Menston: The Scolar Press.
EE = *English Experience*, Amsterdam: Theatrum Orbis Terrarum.
MSN = *Mémoires de la Société Néophilologique de Helsinki*.
(For the corpora referred to, see Chapter 2: Further reading and study resources.)

Abbott, Edwin A. (1870), *A Shakespearian Grammar*, 3rd edn, London: Macmillan and Co.

Adamson, Sylvia (1989), 'With a double tongue: diglossia, stylistics and the teaching of English', in Mick Short (ed.), *Reading, Analysing and Teaching Literature*, London: Longman, 204–40.

Adamson, Sylvia (1999), 'Literary language', in Roger Lass (ed.), *The Cambridge History of the English Language*, vol. 3, *1476–1776*, Cambridge: Cambridge University Press, 539–653.

Adamson, Sylvia, Lynette Hunter, Lynne Magnusson, Ann Thompson and Katie Wales (eds) (2001), *Reading Shakespeare's Dramatic Language* (The Arden Shakespeare), London: Thomson Learning.

Algeo, John (ed.) (2001), *The Cambridge History of the English Language*, vol. 6, *English in North America*, Cambridge: Cambridge University Press.

Altenberg, Bengt (1982), *The Genitive v. the Of-Construction: A Study of Syntactic Variation in 17th Century English* (Lund Studies in English 62), Lund: Gleerup.

Ascham, Roger (1570), *The Scholemaster*, London: Iohn Daye.

Bacon, Nathaniel (1978–9, 1982–3, 1987–8), *The Papers of Nathaniel Bacon of Stiffkey*, ed. A. Hassell Smith, Gillian M. Baker and R. W. Kenny (Norfolk Record Society 46, 49, 53), Norwich: Norfolk Record Society.

Bækken, Bjørg (1998), *Word Order Patterns in Early Modern English*, Oslo: Novus Press.

Bailey, Richard W., James W. Downer, Jay L. Robinson, with Patricia V. Lehman (1975), *Michigan Early Modern English Materials*, Ann Arbor, MI: Xerox University Microfilms and The University of Michigan Press. Online: http://www.hti.umich.edu/m/memem/.

Barber, Charles [1976] (1997), *Early Modern English*, 2nd edn, Edinburgh: Edinburgh University Press.

Bauer, Laurie (2002), *An Introduction to International Varieties of English*, Edinburgh: Edinburgh University Press.

Bennett, Henry S. (1989), *English Books and Readers, 1475–1557*, vol. 1; *1558–1603*, vol. 2, 2nd edn, Cambridge: Cambridge University Press.

Benskin, Michael (2004), 'Chancery Standard', in Christian Kay, Carole Hough and Irené Wotherspoon (eds), *New Perspectives on English Historical Linguistics*, vol. II, Amsterdam and Philadelphia: Benjamins, 1–40.

Biber, Douglas, Susan Conrad and Randi Reppen (1998), *Corpus Linguistics: Investigating Language Structure and Use*, Cambridge: Cambridge University Press.

Biber, Douglas, Stig Johansson, Geoffrey Leech, Susan Conrad and Edward Finegan (1999), *Longman Grammar of Spoken and Written English*, London: Longman.

Blake, Norman F. (2002), *A Grammar of Shakespeare's Language*, Basingstoke: Palgrave.

Blank, Paula (1996), *Broken English: Dialects and the Politics of Language in Renaissance Writings*, London: Routledge.

Blount, Thomas [1656] (1969), *Glossographia*, London: H. Moseley; EL 153.

Bolton, Whitney F. (ed.) (1966), *The English Language: Essays by English and American Men of Letters 1490–1839*, Cambridge: Cambridge University Press.

Boulton, Jeremy (1987), *Neighbourhood and Society: A London Suburb in the Seventeenth Century*, Cambridge: Cambridge University Press.

Britton, Derek (2000), 'Henry Machyn, Axel Wijk and the case of the wrong Riding: the South-West Yorkshire character of the language of Machyn's diary', *Neuphilologische Mitteilungen* 101 (4): 571–96.

Brook, Stella (1965), *The Language of the Book of Common Prayer*, London: André Deutsch.

Bullokar, John [1616] (1967), *An English Expositor*, London: A. Crooke; EL 11.

Bullokar, William (1586), *William Bullokarz Pamphlet for Grammar*, London: Edmund Bollifant.

Burnley, David (1983), *A Guide to Chaucer's Language*, London: Macmillan.

Busse, Ulrich (2002), *Linguistic Variation in the Shakespeare Corpus: Morpho-Syntactic Variability of Second Person Pronouns* (Pragmatics and Beyond 106), Amsterdam: Benjamins.

Butler, Charles (1633), *The English Grammar*, Oxford: William Turner.

Carstairs-McCarthy, Andrew (2002), *An Introduction to English Morphology*, Edinburgh: Edinburgh University Press.

Cawdrey, Robert [1604] (1970), *A Table Alphabeticall*, London: I. R. for Edmund Weauer; EE 226.

Chamberlain, John (1939), *The Letters of John Chamberlain*, ed. Norman Egbert McClure (American Philosophical Society, Memoirs 12, I–II), Philadelphia: American Philosophical Society.

Cockeram, Henry [1623] (1968), *The English Dictionarie*, London: N. Butter; EL 124.

Coles, Elisha [1676] (1971), *An English Dictionary*, London: S. Crouch; EL 268.

Conway, Anne (1992), *The Conway Letters*, ed. Marjorie Hope Nicolson, rev. Sarah Hutton, Oxford: Clarendon Press.

Coote, Edmund [1596] (1968), *The English Schoole-Maister*, London: printed by the Widow Orwin for Ralph Iackson and Robert Dexter; EL 98.

Crawford, Patricia (1985), 'Women's published writings 1600–1700', in Mary Prior (ed.), *Women in English Society 1500–1800*, London and New York: Methuen, 211–82.

Cressy, David (1980), *Literacy and Social Order: Reading and Writing in Tudor and Stuart England*, Cambridge: Cambridge University Press.

Cruttenden, Alan (1994), *Gimson's Pronunciation of English*, London: Edward Arnold.

Crystal, David [1995] (2003), *The Cambridge Encyclopedia of the English Language*, 2nd edn, Cambridge: Cambridge University Press.

Crystal, David (2003), *A Dictionary of Linguistics and Phonetics*, 5th edn, Oxford: Blackwell.

Culpeper, Jonathan and Phoebe Clapham (1996), 'The borrowing of Classical and Romance words into English: a study based on the electronic *Oxford English Dictionary*', *International Journal of Corpus Linguistics* 1(2): 199–218.

Curzan, Anne (2003), *Gender Shifts in the History of English*, Cambridge: Cambridge University Press.

Danielsson, Bror (ed.) (1955, 1963), *John Hart's Works on English Orthography and Pronunciation (1551, 1569, 1570)*, Parts 1–2, Stockholm: Almqvist and Wiksell.

Defoe, Daniel (1697), *An Essay upon Projects*, London: Tho. Cockerill.

Denison, David (1993), *English Historical Syntax: Verbal Constructions*, London: Longman.

Devitt, Amy (1989), *Standardizing Written English: Diffusion in the Case of Scotland 1520–1659*, Cambridge: Cambridge University Press.

Dobson, Eric J. [1957] (1968), *English Pronunciation 1500–1700*, vol. 1, 2nd edn, Oxford: Clarendon Press.

Dons, Ute (2004), *Descriptive Adequacy of Early Modern English Grammars*, Berlin and New York: Mouton de Gruyter.

Ellegård, Alvar (1953), *The Auxiliary 'Do': The Establishment and Regulation of Its Use in English* (Gothenburg Studies in English 2), Stockholm: Almqvist and Wiksell.

Elsness, Johan (1994), 'On the progression of the progressive in early Modern English', *ICAME Journal* 18: 5–25.

Evelyn, John [1951] (2000), *The Diary of John Evelyn*, ed. E. S. de Beer, Oxford: Clarendon Press.

Finkenstaedt, Thomas, Ernst Leisi and Dieter Wolff (1973), *A Chronological English Dictionary*, Heidelberg: Winter.

Finkenstaedt, Thomas and Dieter Wolff (1973), *Ordered Profusion: Studies in Dictionaries and the English Lexicon* (Annales Universitatis Saraviensis, Reihe: Philosophische Fakultät 13), Heidelberg: C. Winter.

Fischer, Andreas (1994), '"Sumer is icumen in': the seasons of the year in Middle English and Early Modern English', in Dieter Kastovsky (ed.), *Studies in Early Modern English*, Berlin and New York: Mouton de Gruyter, 79–95.

Fischer, David H. (1989), *Albion's Seed: Four British Folkways in America*, New York and Oxford: Oxford University Press.

Fisher, John H., Malcolm Richardson and Jane L. Fisher (1984), *An Anthology of Chancery English*, Knoxville: The University of Tennessee Press.

Florio, John (1598), *A Worlde of Words, or Most Copious, and Exact Dictionarie in Italian and English*, London: Edward Blount.

Franz, Wilhelm (1939), *Die Sprache Shakespeares in Vers und Prosa, Shakespeare-Grammatik*, 4th edn, Halle: Niemeyer.

Garner, Bryan A. [1983] (1987), 'Latin-Saxon hybrids in Shakespeare and the Bible', in Vivian Salmon and Edwina Burness (eds), *A Reader in the Language of Shakespearian Drama*, Amsterdam and Philadelphia: Benjamins, 229–234.

Geeraerts, Dirk (1997), *Diachronic Prototype Semantics: A Contribution to Historical Lexicology*, Oxford: Clarendon Press.

Gil, Alexander [1619] (1972), *Logonomia Anglica*, London: J. Beale; Bror Danielsson and Arvid Gabrielson (eds), *Alexander Gill's Logonomia Anglica (1619)*, 2 vols (Stockholm Studies in English, 26, 27), Stockholm: Almqvist and Wiksell.

Gordon, Ian A. (1980), *The Movement of English Prose*, London: Longman.

Görlach, Manfred (1991), *Introduction to Early Modern English*, Cambridge: Cambridge University Press.

Görlach, Manfred (1999), 'Regional and social variation', in Roger Lass (ed.), *The Cambridge History of the English Language*, vol. 3, *1476–1776*, Cambridge: Cambridge University Press, 459–538.

Görlach, Manfred (2001), *Eighteenth-Century English*, Heidelberg: Winter.

Greaves, Paul (1594), *Grammatica Anglicana*, Cambridge: John Legate.

Gustafsson, Larisa O. (2002), *Preterite and Past Participle Forms in English, 1680–1790* (Studia Anglistica Upsaliensia 120), Uppsala: Uppsala University.

Harrison, William [1577] (1965), 'The description of England', in *Holinshed's Chronicles: England, Scotland and Ireland*, vol. I, London: AMS Press, 221–431.

Hart, John [1551] (1955), *The Opening of the Unreasonable Writing of Our Inglish Toung*, London; ed. Bror Danielsson.

Hart, John [1569] (1969), *An Orthographie*, London: W. Serres; EL 209.

Hart, John [1570] (1955), *A Methode or Comfortable Beginning for All Vnlearned*, London: Henrie Denham; ed. Bror Danielsson.

Henry VIII, King of England (1988), *Die Liebesbriefe Heinrichs VIII. an Anna Boleyn*, ed. Theo Stemmler, Zürich: Belser Verlag.

Hofland, Knut and Stig Johansson (1982), *Word Frequencies in British and American English*, Bergen: The Norwegian Computing Centre for the Humanities.

Hogg, Richard (2002), *An Introduction to Old English*, Edinburgh: Edinburgh University Press.

Hope, Jonathan (1993), 'Second person singular pronouns in records of Early Modern "spoken" English', *Neuphilologische Mitteilungen*, 94 (1): 83–100.

Hope, Jonathan (2003), *Shakespeare's Grammar* (The Arden Shakespeare), London: Thomson Learning.

Horobin, Simon and Jeremy Smith (2002), *An Introduction to Middle English*, Edinburgh: Edinburgh University Press.

Huddleston, Rodney and Geoffrey K. Pullum (2002), *The Cambridge Grammar of the English Language*, Cambridge: Cambridge University Press.

Hughes, Geoffrey (1988), *Words in Time: A Social History of the English Vocabulary*, Oxford: Blackwell.

Hussey, Stanley S. (1992), *The Literary Language of Shakespeare*, 2nd edn, London: Longman.

Jacobson, Sven (1981), *Preverbal Adverbs and Auxiliaries: A Study of Word Order Change* (Stockholm Studies in English 55), Stockholm: Almqvist and Wiksell.

Johnson, Samuel (1755), *A Dictionary of the English Language*, London: printed by W. Strahan, for J. and P. Knapton (etc.).

Jones, Charles (ed.) (1997), *The Edinburgh History of the Scots Language*, Edinburgh: Edinburgh University Press.

Jones, Richard F. [1953] (1966), *The Triumph of the English Language*, Stanford, CA: Stanford University Press.

Kastovsky, Dieter (ed.) (1994), *Studies in Early Modern English*, Berlin and New York: Mouton de Gruyter.

Kemp, John A. (transl.) (1972), *John Wallis's Grammar of the English Language*, London: Longman.

Kjellmer, Göran (2000), 'On American personal names: a historical study', *Studia Neophilologica* 72: 142–57.

Kytö, Merja (1991), *Variation and Diachrony, with Early American English in Focus: Studies on* Can/May *and* Shall/Will (Bamberger Beiträge zur englischen Sprachwissenschaft 28), Frankfurt am Main: Lang.

Kytö, Merja (1993), 'Third-person present singular verb inflection in early British and American English', *Language Variation and Change* 5: 113–39.

Kytö, Merja (comp.) (1996), *Manual to the Diachronic Part of the Helsinki Corpus of English Texts*, 3rd edn, Helsinki: Department of English, University of Helsinki.

Kytö, Merja (1997), '*Be/have* + past participle: the choice of the auxiliary with intransitives from Late Middle to Modern English', in Matti Rissanen, Merja Kytö and Kirsi Heikkonen (eds), *English in Transition: Corpus-based Studies in Linguistic Variation and Genre Styles*, Berlin and New York: Mouton de Gruyter, 17–85.

Kytö, Merja and Suzanne Romaine (1997), 'Competing forms of adjective comparison in modern English', in Terttu Nevalainen and Leena Kahlas-Tarkka (eds), *To Explain the Present: Studies in the Changing English Language in Honour of Matti Rissanen* (MSN 52), Helsinki: Société Néophilologique, 329–52.

Labov, William (1995), *Principles of Linguistic Change: Internal Factors*, Cambridge, MA: Blackwell.

Lancashire, Ian (2003), 'The lexicons of Early Modern English', *Computing in the Humanities Working Papers* A 23 (September 2003). Online: http://www.chass.utoronto.ca/~ian/#Papers.

Lass, Roger (1994), 'Proliferation and option-cutting: the strong verb in the fifteenth to eighteenth centuries', in Dieter Stein and Ingrid Tieken-Boon van Ostade (eds), *Towards a Standard English, 1600–1800*, Berlin and New York: Mouton de Gruyter, 81–113.

Lass, Roger (1999), 'Phonology and morphology', in Roger Lass (ed.), *The Cambridge History of the English Language*, vol. 3, *1476–1776*, Cambridge: Cambridge University Press, 56–186.

Lass, Roger (ed.) (1999), *The Cambridge History of the English Language*, vol. 3, *1476–1776*, Cambridge: Cambridge University Press.

Lass, Roger (2000), 'Language periodization and the concept of "middle"', in Irma Taavitsainen, Terttu Nevalainen, Päivi Pahta and Matti Rissanen (eds), *Placing Middle English in Context*, Berlin and New York: Mouton de Gruyter, 7–41.

Lass, Roger (2001), 'Shakespeare's sounds', in Sylvia Adamson, Lynette Hunter, Lynne Magnusson, Ann Thompson and Katie Wales (eds), *Reading Shakespeare's Language: A Guide* (The Arden Shakespeare), London: Thomson Learning, 257–69.

Levins, Peter [1570] (1969), *Manipulus Vocabulorum: A Dictionarie of English and Latine Wordes*, London: Henrie Bynneman, for J. Waley; EL 195.

Lewis, C. S. (1967), *Studies in Words*, 2nd edn, Cambridge: Cambridge University Press.

Lowth, Robert (1762), *A Short Introduction to English Grammar*, London: A. Millar, R. and J. Dodsley.

Marchand, Hans [1960] (1969), *The Categories and Types of Present-Day English Word-Formation: A Synchronic-Diachronic Approach*, 2nd edn, München: Beck'sche.

Mazzon, Gabriella (2004), *A History of English Negation*, London: Longman.

McClure, J. Derrick (1994), 'English in Scotland', in Robert Burchfield (ed.), *The Cambridge History of the English Language*, vol. 5, *English in Britain and Overseas*, Cambridge: Cambridge University Press, 23–93.

McGrath, Alister (2001), *In the Beginning: The Story of the King James Bible*, London: Hodder and Stoughton.

McIntosh, Angus, Michael L. Samuels and Michael Benskin (1986), *A Linguistic Atlas of Late Mediaeval English*, vol. 1, Aberdeen: Aberdeen University Press.

McMahon, April (2002), *An Introduction to English Phonology*, Edinburgh: Edinburgh University Press.

Meurman-Solin, Anneli (1993), *Variation and Change in Early Scottish Prose: Studies Based on the Helsinki Corpus of Older Scots*, Helsinki: Academia Scientiarum Fennica.

Meurman-Solin, Anneli (1995), 'A new tool: the Helsinki Corpus of Older Scots (1450–1700)', *ICAME Journal* 19: 49–62.

Michael, Ian (1970), *English Grammatical Categories and the Tradition to 1800*, Cambridge: Cambridge University Press.

Miller, Jim (2002), *An Introduction to English Syntax*, Edinburgh: Edinburgh University Press.

Milroy, James (1992), *Linguistic Variation and Change*, Oxford: Blackwell.

Milroy, James (2002), 'The legitimate language', in Richard Watts and Peter Trudgill (eds), *Alternative Histories of English*, London: Routledge/ Taylor and Francis, 7–25.

Milroy, James and Lesley Milroy (1999), *Authority in Language: Investigating Standard English*, 3rd edn, London and New York: Routledge.

Moessner, Lilo (2002), 'Who used the subjunctive in the 17th century?', in Sybil Scholz, Monika Klages, Evelyn Hantson and Ute Römer (eds), *Language, Context and Cognition*, München: Langenscheidt-Longman, 227–35.

More, Thomas (1947), *The Correspondence of Sir Thomas More*, ed. Elizabeth Frances Rogers, Princeton: Princeton University Press.

Mulcaster, Richard [1582] (1970), *The First Part of the Elementarie which Entreateth Chefelie of the Right Writing of our English Tung*, London: T. Vautroullier; EL 219.

Mustanoja, Tauno F. (1960), *A Middle English Syntax*, Part 1 (MSN 23), Helsinki: Société Néophilologique.

Nevalainen, Terttu (1991), *BUT, ONLY, JUST: Focusing Adverbial Change in Modern English 1500–1900* (MSN 51), Helsinki: Société Néophilologique.

Nevalainen, Terttu (1997), 'The processes of adverb derivation in Late Middle and Early Modern English', in Matti Rissanen, Merja Kytö and Kirsi Heikkonen (eds), *Grammaticalization at Work: Studies of Long-term Developments in English*, Berlin and New York: Mouton de Gruyter, 145–190.

Nevalainen, Terttu (1999), 'Early Modern English lexis and semantics', in Roger Lass (ed.), *The Cambridge History of the English Language*, vol. 3, *1476–1776*, Cambridge: Cambridge University Press, 332–458.

Nevalainen, Terttu and Helena Raumolin-Brunberg (1993), 'Early Modern British English', in Matti Rissanen, Merja Kytö and Minna Palander-Collin (eds), *Early English in the Computer Age*, Berlin and New York: Mouton de Gruyter, 53–73.

Nevalainen, Terttu and Helena Raumolin-Brunberg (2003), *Historical Sociolinguistics: Language Change in Tudor and Stuart England*, London: Longman.

Nurmi, Arja (1999), *A Social History of Periphrastic DO* (MSN 56), Helsinki: Société Néophilologique.

Nurmi, Arja and Päivi Pahta (2004), 'Social stratification and patterns of code-switching in Early English letters', *Multilingua* 23 (4): 417–56.

Orton, Harold (1962), *Survey of English Dialects: Introduction*, Leeds: E. J. Arnold and Son.

Osborne, Dorothy (1959), *The Letters of Dorothy Osborne to William Temple*, ed. G. C. Moore Smith, Oxford: Clarendon Press.

The Oxford English Dictionary (1989), 2nd edn, ed. J. A. Simpson and E. S. C. Weiner; additions (1993–7), ed. John Simpson and Edmund Weiner with Michael Proffitt; 3rd edn (in progress Mar. 2000), ed. John Simpson; *OED Online* (http://dictionary.oed.com), Oxford: Oxford University Press.

Oxinden, Henry (1933), *The Oxinden Letters 1607–42*, ed. Dorothy Gardiner, London: Constable.

Parkhurst, John (1974–5), *The Letter Book of John Parkhurst Bishop of Norwich*, ed. Ralph A. Houlbrooke (Norfolk Record Society 43), Norwich: Norfolk Record Society.

Partridge, Astley C. (1969), *Tudor to Augustan English: A Study in Syntax and Style from Caxton to Johnson*, London: André Deutsch.

Partridge, Astley C. (1973), *English Biblical Translation*, London: André Deutsch.

Paston, Katherine (1941), *The Correspondence of Lady Katherine Paston, 1603–27*, ed. Ruth Hughey (Norfolk Record Society 14), Norwich: Norfolk Record Society.

Peitsara, Kirsti (1992), 'On the development of the *by*-agent in English', in Matti Rissanen, Ossi Ihalainen, Terttu Nevalainen and Irma Taavitsainen (eds), *History of Englishes*, Berlin: Mouton de Gruyter, 379–400.

Pepys, Samuel (1955), *The Letters of Samuel Pepys and his Family Circle*, ed. Helen Truesdell Heath, Oxford: Clarendon Press.

Phillips, Edward (1658), *The New World of English Words, or a Generall Dictionary*, London: Nath. Brooke.

Pinney, John (1939), *Letters of John Pinney 1679–99*, ed. Geoffrey F. Nuttall, London: Oxford University Press.

Price, Glanville (ed.) (2000), *Languages in Britain and Ireland*, Oxford: Blackwell.

Puttenham, George [1589] (1968), *The Arte of English Poesie*, London: Richard Field; EL 110.

Quirk, Randolph, Sidney Greenbaum, Geoffrey Leech and Jan Svartvik (1985), *A Comprehensive Grammar of the English Language*, London: Longman.

Rastell, John (1523–4), *Exposiciones terminorum legum anglorum*, London: John Rastell.

Raumolin-Brunberg, Helena (1991), *The Noun Phrase in Early Sixteenth-Century English* (MSN 50), Helsinki: Société Néophilologique.

Rissanen, Matti (1999), 'Syntax', in Roger Lass (ed.), *The Cambridge History of the English Language*, vol. 3, *1476–1776*, Cambridge: Cambridge University Press, 187–331.

Romaine, Suzanne (1982), *Socio-Historical Linguistics*, Cambridge: Cambridge University Press.

Rydén, Mats (1966), *Relative Constructions in Early Sixteenth Century English*, Uppsala: Almqvist and Wiksell.

Rydén, Mats (1983), 'The emergence of *who* as relativiser', *Studia Linguistica* 37 (2): 126–34.

Rydén, Mats (1984), *The English Plant Names in 'The Grete Herball' (1526)* (Stockholm Studies in English 71), Stockholm: Almqvist and Wiksell.

Rydén, Mats and Sverker Brorström (1987), *The Be/Have Variation with Intransitives in English* (Stockholm Studies in English 70), Stockholm: Almqvist and Wiksell.

Rydén, Mats, Ingrid Tieken-Boon van Ostade and Merja Kytö (eds) (1998), *A Reader in Early Modern English*, Frankfurt am Main: Narr.

Salmon, Vivian (1999), 'Orthography and punctuation', in Roger Lass (ed.), *The Cambridge History of the English Language*, vol. 3, *1476–1776*, Cambridge: Cambridge University Press, 13–55.

Salmon, Vivian and Edwina Burness (eds) (1987), *A Reader in the Language of Shakespearian Drama*, Amsterdam and Philadelphia, PA: Benjamins.

Samuels, Michael (1963), 'Some applications of Middle English dialectology', *English Studies* 44: 81–94.

Schäfer, Jürgen (1980), *Documentation in the OED: Shakespeare and Nashe as Test Cases*, Oxford: Clarendon Press.

Schäfer, Jürgen (1989), *Early Modern English Lexicography*, 2 vols, Oxford: Clarendon Press.

Scheler, Manfred (1977), *Der englische Wortschatz* (Grundlagen der Anglistik und Amerikanistik 9), Berlin: Schmidt.

Scheler, Manfred (1982), *Shakespeares Englisch* (Grundlagen der Anglistik und Amerikanistik 12), Berlin: Schmidt.

Schneider, Edgar W. (1992), '*Who(m)?* Constraints on the loss of case marking of *wh*-pronouns in the English of Shakespeare and other poets of the Early Modern English period', in Matti Rissanen, Ossi Ihalainen, Terttu Nevalainen and Irma Taavitsainen (eds), *History of Englishes*, Berlin and New York: Mouton de Gruyter, 437–42.

Scragg, Donald G. (1974), *A History of English Spelling*, Manchester: Manchester University Press.

Serjeantson, Mary S. [1935] (1961), *A History of Foreign Words in English*, London: Routledge and Kegan Paul.

Shakespeare, William [1623] (1998), *Mr. William Shakespeares Comedies, Histories, & Tragedies, A Facsimile of the First Folio, 1623*, ed. Doug Moston, New York and London: Routledge.

Sharpe, James A. (1990), *Early Modern England: A Social History 1550–1760*, London: Edward Arnold.

Shipley, Joseph T. (1977), *In Praise of English: The Growth and Use of Language*, New York: Times Books.

Smith, Jeremy (1996), *An Historical Study of English*, London: Routledge.

Smith-Bannister, Scott (1997), *Names and Naming Patterns in England, 1538–1700*, Oxford: Clarendon Press.

Spevack, Marvin (1973), *The Harvard Concordance to Shakespeare*, Cambridge, MA: The Bellknap Press of Harvard University Press.

Starnes, De Witt T. and Gertrude E. Noyes [1946] (1991), *The English Dictionary from Cawdrey to Johnson 1604–1755*, new ed. Gabriele Stein, Amsterdam and Philadelphia, PA: Benjamins.

Stein, Gabriele (1985), *The English Dictionary before Cawdrey*, Tübingen: Narr.

Strang, Barbara M. H. (1970), *A History of English*, London and New York: Methuen.

Stuart, Arabella (1994), *The Letters of Lady Arbella Stuart*, ed. Sara Jayne Steen, Oxford: Oxford University Press.

Sundby, Bertil, Anne K. Bjørge and Kari E. Haugland (1991), *A Dictionary of English Normative Grammar 1700–1800*, Amsterdam and Philadelphia, PA: Benjamins.

Swift, Jonathan (1712), *A Proposal for Correcting, Improving and Ascertaining the English Tongue*, London: Benj. Tooke.

Thompson, Roger (ed.) (1976), *Samuel Pepys' Penny Merriments*, London: Constable.

Trudgill, Peter [1990] (1999), *The Dialects of England*, 2nd edn, Oxford: Blackwell.

Vickers, Brian (ed.) (1987), *English Science, Bacon to Newton*, Cambridge: Cambridge University Press.

Vorlat, Emma (1975), *The Development of English Grammatical Theory, 1586–1737*, Leuven: Leuven University Press.

Wallis, John [1653] (1969), *Grammatica Linguae Anglicanae*, Oxford: Leon. Lichfield; EL 142.

Wells, John C. (1982), *Accents of English*, 3 vols, Cambridge: Cambridge University Press.

Whythorne, Thomas [c. 1576] (1961), *The Autobiography of Thomas Whythorne*, ed. James M. Osborn, Oxford: Clarendon Press.

Winchester, Barbara (ed.) (1953), *The Johnson Letters, 1542–52*, (unpublished doctoral dissertation), University of London.

Wrightson, Keith (1982), *English Society 1580–1680*, London: Hutchinson.

Wrightson, Keith (1991), 'Estates, degrees, and sorts: changing perceptions of society in Tudor and Stuart England', in Penelope J. Corfield (ed.), *Language, History and Class*, Oxford: Blackwell, 30–52.

Wrightson, Keith (2002), *Earthly Necessities: Economic Lives in Early Modern Britain, 1470–1750*, London: Penguin Books.

Wrigley, Edward A. and Roger S. Schofield (1981), *The Population History of England 1541–1871: A Reconstruction*, London: Edward Arnold.

Wyld, Henry C. (1936), *A History of Modern Colloquial English*, 3rd edn, Oxford: Blackwell.

Index

Note: major references are given in **bold**.